MALE FEMALING

The glamour of transvestite fashion is the epitome of 1990s style, but the significance of cross-dressing and sex-changing goes much deeper than the annals of fashion. Ekins vividly details the innermost desires and the varied practices of males who wear the clothes of women for the pleasure it gives them (cross-dressers), or who wish to change sex and are actively going about it (sex-changers).

This unique and fascinating book transforms an area of study previously dominated by clinical models to look instead at cross-dressing and sex-changing as a highly variable social process. Giving precedence to the processual and emergent nature of much cross-dressing and sex-changing phenomena, the book traces the phased femaling career path of the 'male femaler' from 'beginning femaling' through to 'consolidating femaling'. Based upon seventeen years of fieldwork, life history work, qualitative analysis, archival work and contact with several thousand cross-dressers and sex-changers, the book meticulously and systematically develops a theory of 'male femaling' which has major ramifications for both the field of 'transvestism' and 'transsexualism', and for the analysis of sex and gender more generally.

Male Femaling provides social and cultural theorists with a lively case study for the generation of new theory. Social psychologists and sociologists interested in seeing grounded theory applied to a particular case study will be well rewarded. It will be essential reading for students of gender studies who seek to explore the interrelations between sex, sexuality and gender from the informant's point of view.

Richard Ekins is Senior Lecturer in Social Psychology at the University of Ulster at Coleraine.

MALE FEMALING

A grounded theory approach to cross-dressing
and sex-changing

Richard Ekins

Foreword by
Anselm Strauss

London and New York

First published 1997
by Routledge
11 New Fetter Lane, London EC4P 4EE

Simultaneously published in the USA and Canada
by Routledge
29 West 35th Street, New York, NY 10001

Reprinted 1998

© 1997 Richard Ekins

Typeset in Garamond by
Ponting-Green Publishing Services, Chesham,
Buckinghamshire

Printed and bound in Great Britain by
Biddles Ltd, Guildford and King's Lynn

British Library Cataloguing in Publication Data
A catalogue record for this book is available from the
British Library

Library of Congress Cataloguing in Publication Data
Ekins, Richard, 1945–
Male femaling: a grounded theory approach to cross-dressing and
sex-changing / Richard Ekins; foreword by Anselm Strauss
p.   cm.
Includes bibliographical references and index.
1. Transvestism.   2. Transsexualism.   3. Social psychology.
4. Sex role.   I. Title.
HQ77.E45   1996
305.3–dc20   96–16356
CIP

ISBN 0–415–10624–9 (hbk)
ISBN 0–415–10625–7 (pbk)

The SI [symbolic interaction] focus on people's 'definitions' and 'naming' is not a call for subjectivism, individualism and the rest but rather a 'respect' for the subject matter of sociology – the meaningful (to the actors involved) social process. This inductive approach thus calls for emphasis on the *experience* of the participants in that process and is not a glorification of subjectivity. It seeks to stay on the level of social experience and thereby to exclude 'foreign matter' to that experience – such as causes, inferred personality variables, a preset methodology, and an a priori theory.

(Warshay 1980 3 (1): 6)

The goal of grounded theory is to generate a theory that accounts for a pattern of behaviour which is relevant and problematic for those involved. The goal is not voluminous description, nor clever verification.

(Glaser 1978: 93)

To Wendy, Matthew and Luke

CONTENTS

CONTENTS

FIGURES

FOREWORD

Questionnaires and government forms always seem to include queries about personal identity that make no sense whatever. 'Please check the proper answer: Race (White, Black, Yellow), Sex (Male, Female), etc.' Race reduced to one of three or four boxes! What if you are Hawaiian born, with a Spanish/Philippine father and a Japanese/Chinese mother, each of whom in turn had mixed combinations of parents? And the bodies of American 'Blacks' are constituted of indeterminate amounts of whiteness, but they are asked to ignore that when filling out the questionnaire. As for sex: the assumption here is that we are either male or female, that all life forms, including the human, come down to just those two classes of beings. Life is scarcely that simple – and my own prejudice is anyhow, then it would be boring – but, on the contrary, is immensely complex. To know just how complicated sexual matters are takes both experience and careful research.

One of the virtues of this systematically ordered and beautifully written account of what are commonly termed 'transvestite' and 'transsexual' men is that it is based on meticulous research, done by someone who has spent many years in close contact with the people whom he has studied. Rather than rely on distancing research methods, Richard Ekins has used a combination of methods that have brought him into close and greatly varied contact with what he has written about here. He has used not just interviews and documents, but made close observations in a host of sites that give him the data for his analyses.

One of the great virtues of the book is the vividness of that data, some of which he uses as illustrations of analytic commentaries and others which provide extended or focused data that allow for direct analyses. None of those interpretations express moral opinions, either damning or extolling the all too human behaviour about which he is writing. Inevitably you will come away from this book, whatever else your reactions might be, with an appreciation for the enormously varied forms of action that human life takes. Like it or not, condemn it or not, Ekins is saying, that is the way of the world, and he is trying to describe and understand it.

His mode of presentation consists largely of descriptions of situations, of quotations both short and extended, of longer case histories that seem less like 'cases' than life stories, and of analytic interpretations of these ethnographic and documentary materials. The interpretations are guided by 'grounded theory methodology', which is now increasingly being used by social scientists who do so-called qualitative research. The methodology emphasises building systematic interpretations in close interplay between yourself as researcher and the data that you collect, rather than being too much guided or indeed constrained by prior theories. For Ekins the methodology works very well, since the people whom he has studied have very rarely been studied by anyone who has been in such close extensive contact with them nor participated (in his case as a privileged observer) in so many of their social worlds. (Social worlds is one of his major concepts.)

Among Ekins' key ordering conceptualisations is 'male femaling', a process he traces in a series of steps from beginning awareness to a consolidating of identity. These steps are 'ideal types', for not everybody passes through all of them, nor are they irreversible. People can be quite into cross-dressing, for instance, but then leave the practice totally or in part; nor does everybody have the same sexual career – not at all. Moreover, to the variety of responses and identities a major contributor is which of three issues (or their combinations) is foremost? The first is the matter of sex (that is, the body itself). The second is sexuality (that is, genital feelings and responses). The third is gender (that is, the social and cultural accompaniments, like dress, posture, gesture and speech style). Men can have female sexual responses but be uninterested in feminine styles or in changing their sexual equipment. Or the emphasis may be on gender but not body or sexuality; or on combinations – and not forever, but changeable. All of this is tied to the development of associated identities and selves, in a sophisticated and systematic social psychological analysis.

Accompanying this are Ekins' observations about medical diagnoses and interpretations, of which he is critical but neither sarcastic nor blaming. He is just interested in observing what they are, and why, and their differences to those of the men themselves, and various consequences for medical treatment and for public opinion. Of the latter he is more openly critical not just for its overly simplistic character but because it is unceasingly negative. (Here he does understandably show moral indignation though trying to understand why it exists.)

As an additional feature, Ekins makes various suggestions for areas of future research. It struck me, also, that his theoretical framework could just as well be used for studying aspects of [more conventional] heterosexual life, since they too can be viewed as having not so unchanging perspectives on body, sexuality and gender – whatever their actual sexual behaviour or choice of sexual objects may be. Not incidentally, there are other implications in

Ekins' work for the study of the human body, a topic on which a great many words, not all correct or profound, have been written in the last decade or so by psychologists and other behavioural scientists.

All in all, I have found this a quite exciting book.

Anselm Strauss
Emeritus Professor of Sociology
University of California
San Francisco, CA
22 December 1995

PROLOGUE

'When you meet a human being the first distinction you make is "male or female?" and you are accustomed to making the distinction with unhesitating certainty', wrote Sigmund Freud (1933: 113). This book is about males who make us hesitate. It is the outcome of seventeen years of sociological and social psychological research with males who either wear the clothes of the opposite sex for the pleasure it gives them (cross-dressers), or who wish to change sex and are actively going about it (sex-changers).

My initial fieldwork was carried out during periods of research in major British cities between 1979 and 1985 – sometimes as a casual participant, sometimes as an overt observer. During this period I gained access to all the major subcultural settings – drag balls, bars and clubs, 'transvestite' weekends, private parties and contact magazine and erotica networks throughout the United Kingdom. A further period of fieldwork followed between 1993 and 1995. From 1984 onwards, my focus has been on intensive life history work with selected informants. Since 1986, the research has taken an increasingly international flavour. From that date, I have directed the Trans-Gender Archive at the University of Ulster, Northern Ireland. The Archive is supported by the major 'transvestite' and 'transsexual' organisations through-out the world – most notably throughout the United Kingdom, North Western Europe, the USA, Australia, New Zealand and South Africa. It contains a comprehensive collection of material on cross-dressing and sex-changing, and is the first public collection of its type in the world (Ekins 1988; 1989a; 1990b). Moreover, as the Archive's Director, I have maintained access to a mass of unpublished and hitherto unavailable material.

Over the seventeen year period, I have observed several thousand cross-dressers and sex-changers; several hundred became my informants; several score were followed up over a period of years and were accompanied in the full range of settings – at home, at clinics, at work, at leisure; and several dozen became the subject of detailed life history work which is still continuing. At all stages I discussed my developing thoughts with selected informants and applied my developing ideas in the full range of settings.

1

I first mapped the various scientific, subcultural and lay conceptualisations and theorisations of cross-dressing and sex-changing phenomena and their interrelations from the standpoint of a sociology of knowledge informed principally by symbolic interactionism (Curtis and Petras 1970; Blumer 1969; Ekins 1978). I then focused on individual and group participation in the social worlds (Strauss 1978; 1982; 1993; Unruh 1979; 1980) of cross-dressers and sex-changers. The mass of observations were ordered in terms of grounded theory, which is the discovery of theory from data systematically obtained and analysed in social research, following the basic methodology set forth in Glaser and Strauss (1967b), expanded in Glaser (1978), Bigus, Hadden and Glaser (1982) and Strauss (1987), and clarified in Strauss and Corbin (1990) and Glaser (1992).

Within a couple of years of simultaneous data collection, coding and analysis, I had generated the core category 'male femaling'. Not long afterwards, it emerged as the single major social process being researched. It was pervasive and fundamental. It was patterned. It occurred over time and went on irrespective of the conditional variation of place. From then on, I found it increasingly illuminating to conceptualise male cross-dressers and sex-changers as males who 'female' in various ways, in various contexts, at various times, with various stagings and with various consequences. The emphasis could be on typing behaviour, not people (Glaser, 1978: 69). In particular, this re-conceptualisation showed the proper respect for the ambiguous, ambivalent, multi-contextual, multi-dimensional, emergent nature of much cross-dressing and sex-changing phenomena. The next step was the delineation of three major modes of femaling – those of 'body femaling', 'erotic femaling' and 'gender femaling', and an exploration of their interrelations in terms of the various facets of sex, sexuality and gender that emerged from the data.

For a basic social process to be genuinely processual it must have a minimum 'process out' requirement of two clear, emergent stages which should differentiate and account for variations in problematic patterns of behaviour (Glaser, 1978: 97). I found that the staged career paths of male femalers processed out into five major phases – 'beginning femaling', 'fantasying femaling', 'doing femaling', 'constituting femaling' and 'consolidating femaling'. In terms of grounded theory these phases are stages *in vivo*, that is, perceivable by the persons involved, but demarcated by the sociologist for theoretical reasons (Glaser 1978: 98). This led me to construct an ideal-typical career path within which I was able to use the 'constant comparative method' (Glaser and Strauss, 1967b: 101–15) to explore the interrelations between the three modes of femaling and the interrelations between sex, sexuality and gender as they developed in individual biographies over time.

This book should be of interest to a varied readership. Social psychologists and sociologists interested in seeing grounded theory applied to a particular 'case study' will be well rewarded. Sexologists might also find its approach appealing. It should, moreover, be of value to students, from varied disciplines, because it sets forth, for the first time, the detailed interrelations of sex, sexuality and gender from the informant's point of view. Such an approach is particularly timely in a period when ethnographic work is again becoming so popular in the social sciences. More ambitiously, the book's theoretical reconceptualisation of the area in terms of 'male femaling' provides sex, sexuality and gender researchers with an original theoretical framework to develop their own theory and research, both inside and outside of the specific area of male femaling. Finally, cross-dressers and sex-changers themselves should find it of interest, because much of the detail it reports has hitherto been unavailable outside of the medico-psychiatric specialist literature, where it has previously been theorised from an entirely different point of view – a point of view seen as largely hostile to 'male femalers', and not, therefore, of much interest to most of them.

Grounded theory is a method of research which demands intimate appreciation of the arena studied, but which writes up that intimate appreciation in terms of theoretical analyses. In consequence, grounded theory writings are frequently read *either* for their 'findings', *or* for their theory, notwithstanding the fact that grounded theorists see themselves as writing theory accompanied by theory-informed data (Strauss 1987: 217).

Moreover, I take the post-positivist view that theory emerges in *interplay* between the researcher and the data and that grounded theorists, it follows, must be explicit about their ontological and epistemological point of view. It must be recognised, however, that the detailing of my standpoint on this – rooted as it is in symbolic interactionism, the 'double hermeneutic' and structuration theory – is likely to be of little interest to the transgender community, to most sexologists and to those working in cultural studies or queer theory where there is currently a growing interest in theorising transgender identities (Whittle 1996), but from a different point of view.

I have, therefore, divided the book into three parts – Part I: Introduction, Part II: Mainly theory and Part III: Mainly practice. Readers who wish to skip the bulk of the sociological theorising are invited to turn directly from Part I to Part III. On the other hand, I would hope that a careful reading of Part II would be rewarding for sociological theorists in so far as it attempts to show the links between symbolic interactionism, grounded theory and structuration theory. Psychologists, too, who are beginning to turn to symbolic interactionism and grounded theory as part of their 'rethinking psychology' (Smith, Harré and Van Langenhove 1995a; 1995b) might find Part II an enlightening summary of a major post-positivist ontology, epistemology and methodology.

It has become fashionable recently to argue that researchers must be clear about their relationships – especially sexual – with their informants (Kulick and Willson, 1995). My own position on these matters broadly follows Warren (1977). Writing in the context of the 'research bargain' and research into the stigmatised and secret 'gay world' of the 1970s, Warren (1977: 93) argues as follows:

> Researchers cannot select and play a role, since others cast them into a variety of roles. Entrée into public gay settings is easy; entrée into more private arenas depends on the establishment of interpersonal relationships. The major research bargain in informal relations is identical to that of everyday life: a mutual exchange of interest and interaction.

In the course of that mutual exchange I have earned the confidence of the transgender community. I trust that this book will enable me to maintain that confidence and further develop the mutual exchange.

Cross-dressing and sex-changing evoke in many people a generalised uneasy mix between fascination and repulsion. I consider this issue in Chapter 1 with reference to a number of vignettes which serve also to introduce the particular social psychological and sociological emphases of this study. In particular, the chapter introduces the book's concern to explore the interrelations between the public and private faces of cross-dressing and sex-changing in terms of three main problems: the interrelations between sex, sexuality and gender; between self, identity and world; and between the formulations of different experts, members and lay people.

The body of academic literature on cross-dressing and sex-changing is now a large one (Denny 1994). The vast majority of this literature declares its allegiance to positivist science and continues to work within what Gagnon and Parker (1995: 3) refer to as 'the sexological period dating from 1890–1980'. In so doing, it simply ignores the epistemological crisis that has taken place in the human sciences over the last couple of decades – a time of paradigm shift when the knowledge claims of positivist science have become increasingly problematic. This is not the whole story, however. From Garfinkel's classic paper, 'Passing and the managed achievement of sex status in an intersexed person' (1967), onwards, a small literature on cross-dressing and sex-changing has emerged that has grappled with the crisis in various ways. Chapter 2 considers both literatures from the standpoint of grounded theory.

Grounded theory has, itself, been caught up in the epistemological crisis (Charmaz 1995). Indeed, its founders, Glaser and Strauss, are in deep disagreement about the issue. Glaser 'seems to take the extreme position that theory will emerge if you work with the data, like reality is out there and you work to get at it' (Strauss, 1995). Strauss, on the other hand, takes 'the classic Pragmatist metaphysical and epistemological positions on "reality" and "truth" . . . emerging theory "emerges" in *interplay* between the researcher and the data (which get to us by various routes including our own efforts)' (ibid. 1995). I follow Strauss here, and it is the intent of Chapter 3 to set forth my own particular response to the crisis.

Chapter 4 may be taken as an extension of Chapter 3. It outlines the framework for the study with reference to the re-conceptualisation of the research arena in terms of 'male femaling', and its modes, facets and variations. Male femaling is a basic social process. It does, however, need to be set within social structure if we are to understand and explain the manifold ways in which male femalers process problems consequent upon their engaging in behaviour commonly regarded as deviant in contemporary Western societies. I came to see what I term the 'masked awareness context' as the social structural unit within which male femaling is best understood. Chapter 4 unpacks this social structural unit with reference to a number of illustrative vignettes. It then sets forth the five phases in an ideal-typical career path of the male femaler – those of 'beginning femaling', 'fantasying femaling', 'doing femaling', 'constituting femaling' and 'consolidating femaling' – which form the basis and organising principle of the chapters that follow in Part III.

'Beginning femaling' is the focus of Chapter 5. Examples of beginning femaling are elaborated with reference to the interrelations between the three modes of femaling – body femaling, gender femaling and erotic femaling (3MF) – and the interrelations between sex, sexuality and gender (SSG). The chapter goes on to detail how the beginning femaler is soon confronted with problems of stigma, secrecy and information management, and considers these problems in terms of the masked awareness context.

'Fantasying femaling', with reference to the 3MF and SSG, is the focus of Chapter 6. In this phase, the accent is on the elaboration of fantasies involving femaling. The chapter examines the recently emerged male femaling telephone sex lines and indicates how they provide excellent material for the under-standing and explanation of an 'erotic fantasy femaling' emphasis, within which 'body femaling' and 'gender femaling' are variously co-opted in the service of orgasm. The emphasis in this chapter is on femaling which does not entail manifest display and disclosure to others, that is, a private awareness context.

'Doing femaling', again with reference to the 3MF and SSG, is the focus of Chapter 7. This phase may include more sustained cross-dressing, or the acting out of aspects of fantasy body femaling. The emphasis is placed on male femaling practices, 'purges' (the periodic throwing away of offending clothes, cosmetics and jewellery), guilt and personal confusion, as well as the development of different 'doing' styles. The masked awareness types – 'closed', 'suspicion', 'open' and 'pretence', and the processes within them – 'masking', 'displaying', 'reading', 'pretending' and 'disclosing' – are developed with reference to numerous vignettes. The emphasis in this chapter is on displaying as female, with its attendant fear of consequences.

'Constituting femaling' – the focus of Chapter 8 – is the phase that marks the period where the femaler begins to constitute the meaning of his activities in a more serious and sustained way. The major permutations of constituting are outlined, using selected material to illustrate the major constitutions available to the contemporary male femaler. Consideration is given to the private constituting of a lone male femaler, the constitution of a 'cure' within the dyad of the psychoanalytic situation, the making of a modern transsexual, and the constitution of meanings within the private networking that takes place between male femalers who use contact columns.

'Consolidating femaling' – the phase that marks the period where a more full-blown constitution of femaling self and world is established – is the focus of Chapter 9. Again, the material is presented with particular reference to the interrelations between the 3MF and SSG. Here, the emphasis is on particular outcomes, meanings, end-points and the reconstructions of pasts. The chapter considers consolidating in terms of its three major modes – those of 'aparting', 'substituting' and 'integrating', and illustrates each with reference to detailed life history material collected from three selected informants who have consolidated, respectively, around each different mode.

Use of the concept of the career path is sometimes said to impose too much order on lives which, both to outsiders and to those who have lived them, may appear to have 'been more confused and chaotic' (King 1993: 160–1). The reader should remember, however, that the phases do not delineate fixed sequences and stages through which male femalers move from less serious involvement in femaling in the way sometimes suggested for deviant careers (Lemert 1972: 79). Rather, it is the minority who proceed through all the phases of male femaling to a 'consolidated' end state. Most male femalers will circle and cycle all or parts of the phases again and again. They may stop off at different points, and for different periods, on different occasions.

Finally, in a short conclusion, I summarise the major interrelated themes of the book, highlight the contemporary significance of male femaling and make a number of suggestions for areas of future research. In particular, male femalers are seen to be a particularly fruitful resource for social psychologists and sociologists of sex, sexuality and gender who are seeking firmer foundations for their work. I end with the provocative question: to what extent would our understanding and explanation of the behaviour of all males and females be enhanced by a utilisation of the sort of conceptual framework proposed in this study?

A book like this accumulates a great many debts. The fieldwork upon which it was based was enabled by funding from the Faculty of Social and Health Sciences, University of Ulster, between 1980 and 1985, and from the Sociology Research Unit, University of Ulster, between 1993 and 1995. I thank Roger Ellis, Arthur McCullough and Lindsay Prior, particularly, in this regard. Significant funding was also provided by a McCrea Research Award (1985–6), and by grants from the Self Help Association for Transsexuals (1985–6) and from Schering Laboratories (1986).

I thank the many cross-dressers and sex-changers who have so readily shared their time and thoughts with me, particularly, Johnny Brown, Erica, Cheryl, Lynn, David, Martine Rose, Mark Rees, Heather, Val, Vicki, Norma, John, Tom, George Lewis, Terri Webb, Tish, Kathryn, Michelle, Christine-Jane Wilson, Kris Clarke, Alice, Millie, Daphne, Jennifer, Carole, Barbara,

Adèle Anderson, Gary, Rachel O'Connor, Vicky Lee, Tony, Stephen, Gail Hill and Bruce Laker/Phaedra Kelly.

Mrs Silk, Alan and Ann Beamish, Hazel Jones, Stacy Novak, Christienne, Peter Farrer, Jutta Witzel, David Burgess, John Berry, Nicholas Dodge, Peter Mills, Jackie Granleese, Ethna O'Gorman and Michael Haslam were also a great help.

Special thanks go to Chris Rojek who commissioned the book, Thomas Freeman who made it possible for me to write it, Dave King and Anselm Strauss who suggested a number of significant refinements, and most of all to Wendy Saunderson, my mentor and support throughout the entire proceedings.

I also acknowledge *Sociological Review* for extracts from 'On male femaling: a grounded theory approach to cross-dressing and sex-changing' by Richard Ekins; Routledge for extracts from *Blending Genders: Social Aspects of Cross-Dressing and Sex-Changing* edited by Richard Ekins and Dave King; *Female Impersonators* for the photograph of Holli White; and Debbie Humphry for the photograph of Vicky Lee.

Writing about male femalers poses particular problems concerning the use of personal pronouns. To place scare quotes around 'she', 'her' (and so on), when referring to male femalers, is offensive to many cross-dressers and sex-changers. Throughout this book, therefore, I have used she, her (and so on), to refer to the female identities of male femalers, except in those rare cases where the male femaler has specifically suggested that it is more authentic in his case to refer only to his male identity, notwithstanding his male femaling. Femme names (the female names adopted by male femalers) have been changed to preserve anonymity where appropriate.

Part I
INTRODUCTION

1

THE PUBLIC AND PRIVATE FACES OF CROSS-DRESSING AND SEX-CHANGING

THE PUBLIC FACE OF CROSS-DRESSING AND SEX-CHANGING

Some personal observations

As I sit on the Belfast–London shuttle, shortly after signing the contract to write this book, cross-dressing and sex-changing seem far removed. The officers, crew and passengers are clearly either male or female. The pilot looks masculine, vigorous and authoritative. The hostesses are elegant, well groomed and made-up. They seem to be enjoying their femininity. I seem to be set within a firmly dichotomised world. Every page of the inflight reading material confirms it. Every stage of interaction I observe reinforces it and as I continue my journey it is confirmed over and over again.

However, if I take the trouble to look, a quite different world reveals itself. Although cross-dressing and sex-changing appear to be nowhere, actually they are everywhere. Fixing my gaze on a billboard as I descend the escalators into the London Underground, the image of a rather odd masculine 'woman' stares back at me. *Just Like a Woman* has been released in London. The internationally acclaimed Julie Walters stars as the landlady who falls in love with her transvestite lodger. A short while later, telephoning for a hotel reservation from a booth in Earl's Court station, I see something which attracts my attention. Set amongst the dozens of prostitutes' advertising cards, dotted about the telephone booth, are many which feature sketches of men in various stages of feminine undress: 'New Young Mistress Loves Slaves – For TV [Transvestite] and CP [Corporal Punishment] Uniforms – 546 029'; 'Transformation – From *He* to *She* – Time and Care Taken – 643 3191; 'Young Mistress Wants TV Submissive Slave to Report Now – 515 1558'; 'Transvestite Gina – 0171–240–5077 – Uniform Fantasies – Massage'; Even, 'Pre-Op Transexual Gina – Transforms, Dominates, Ties U Up – 0171–511–2399'.

Withdrawing from the fascinations of this telephone booth, I go to buy an evening newspaper on the underground news-stand. Again I am distracted by

11

yet another aspect of cross-dressing and sex-changing: *Marie Claire*, the women's magazine and 'winner of nine major awards' is featuring 'Samoa: Where Men Live as Women' (Haworth 1993). Inside, the title becomes 'Samoa: Where Men Think They are Women'.

> In the South Pacific islands of Samoa, as many as one family in five has a son who lives as a woman. They are totally accepted by society, are usually highly educated and hold many key jobs. In their spare time they even date boys; they even enter beauty competitions.

I could go on for a very long time: entering the HMV Shop on Oxford Street I am met by a special 'three for the price of two' offer, which invites me to take home *Victor/Victoria*, *Tootsie* and *Some Like it Hot* (all major box office hits, based upon cross-dressing themes). As I enter Waterstones, I see a display of Andy Warhol books: *A Low Life in High Heels* is the biography of Andy Warhol's transvestite protégé Holly Woodlawn (1991), immortalised in the Lou Reed song, 'Walk on the Wild Side'. Back on the tube, and a woman reads a magazine article titled 'Gossip! Gossip! Gossip! Madonna is to change sex and play a man in her next film'. Madonna is to play Holly who 'came from Miami, FLA, hitchhiked her way across the USA, plucked her eyebrows on the way, shaved her legs then he was a she . . .'.

Also in Waterstones was the prominent display of New York photographer Nan Goldin's (1993) book *The Other Side*. The cover blurb reads:

> After years of experiencing and photographing the struggle of the two genders with their codes and definitions and their difficulties in relating to each other, it was liberating to meet people who had crossed these gender boundaries. Most people get scared when they can't categorize others – by race, by age, and, most of all, by gender. It takes nerve to walk down the street when you fall between the racks. Some of my friends shift genders daily from boy to girl and back again. Some are transsexual before or after surgery, and among them some live entirely as women while others identify themselves as transsexuals. Others dress up openly for stage performances and live as gay boys by day. And still others make no attempt at all to fit in anywhere, but live in a gender-free zone, flaunting their third sex status. The pictures in this book are not of people suffering gender dysphoria but rather expressing gender euphoria. This book is about new possibilities and transcendence. The people in this book are truly revolutionary; they are the real winners of the battle of the sexes because they have stepped out of the ring.

It is striking just how publicly and openly this quite different world of sex-changing and cross-dressing reveals itself, once we take the trouble to look. It even pervades the private space of the public convenience I later use: on the wall beside me, written in an untidy childish hand, 'TV Baby Susan likes to be treated like a baby girl for sex fun. Tel. 0181–857–8103. Ask for "Babs Susan"'.

Some popular press treatments

The 'public face' of cross-dressing and sex-changing is variously acceptable and unacceptable in different social contexts. However, though it may be celebrated by some, it is more likely to evoke a generalised uneasy mix between fascination and repulsion in others.

Many people, probably the vast majority, will never, knowingly, meet a cross-dresser or sex-changer. Yet, mass communication makes them available to everyone (King 1990). It is, perhaps, the mix of fascination and repulsion which explains the popularity of cross-dressing and sex-changing as themes dealt with again and again by the mass media. The *News of the World* of the 1940s and 1950s, for example, regularly featured legal cases in which cross-dressing featured (Ekins 1990c; 1992a). What unites them all is that the reader is being invited to share in a sense of wonderment, to be amused, to be titillated, to be sympathetic, perhaps, even to feel admiration (King 1990).

From thousands of press cuttings in the Trans-Gender Archive, the following two have been chosen to illustrate typical treatments of cross-dressing and sex-changing. One dates from the late 1940s, the period immediately prior to the emergence of sex-changing as a practical possibility; the other, from the 1980s, a contemporary report from a period in which sex-changing is relatively commonplace.

Headline: Barmaid Crooner was a Man: Wearing the New Look and Nylons on Night of Arrest

This week-end a man, aged 22, who had a flair for dressing up as an attractive girl, is in Wandsworth Gaol, starting to serve a sentence of 18 months' imprisonment passed on him at Middlesex Sessions for house-breaking. Many people will remember him as 'the charming Miss Pamela'.

In the course of his amazing female masquerade, Bird used to dress in the height of fashion, swathed in expensive furs and more recently wearing the new look.

He had been a bus conductress, barmaid and woman dance-band crooner. When he was employed as a barmaid at a public-house his hair was long and bleached and his finger nails were painted red.

It was stated by the prosecution that Bird was sent to a house by a domestic agency. He stole clothes belonging to Mr Roberts, and three days later broke into the house when it was unoccupied, discarded Mr Roberts's clothes, and changed into Mrs Roberts's attire, including her best underwear, and then walked out with property worth £800.

Bird's first conviction was in 1943, when, at the age of 16, he embarked on a career of crime and decided to become a blonde 'girl' in a dual character role.

He had many jobs ranging from cook to crooner, but his favourite was that of domestic servant, working in different houses three or four hours a day.

On such occasions Bird always told the lady of the house: 'Just call me Pamela'.

Carefully shaven and using powder and the right amount of lipstick, as well as a certain amount of padding in his woman's dress, Bird always passed as an attractive young woman.

A fair singer, he persuaded various bands to give him a job as a woman crooner and actually attracted a flock of male admirers.

But Bird was not always in the glamorous limelight when he dressed as a girl. On one occasion, he was taken to a girl's rescue home. There he actually shared a bedroom with another girl until suspicion was aroused.

Bird's last job, before his arrest, was in a public-house, where he reigned as 'queen of the bar' for several weeks.

Here, too, he deceived a number of 'admirers' who liked to talk to the tall, slim, fashionably dressed and attractive 'Pamela'.

One night, however, the attractive 'Pamela' decided to take a walk. 'She' was dressed in a new look blue frock, fur coat, black nylons and elbow-length black gloves. Round 'her' head was a scarf and 'she' wore ankle-strap white high-heeled shoes and carried a white leather hand-bag. All these fineries had been stolen.

This evening promenade was brought to a shattering stop when Sergt. Lindsay touched 'Pamela' on the arm. At the police station 'she' was charged as Mr Denis Bird.

(News of the World 3 July 1949)

The time-lapse since 'Miss Pamela's' day has brought with it the practical possibility of 'sex-change' surgery as illustrated in the following report. The report is also more explicit and the deception more advanced. For all that, though, the close attention to detail and the prurience of the reporting makes the appeal of the two stories similar.

Headline: Boy Who Fooled The Top Women's Prison

A man revealed yesterday that he had fooled police and medical authorities into believing he is a girl and admitting him to Holloway Prison, Britain's top women's jail.

Inside the jail he was made to strip for a medical and take a bath, guarded by a woman prison officer.

But the man, who uses the name Claire Morley and has taken hormone pills for three years to get a 36–24–36 figure, told me: 'No-one had the slightest idea I was not really a girl'.

Blond, blue-eyed Mr Morley, who will be 20 next month, added: 'In all respects except the vital one, I'm a girl.

I look like a girl, feel like a girl, think like a girl'.

His audacious deception started when he was accused of stealing skirts from a London store and was taken to Marlborough Street police-station.

Morley told me: 'I was put in a room and told to take all my clothes off. A police matron looked at me but didn't notice anything. When she asked me to take my panties down I just pulled them down a short way, then pulled them up quickly again'.

After a few hours he was allowed to leave. Next day he appeared before magistrates on the shoplifting charge and was remanded on bail.

Morley, who hopes to have a full sex-change operation later this year, then told me how he has always been haunted by the desire to be a woman.

'I've felt myself to be a girl as long as I can remember', he said. 'Though I went to school as a boy I never played with other boys.

At 15 I left school and my home and have lived as a girl ever since. I don't ever think of myself as a boy now.

I'm desperately hoping for the operation so I can complete the change and become a girl in the real sense of the word.

I know it isn't possible under English law at present for a sex-change person to get married but it is possible abroad and this is what I shall do'.

(Source unknown)

Embedded within the above two media presentations are various aspects of the three central themes of the book: aspects of sex, sexuality and gender; self, identity and world; and the differing formulations of experts, members and lay folk. The remainder of this chapter introduces the interrelations between these three problems with a focus on the 'private' face of cross-dressing and sex-changing where the emphasis is upon 'subjective' private experience.

THE PRIVATE FACE OF CROSS-DRESSING AND SEX-CHANGING

Despite the desire to titillate, or, perhaps, because of it, press reports such as these are noticeably coy about the subjective erotic state of those they report. They may not mind if readers find their reporting sexually stimulating, but we learn nothing of the details of the private face of their subject's erotic sexual life. The feature of the 'public face' of cross-dressing and sex-changing is its tendency to studiously avoid the issue.

Sex, sexuality and gender

To make the above point explicit, it is important to introduce the first three-fold distinction which is absolutely central to the organisation of this book.

15

This is the distinction between 'sex', 'sexuality' and 'gender'. This study restricts the term 'sex' to the biological and physiological aspects of the division of humans into males and females; 'sexuality' to 'those matters pertaining to the potential arousability and engorgement of the genitals' (Plummer 1979: 53); and 'gender' to the socio-cultural correlates of the division of the sexes. These definitions are sensitising rather than definitive. In particular, what follows is concerned to explore the neglected interrelations between them.

Once this distinction is made, it is evident that the particular feature of the 'Miss Pamela' piece is its preoccupation with 'gender'. The emphasis is upon the accoutrements of femininity. The titillation comes from the fact that it is someone of the male sex who is so preoccupied with such things, *for himself*. On the other hand, the 'Claire Morley' piece is preoccupied with 'sex'. The emphasis is upon a hinted – rather than stated – preoccupation with Mr Morley's biology and physiology. We know he is male. He has, however, acquired a 36–24–36 figure in three years. He is 'in all respects but one', a girl. The bulk of the piece is taken up with the fact that his custodians repeatedly fail to see this one respect. He sees his sex-change operation as settling that last detail.

If, however, we approach the topic from the personal standpoint of the cross-dresser and sex-changer, himself, a very different emphasis is likely to emerge. Certainly, cross-dressers and sex-changers are likely to be pre-occupied with sex and gender. However, from their standpoint, it is quite inappropriate to ignore the question of sexuality. This more private face of cross-dressing and sex-changing is well illustrated by the following case of Barry. Unfolding with the various stages of Barry's emerging sexuality is his increasing fascination and deepening involvement with various aspects of cross-dressing and sex-changing.

Barry was brought up in a conventional middle-class family in Cambridge, England. He recalls his first 'cross-dressing incident' as taking place when he was 5 years old. He was playing 'schools' with his sister. They were the 'Browns' and he was Anna Brown. What more natural than he should put on his sister's school skirt and blouse? Lost in the game, and attaching no particular significance to it, the children are called to lunch by their mother. They bound into the dining room, to be met by the stony gaze of their father, seated at the head of the table. Barry becomes acutely aware of the tension in the air. He shuffles nervously, feeling the cold of the seat on his bare thighs. He looks down at 'his' skirt. Nothing is said. He knows he has done something dreadfully wrong. His parents disapprove. This is taboo. He will not do it again. Or will he?

Barry is now 12 and on a trip with his local Boy Scout troop. As they are supposed to be settling down to bed, one of the boys places a handkerchief on the bed and folds it over in various complicated ways. 'Abracadabra', he says as he flashes before the other boys eyes, what looks like a brassiere. He places his handkerchief bra over his bare nipples, and cavorts about in mimicry of a strip-tease artist. A little while later, Barry, now tucked up in bed, finds the image of the handkerchief bra coming into his mind, while his penis stiffens. That night he masturbates with the thought of it firmly at the forefront of his mind. Afterwards, he feels guilty and tries to forget the incident, but he cannot.

Barry is now 15. He has been becoming increasingly preoccupied with girls, but more so with their clothing. He finds himself becoming increasingly drawn to the window displays in women's shops, particularly to the women's underwear. One Christmas, during his first holiday job, he finds himself plucking up the courage to buy a baby-doll pyjama set displayed enticingly in a shop window. 'You certainly know what you want!' says the assistant, as Barry takes his precious pyjama set home. Actually, he does not quite know what he wants. Nor does he quite know what he is doing, or why. But he does know he must not tell a soul. No one must find out. He hides the pyjama set under the floorboards of his bedroom. Now, when he masturbates, he often wears his baby-doll set. Afterwards, he is very guilty. One day he determines to have no more of this nonsense, and throws it away. He feels great relief. Very soon, however, he is buying more women's clothes. He does not know why.

Barry is now 17. He is flipping through a newspaper and his eyes alight on a beautiful blonde, full-bosomed woman. He feasts on the sight. There is some banter with his friend. But wait! This woman is a man! It transpires this beautiful 'model' is the celebrated Coccinelle, who has had a sex-change operation in Casablanca and now, looking for all the world like Brigitte Bardot, has become the bride of her male secretary, a very masculine looking Francis Bonnet. Barry looks lingeringly and in disbelief. She looks so enticing. How can such a thing come to pass?

Barry is now at university. 'Let's go down to the "King Henry"', says a fellow student, 'It's a right laugh there'. As they enter the bar, Barry is aware of a strange feel to the place. There are men wearing make-up and women's clothes. His mates joke about it all, particularly about the 'pansy' with dyed blonde hair, leopard skin pants and a feather boa round his neck. Barry feels unsettled. Is he fascinated? Or is he repulsed? He's not sure, but he cannot forget what he has seen.

Barry has left university now. He's on holiday alone in New York. What will he do to tonight? His eyes alight on an advertisement for a 'Cabaret show with a difference': all the glamorous performers are men – female impersonators. He finds the prospect intriguing. While at the show, the compère joins him at his table. She is attractive. What the hell? They get talking. He finds her appealing. She's young and slim. She's saving up her dollars, to get her 'sex-change' in Casablanca (Ekins 1990a). She's so feminine. He walks her home, and as he does so places his arm around her body. He feels the boniness of a male physique. He is a little alarmed. He does not take it any further.

Nevertheless, in the privacy of his bedroom, he dresses in some women's underclothes that he always takes with him on his travels. He masturbates to orgasm, thinking of this exciting and beautiful creature he has just met.

Back in London now, he has become increasingly aware of the network of drag shows dotted around the bars and clubs. He finds himself increasingly drawn to the bohemian glamour and sleaze of these drag bars. There he begins to meet 'transvestites' and 'transsexuals'. Soon he will have his first 'transsexual' girlfriend. But Barry is still cross-dressing in private, alone. What does this make him? He wonders. Barry's confusion as to who and what he is leads us to the second central theme: that of the interrelations between self, identity and world.

Self, identity and world

From the symbolic interactionist perspective of this study, senses of self, identity and world arise *pari passu* within interaction with others and the physical world (Weigart 1983). More specifically, individuals are social individuals inhabiting social worlds (Mead 1934; Strauss 1993). Identity is a meaning that self acquires when '*situated* – that is, cast in the shape of a social object by the acknowledgement of his participation or membership in social relations' (Stone 1962: 93). Following Strauss (1977), I use self and identity as sensitising concepts, admittedly ambiguous and diffuse, in order to 'better look around the corners of the problems, and be less likely to slide down the well-worn grooves of other men's thoughts' (ibid. pp. 9–10). But I am particularly mindful that 'within the framework of the social construction of human reality, identity is conceptualised as a social meaning constructed like other meanings, *but* with the uniquely existential dimension of being anchored in an individual's body' (Weigart 1983: 190). Thus, whereas types of identity are purely social realities, actual personal identity 'is a social reality vivified in individual experience and anchored in individual bodies' (Weigart 1983: 191).

The conventional male is assigned as such at birth on the basis of a visual inspection of his body. In due course, he comes to have a sense of himself as male, he develops a male identity, presents himself accordingly, finds himself sexually attracted to the opposite sex and in the fullness of time develops a sexual relationship with a female, who presents herself as such, finds males sexually attractive and so on.

Throughout this process, selves, identities and worlds are being constantly renegotiated, and when things proceed relatively straightforwardly, their development may appear unproblematic. This is the natural 'taken for granted' course of things. With cross-dressers and sex-changers, however, this 'taken for granted' course of things is being variously rendered problematic, at different times, in different contexts and with various consequences.

Barry has been assigned male at birth, comes to have a sense of himself as male, develops a male identity and presents himself accordingly. But then come problems. He finds himself increasingly drawn to the gendered accoutrements of femininity. Later he finds himself sexually attracted to biological males who dress as females and seek to become like females. The effect of all this is that he begins to question his sense of self and his identity. At the same time, the conventionally dichotomised worlds of men and of women become increasingly problematic for him.

Other male cross-dressers and sex-changers may never develop a sense of themselves as males or develop a male identity. The celebrated 'transsexual' writer Jan Morris, for instance, made sense of her predicament very early in life (Morris, 1975: 11). She concluded at a very young age that she was born into the wrong body:

> I was three or perhaps four years old when I realized that I had been born into the wrong body, and should really be a girl. I remember the moment well, and it is the earliest memory of my life.

In *Conundrum*, she details how she presented a false sense of herself as male for many years, and how, after years of marriage and fatherhood, she finally sought the sex re-assignment surgery that enabled her to be at ease with her 'real' self.

Others may develop dual identities. Since being widowed in his 60s, Ben/Deirdre is Ben outside his home and Deirdre inside it. Deirdre is involved in various transvestite groups. Ben is involved in various church activities. Deirdre has her own personality and 'femme' style, quite separate from Ben. She is, she explains, 'a much nicer person than Ben', more tolerant, more forgiving. Deirdre enjoys sewing and home-making. Ben enjoys cars. As Deirdre potters around the house doing the housework she finds herself thinking: 'I must wash Ben's socks'.

Coccinelle, whom Barry was so taken with when he was 17, wrote her first autobiography, shortly after her marriage in 1962 (Costa 1962). In it she describes how as a young boy he looked feminine:

> As a small child I looked very much like a little girl, but I was born a boy and my mother had to dress me as one. And after all who could blame her? When inquisitive people or friends talked about me, she always had to point out to them the mistake they were making and to tell them to which sex I really belonged. This never failed to astonish them considerably and at once there was a flood of complimentary remarks about the extreme delicacy of my features, the silky texture of hair and my general appearance as a pampered doll.
>
> (ibid. p. 16)

Coccinelle then finds herself increasingly drawn to the world of girls:

> And besides my face there was also my temperament ... Instead of playing with toy soldiers like other boys of my age, I found it much

more interesting to play with dolls. I particularly enjoyed dressing and undressing them, sewing for them and making them tiny bonnets and petticoats. I didn't like to run about in the street and I had no wish to associate with other small boys. They were too boisterous and they went in for games too rough for my liking. I sought the company of girls and *only* girls ... I must add that the feeling was mutual: little girls enjoyed being with me, unlike the boys, who disliked my gentle manner and, for their part, preferred to avoid me.

(ibid. pp. 16–17)

As she develops into adolescence, she finds herself drawn to boys as potential sexual partners. Increasingly, she feels different and alone. Is she a freak? She recounts how when a group of prostitutes dress her as a woman, for a laugh, she begins to feel herself as a woman. Later, she tries to destroy the past evidence of her boyhood, and increasingly affirms her feminine identity. She was 'really' female all along, and obtains medical assistance to confirm that 'fact'. 'Undecisive nature' has been 'finally overruled' with the assistance of hormonal treatment and the surgeon's knife.

Expert, member and lay knowledge

In making sense of self, identity and world, there is a constant interplay between private experiences and public knowledge. The third central theme of this book is the exploration of this interplay. Rooted, as it is, in a sociology of knowledge approach, informed principally by symbolic interactionism, this book considers the impact of publicly available knowledge about sex, sexuality and gender on the developing senses of self, identity and the world of cross-dressers and sex-changers. In particular, it considers the inter-relations between scientific, subcultural and lay conceptualisations and theorisations of cross-dressing and sex-changing, and their impact on the selves, identities and worlds of male cross-dressers and sex-changers themselves.

Following Goffman, Mead and Schutz, I take it that meaning frames (Goffman 1974), their constituent objects, and knowledge of both, emerge from a world 'taken for granted' (Schutz 1967), a 'world that is there' (Mead 1938). I then find it instructive to distinguish the meaning frames of science from those of 'members' (in my case cross-dressers and sex-changers themselves) and those of lay people. The empirical task then becomes to plot the interrelations between three meaning frames – more specifically to plot the interrelations between three 'knowledges': 'scientific' or 'expert' knowledge (the latter term includes legal knowledge, for example); 'member' knowledge (which would include subcultural knowledge); and 'common-sense' or 'lay' knowledge.

Maria/Anthony's case provides something of the flavour of the impact of these various interrelations. Anthony has cross-dressed sporadically through-out his adolescence, as an aid to masturbation. It is his secret. At 17, he is fascinated by the female impersonator star, Danny La Rue.

When Danny La Rue is appearing at his local theatre in the early 1970s Anthony decides to see the show. However, he himself feels compelled to go dressed as a woman. Inexperienced in the art of make-up and dress sense, he looks very obviously a young man dressed as a woman. He is apprehended by the police. His family is informed and he is told that unless he agrees to see a psychiatrist he will be charged with conduct likely to cause a breach of the peace. His parents are appalled. He is devastated by the humiliation of the events and agrees to undergo a course of aversion therapy to 'cure' him of his 'illness'. Electrodes are attached to his body, and he is shown slides of women's clothes and given concurrent electric shocks. This procedure is intended to 'cure' him of his 'sexual perversion'. It might have done, but it didn't. Later, he tells me he only went through with the treatment in order to avoid the legal proceedings.

Some fifteen years later, I meet Maria at a transvestite/transsexual support group meeting. She appears feminine and convincing as a woman, from a distance. She feels flattered and 'feminine' when I offer her my chair. Her most recent relationship has gone the same way as several of the others. After living for a while with a woman, Maria is unable to keep her envy of the woman at bay. She wants to dress in her clothes, behave as she does, have her interests, and so on. She is now at the point of visiting a Consultant Psychiatrist. She is not sure what she wants. Cross-dressing still sexually arouses Maria. She fears that the psychiatrist will give her short shrift and dismiss her as a 'fetishistic transvestite' (a term taken from the medical literature and in regular use at the support group). She is not sure how persistent her 'transsexual' feelings are. She is euphoric when she is given forty-five minutes of the psychiatrist's time. Within a couple of visits, she is re-defining herself, is on a course of hormone treatment and is seeing herself with widening options for the future. My research notes, taken a number of months after the initial interview with the psychiatrist, give the flavour of the re-negotiation of meanings as a result of the interaction between various private and public meanings attached to Maria's feelings and actions. Out-comes at this stage remain uncertain.

Researcher: You see yourself as a transsexual now, then?
Maria: (Laughs) Well I'm taking hormones now; that's one way of defining a transsexual.
R: I rather got the impression you saw yourself as TV (transvestite) before?
M: There are two sorts of transsexual. There are those like Helen, who see their appendage as an accident. They see themselves as women, who have some mistake as regards their bodies. And then there are

21

the other sort, who know that they are men, but still want to be women.

R: Isn't that a bit odd? Going through the change, but still thinking you're male?

M: Well, I don't know. As I keep on with this, I find that I'm like stripping away what I have learned in being male. It's like peeling away the layers of an onion.

R: So, what is underneath?

M: I don't know, but I'm finding out. All I can say is that whenever I act the female role, I feel more myself. It might be that underneath all the layers is a female identity.

As I write now, some ten years later, Maria is a celebrated and successful entertainer. She set about building her new career with the same determination as she had built her previous career as a man. Some know her as a transsexual, some know her only as the female entertainer she appears to be. She, herself, now identifies as a post-operative transsexual and 'new woman'.

Part II

MAINLY THEORY

2

A REVIEW OF THE LITERATURE FROM THE STANDPOINT OF GROUNDED THEORY

As I have intimated in Chapter 1, cross-dressing and sex-changing in contemporary advanced industrialised societies are variously considered as shocking: a media spectacle of prurient and endless fascination; a medical problem to be understood, managed and treated; and an alternative way of life for a misunderstood minority, who are often increasingly concerned to proselytise, and to politicise their predicament.

Each aspect has generated its own literature – in terms of curiosity and sensationalism in the popular press (Ekins 1990c; 1992a; King 1996a); in terms of specialist texts on 'transvestism', 'transsexuality' and 'gender dysphoria' in the psychiatric-psychological-medical arena (Benjamin 1966; Green and Money 1969; Steiner 1985; Docter 1988, Bockting and Coleman 1992); and in terms of world-wide information networks for cross-dressers and sex-changers themselves (Kelly 1987–90; Neil 1987–93; Renaissance Education Association 1987–96). Infrequently, social scientists have attended to the area, most typically from the specialist standpoints of ethnomethodology (Garfinkel 1967; Kessler and McKenna 1978; Hirschauer 1996), the sociology of deviance (Talamini 1982; Sagarin 1969; Feinbloom 1976), the medical-isation of gender roles (Raymond 1980; Billings and Urban 1982), or feminism (Woodhouse 1989). Studies such as these have invariably underplayed the erotic, in both its subjective and social features. Only Lewins (1995) and the occasional serious piece of journalism in the quality press have attempted to bridge the gap between the disparate and discrete literatures.

From a quite different standpoint, the phenomenon dubbed 'gender bending' in the 1980s focused attention on cross-dressing as an aspect of youth style (McGoldrick 1985). Further, a more widespread questioning of gender role stereotypes has led many commentators to touch on 'transsexuals' and 'transvestites' as part of a general consideration of contemporary gender options. These writers suggest that cross-dressers and sex-changers may have a lot to teach us all, about the most fundamental questions of our natures, as being variously sexed and gendered. More recently, these issues have been taken up by cultural and queer theorists (Epstein and Straub 1991; Garber 1992; Kroker and Kroker 1993; Whittle 1996). Garber (1992), particularly, is important in indicating the ubiquity of cross-dressing phenomena, from the standpoint of cultural criticism. Such studies, for the most part, however, remain at the level of textual analysis and evidence a lack of intimate and wide-ranging knowledge of the experiences of cross-dressers and sex-changers themselves. As Anne (1993) puts it, in her review of Garber (1992):

> While mercifully free of the near paranoia towards TVs and TSs which afflicts so many American feminists, there's no clear evidence that she has met any in the flesh. To judge from her text, the nearest she's come is in watching Donahue and his peers on US network television and reading the odd TV group magazine.
>
> Predictably, the weakest parts of the book are those in which she tries to deal with non-literary evidence and get closer to what makes TVs and TSs tick in 'real life'; these come out as a clotted mix of psychological and literary criticism jargon, quoting quite uncritically the rather odd views of a so-called psychological 'expert'.
>
> (Anne 1993)

Stein and Plummer (1994: 184 and n. 10) make much the same point about queer theory:

> There is a dangerous tendency for the new queer theorists to ignore 'real' queer life as it is materially experienced ... while they play with the free-floating signifiers of texts ... Resolutely and unapologetically laden with theoretical jargon, it limits its audience to only the most theory-literate.

What remains to be addressed, then, is a consideration of cross-dressing and sex-changing from the standpoint of a *systematic* and *empirical* exploration of the interrelations between sex, sexuality and gender. This is a matter of fundamental importance for the social sciences and its neglect speaks volumes about the underdeveloped state of the area. Certainly, if any sociology of sex, sexuality and gender is to be based upon firm foundations, we need to know much more about the process whereby identities, selves and objects become variously and with varying degrees of interconnectedness sexed, sexualised and gendered (both inside and outside of the specific area of cross-dressing and sex-changing).

Feminist writers have begun to take female cross-dressing more seriously, thereby appropriating another domain for feminist scholarship (Dekker and van de Pol 1989; Devor 1989; Wheelwright 1989; Epstein and Straub 1991). Male cross-dressing and sex-changing, however, when not ignored as is usually the case in the serious literature, remains largely either medicalised or ghettoised, notwithstanding the growth of men's studies and contemporary treatments of masculinity (Berger and Watson 1995; Cornwall and Lindisfarne 1994).

Arguably, the reason for the neglect is that the literature lacks a serious, non-medicalised treatment of cross-dressers and sex-changers based on extensive and first-hand knowledge of informants, considered as equals and co-workers, as they relate over time and place with their families, friends and associates in the full range of domestic, leisure, work, medical and subcultural settings. It is the purpose of this study to rectify this gap in the literature.

It is instructive to distinguish the grounded theory approach from others used in the psychiatric and social scientific literature. The following review will serve both as a summary of the cognate work and an introduction to the research methodology which generated this study.

THE MEDICAL MODEL AND THE APPROACH FROM GROUNDED THEORY

The vast majority of work in the area follows 'The Medical Model' (Kando 1973: 139–40). Collection of biographical and in-depth psychological data is followed by classification, diagnosis and etiological theorising.

Hirschfeld (1910) collected case histories and then coined the term 'transvestite' for cross-dressers, distinguishing them from homosexuals. He stressed that transvestites most typically are heterosexual in overt object choice, though may be homosexual, bisexual, monosexual or asexual. Benjamin (1966) popularised the term 'transsexual' for sex-changers, distinguished transsexuals from transvestites, and obtained hormonal and surgical intervention for them. Person and Ovesey (1974a; 1974b) distinguished primary and secondary transsexuals. Primary transsexuals are seen to have a gender identity at variance with biology from an early age; secondary transsexuals are seen to take a transsexual route after following a career path (Buckner 1970) more typically associated with transvestites who are seen to cross-dress for sexual gratification or to achieve pleasure associated with the adoption of the opposite gender role. Contemporary emphasis on the incongruent gender identity of transsexuals is marked by the increasing use of the term 'gender dysphoria' to refer to a profound sense of unease or discomfort about one's identity as a male or female which is felt to be in opposition to one's physical sex (Gender Trust, UK 1990: 2). Koranyi (1980: 29–30) gives the flavour:

While the typical fetishist, transvestite or male homosexual will never give up his pleasure-providing sexual organ, the transsexual, the rare atypical transvestite and the effeminate passive homosexual will gladly exchange his usually low sexual potency for the identification pleasure he gains by the complete surgical transformation. Differentiation within that group of people is sometimes a futile academic exercise, which is why the term *gender dysphoria* (Stoller, 1973; Fisk, 1974), an intense displeasure with one's own physical and sexual role, was introduced.

27

Writers and practitioners within the medical model most typically work within biological or psychological perspectives already developed to explain the development of gender identity and sex role more generally. Thus the 'pathology' is understood and explained in terms of a favoured biologic, psycho-analytic, social learning or cognitive developmental theory (Kessler and McKenna 1978: 42–111), with the most prolific writers frequently developing their own particular combination of these traditions (Green 1974; 1987; Money and Ehrhardt 1972; Stoller 1968; 1985).

From the grounded theory perspective, three main points need highlighting. In the first place, the definitions of the situation (Thomas 1923: 14) of cross-dressers and sex-changers themselves (member definitions) are never explored as social constructions of reality (Berger and Luckmann 1966) with their own legitimacy. In particular, the focus on doctor–patient encounters precludes systematic exploration of the social worlds of cross-dressers and sex-changers outside the clinic and consulting room. Second, the terms in which the 'pathology' is viewed tend to preclude serious attention being given to radically different formulations. Feminist writers, for instance, have described gender dissatisfaction in terms of sex-role oppression. Thus Raymond (1980: 9) writes:

> It is significant that there is no specialised or therapeutic vocabulary of *black dissatisfaction, black discomfort*, or *black dysphoria* that have been institutionalised in black identity clinics. Likewise, it would be rather difficult and somewhat humorous to talk about *sex-role oppression clinics*. What the word *gender* (when used in conjunction with *gender dissatisfaction, gender discomfort* or *gender dysphoria*) ultimately achieves is a classification of sex-role oppression as a therapeutic problem, amenable to therapeutic solutions.

Third, and most fundamentally, writers and practitioners working within the medical model inevitably reify existing 'taken for granted', 'common-sense' notions of sex and gender role appropriate behaviour (Berger and Luckmann 1966; Kessler and McKenna 1978). It is not so much that they are unaware of sex and gender role stereotyping, rather that their focus of concern on the patient's well-being precludes systematic consideration of their own presuppositions (Greenson 1966).

Following a grounded theory methodology inevitably leads to a grounded exploration of these gaps in the medical model. Emergents from doctor–patient encounters are seen as just one species of data amongst others. The researcher using the grounded theory procedures of 'theoretical sampling' and 'constant comparisons' (Glaser 1978: 36–54) is inevitably led to research cross-dressers and sex-changers as they make sense of their situations in work, family, medical and member settings. S/he is soon confronted with the complex ways in which various expert, member and common-sense meanings interrelate. Further, s/he is led to consider alternative formulations of different experts, members and lay folk in terms of their settings, interests and presuppositions.

CLASSICAL VARIABLE ANALYSIS AND THE APPROACH FROM GROUNDED THEORY

Classical variable analysis is the sociological approach which is most compatible with the medical model in terms of many of its underlying presuppositions. It tends to presuppose the legitimacy of existing sex and gender roles. The 'what it is' of cross-dressing and sex-changing is largely taken for granted. There is the same tendency to conflate the rule-violating behaviour with the people who break the rules (Rubington and Weinberg 1973: 1–10). At the crudest level, work within this tradition simply lists some of the variables associated with the 'condition' (Hoenig, Kenna and Youd 1970). More usually, it is endeavouring to discover regularities in the patterning of stimuli-and-response that suggest a causal relationship (Wålinder 1967). More sophisticated approaches within this tradition start off with some sociological paradigm, deduce formal hypotheses from it and then test them (Kando 1973: 140–2).

From the perspective of grounded theory the weaknesses of such approaches are many. In addition to the problems raised concerning the medical model, the following points might be made. The variables chosen are divorced from context. Their selection frequently has its origins in the presuppositions of the researcher, not the data. The meanings of the variables are rendered static. The nature of the relationships between variables is not specified. In this sense nothing is understood or explained (Blumer 1956). Furthermore, the hypothesis testing version deduces its hypotheses not from the data, but from the paradigm, and in consequence, closes enquiry. Kando, who has researched sex-changers extensively using a variety of perspectives writes:

> The problem with this procedure is that, since the paradigm only allows for those articulations which the conceptual framework permits, therefore a wide variety of findings is totally beyond its vision. While earlier in the development of the current body of sociological knowledge this paradigm may have provided the necessary articulations to lead researchers in constructive research, an increasing number of sociologists experience it as an obstacle to the open-minded approach to new phenomena, the possible discovery of new processes and the creative formulation of new questions and new sociological interpretations of behaviour.
>
> (Kando 1973: 141)

Significantly, Kando found classical variable analysis to be particularly inappropriate in the understanding and explanation of sex-changing.

THE CRITICAL TRADITION AND THE APPROACH FROM GROUNDED THEORY

The critical tradition in social theory sees social science as coterminous with ethics and social philosophy (Bernstein 1976). Through the method of ideology-critique, it examines the ideological basis and presuppositions of both scientific and common-sense thought (Billings and Urban 1982). Contemporary work on cross-dressing and sex-changing within this tradition most frequently has a radical feminist tone (Birrell and Cole 1990). The particular strength of the approach lies in its ability to reveal societal stereotypes as regards what counts as masculine and feminine and how these are linked with patriarchy, the exploitation of women and the restriction of human possibility more generally. Raymond's (1980) 'transsexual empire' gives the flavour. The possibilities of transsexualism are rooted in sex and gender role stereotyping, she argues, but its actuality is the creation of the 'transsexers': the empire of male medics and paramedics who steer the individual through the change. A trinity of men are seen to dominate the field, namely, Money, Green and Stoller. The operation is only performed if the client can prove that he can 'pass' as a woman. It is 'a male supremacist obscenity' (Raymond 1980).

This approach has considerable merit from the standpoint of grounded theory. Common-sense and scientific definitions of sex and gender role appropriate behaviour are inevitably rendered problematic (Seeley 1966) by the grounded theorist as s/he attempts to understand and explain competing constructions of reality in the area. In this regard the critical tradition marks a considerable sociological advance on the medical model and classical variable analysis. Furthermore, the tradition provides a clear articulation of a radically distinct definition of the situation which constitutes valuable data in its own right. However, as grounded theory and as social science, it is defective. It is a version of 'grand' theory which provides a version of data as filtered through an imposed theoretical framework. In the language of grounded theory, it does not 'fit and work' adequately (Glaser and Strauss 1967b: 10–11). In particular, the theory is not readily modifiable. Raymond's brief treatment of female to male sex-changers is revealing:

> The female-to-constructed-male transsexual is the *token* that saves face for the male 'transsexual empire'. She is the buffer zone who can be used to promote the universalist argument that transsexualism is a supposed 'human' problem, not uniquely restricted to men. She is the living 'proof' that some women supposedly want the same thing. However, 'proof' wanes when it is observed that women were not the original nor are they the present agents of the process. Nor are the stereotypes of masculinity that a female-to-constructed-male transsexual incarnates products of a female-directed culture. Rather women have been assimilated into the transsexual world, as women are assimilated into other

male-defined worlds, institutions, and roles, that is, on men's terms, and thus as tokens.

(Raymond 1980: 27)

For grounded theory, since most of the categories are generated directly from the data, the criteria of fit is automatically met and does not constitute an unsatisfactory struggle of half fits (Glaser 1978: 4).

Significantly, others working within the critical tradition see cross-dressers and sex-changers very differently from Raymond. To Brake (1976), for example, they are mould-breaking sexual radicals with revolutionary potential. Grounded theory enables a detailed look at the features of cross-dressing and sex-changing that provide evidence for these alternative formulations. 'Categories are not precious, just captivating. The analyst should readily modify them as successive data may demand. The analyst's goal is to ground the fit of categories as close as he can' (Glaser 1978: 4).

THE INTERACTIONIST TRADITION, ETHNOMETHODOLOGY AND THE APPROACH FROM GROUNDED THEORY

It is the interactionist tradition that looks most promising when the aim is the understanding and explanation of phenomena through detailed analysis of concrete empirical situations. I take this tradition to include those perspectives which focus on the emergence of meanings and social realities within social interaction. This definition would include historical analysis which seeks to show how social constructions have emerged and changed within social interaction over time (King 1981; Foucault 1979).

The place of grounded theory within this tradition can best be seen by placing it in the middle range of a continuum which moves from ethnography on the one hand to ethnomethodology on the other. The ethnographic approach relies heavily on description. Newton (1979) researches the world of female impersonators (male entertainers who cross-dress) using descriptive and unstructured methods to 'tell it as it is'. This is traditional anthropological field work in an urban setting. Certainly, it is not theory. For the grounded theorist it is not even adequate as preliminary work upon which to base subsequent theorising. Had Newton used the grounded theory procedures of theoretical sampling and constant comparisons she would have have been led into research settings outside the narrow world of the 'drag' artists and their audiences. This, in turn, would have led her to more sophisticated conceptualisations.

Similarly, it is noteworthy that interactionist subcultural studies of cross-dressers and sex-changers and their organisations provide little or no detail of the role of the erotic in either its subjective or social aspects (Sagarin 1969; Feinbloom 1976; Talamini 1982). Grounded theory data collection and sampling procedures so quickly and frequently lead into this domain that it is presumably only the a priori assumptions, preconceived problems or personal predilections of these writers that have led to its neglect in these studies.

In so far as grounded theory is generating theoretical categories which transcend particular examples of data, it can be seen as doing 'formal' sociology.[1] In this sense it is engaged in the same sort of activity as Simmel (Zerubavel 1980) and Goffman (1968). Goffman has discovered the 'form' of stigma situations which is operative whatever the particular 'content' of the stigma. However, Goffman does not provide us with an account of the method which leads us to the insight. It is difficult to know to what degree it is grounded and how (Glaser and Strauss 1967b: 139).

The differences with ethnomethodology are more marked. Grounded theory enables the exploration of a substantive area or set of problems having a direct reference and application to a substantive area in a way that ethnomethodology does not. Here, Garfinkel's study of the sex-changing Agnes is pertinent (Garfinkel 1967). Empirical work on Agnes illuminates the 'taken for granted' world of 'normals' as to common-sense constructions of sex and gender. Ethnomethodology studies 'doing gender' as an ongoing accomplishment (Kessler and McKenna 1978). This is well-grounded theory. However, following Heap and Roth (1973), I take the particular contribution of ethnomethodology to be its move away from a concern with trans-situational phenomena to the question of the phenomenon of transsituation-ality itself. Ethnomethodology's central problem is 'how *members* produce and sustain the sense of objective phenomena taken to exist outside the occasion where that sense is made collectively available' (Heap and Roth 1973: 364). For grounded theory, this takes us too far away from the empirical social worlds of cross-dressers and sex-changers themselves. Grounded theory will always emerge from empirical social worlds and be referable back to them in a way that enables explanation and prediction.

3

THE SOCIAL WORLDS
OF CROSS-DRESSING AND
SEX-CHANGING

For the sociologist and sociological social psychologist, all worlds are social worlds (Mead 1934; Winch 1958) whether private, imaginary (Caughey 1984) or public. Social worlds refer to a form of organisation which cannot be accurately delineated by spatial, territorial, formal or membership boundaries (Unruh 1980), though these may be important components of them. Centrally, their boundaries are determined by interaction and communication which transcend and cross over the more formal and traditional delineators of organisation such as behaviour systems, subcultures and social circles.

Social world analysts will be particularly sensitised to forms of communication, symbolisation and universes of discourse, but they will also examine those 'palpable matters' within the boundaries such as the various activities, memberships, sites, technologies and organisations typical of particular social worlds (Strauss 1978: 121). They will seek to map the social worlds themselves, and individual and group participation within them (Unruh 1980).

There are a number of published guides to the global worlds of cross-dressing and sex-changing which give something of the flavour of both their 'universes of discourse' and their 'palpable matters'. Some, like the *1995 Who's Who & Resource Guide to the Transgender Community*, focus on social world 'celebrities', 'groups' (136 in fourteen different countries) and 'businesses' which cater for cross-dressers and sex-changers. Others have a more specific focus, like the *Crossdresser's International Shopping Guide* (1995). Others, like *The Tranny Guide 1996: The World's Best International Listings Guide For Cross-Dressers and Their Friends*, cover a large range of 'palpable matters'. This latter publication, for instance, includes separate sections on 'Support Groups' (memberships and organisations), 'The Cyber-Tranny's Guide to the Internet' (technologies), 'Getting Out and About' (sites) and 'So You Wannabe in Pictures' (activities).

It is not my purpose to provide a detailed geography of these global worlds. Rather, in this chapter, I first outline what I term the 'social psychology of co-opting' engaged in by cross-dressers and sex-changers indicating how spaces and places are colonised in the service of that co-opting. This conceptualisation calls for an *extension* of existing formulations of social world analysis. I then detail the theoretical and methodological approaches which underlay my mapping of this co-option of social worlds. Finally, I describe my entrance into the various types of private and public worlds inhabited by male cross-dressers and sex-changers. It is left to Chapter 4 to consider the methodology of grounded theory that provides the framework for the more detailed grounded theory analysis that follows in Part III.

THE SOCIAL PSYCHOLOGY OF CO-OPTING

Social worlds of male cross-dressing and sex-changing arise whenever male cross-dressers and sex-changers co-opt the social worlds of females and their constituent objects. In doing so, they become 'male femalers' who are male femaling (see Chapter 4) within male femaling social worlds. These individual and collective male femaling worlds will be variously set within male, female, male/female and male femaling worlds.

Angie's account of SHE – the 'girl' within (Angie, 1991: 15) – provides a peculiarly sensitive illustration of the particular way in which individual male femalers co-opt objects from the world of women, and by virtue of doing so, come to inhabit a male femaling world. Two examples follow. In her first example, Angie comes to inhabit an entirely private, imaginary world set within and triggered by a conventional male/female world of work and employment. In her second example, she is between the worlds of work and home when another input from a female world triggers a male femaling world. In this case, her private world begins to become public.

> Imagine it, there I am in an important meeting, trying to make a very difficult technical point, and the customer's secretary comes in wearing a skirt just like hers (Angie's). She takes over instantly: no longer am I the technical boffin knowing all the fine nuances of my profession. I'm thinking about deniers and dancing, peplums and pleats, and I'm feeling decidedly uncomfortable in these great clod-hopping shoes. Worse still, I'm trying to make my point not now with forceful, manly gestures, but with ever-so-elegant hand movements that don't work without the accompanying red finger nails! I drag myself back to the real world, but the damage is done, she's here and that's it for a while . . . I'm not at my professional best until 'she' gives up and returns to her hiding place.
>
> It's not just at work. It can happen anywhere. I'm stuck in a jam . . . and in the flow of traffic this neat little Peugeot 205 creeps past me. I glance at the driver thinking that her hair looks nice. WHAM! Here she comes again. All of a sudden I'm trying to decide if that style would suit me, and if the colour isn't a shade too red for the girl in the Peugeot, but mightn't it look better on me. My hands slide from their normal firm grasp on the wheel, at ten-to-two just as in all the best driving

manuals, and they assume a sort of casual but ever-so-elegant grip that doesn't fit at all with the driver's appearance. I find myself pressing the search button on the radio, not content until I find some up-beat, decidedly dancing type music that's just her style. I'll just have to drive like her for a while.

In this second example, Angie's emergence is involuntary. Despite herself, Angie finds herself becoming and acting as a woman in a way that might have been recognised as such by observers. On other occasions, however, her male femaling will be variously deliberate, variously enacted and variously private or public.

Let us suppose that Angie's appearance led her to go home and spend the evening on her own, male femaling, before retiring to bed as 'Angie'. Here we would have an example of purely private male femaling within a privately co-opted and enacted male femaling world. On another occasion, she may go out to a local restaurant dressed as 'Angie' in the company of a male friend who knows of her enthusiasm for male femaling in 'straight' settings (male femaling within male/female worlds). She might have prepared for her restaurant evening by visiting her local beauty salon for 'private' treatments in an exclusively female world (male femaling within female worlds).

Alternatively, she may dress as 'Angie' and attend her local transvestite group in the company of other male femalers. This group hires a local hall for its exclusive use one evening a month (group participation in exclusively male femaling worlds). On another occasion she might join a group of cross-dressers and sex-changers who have colonised an enclave in a wine bar in a nearby city for their twice monthly meetings. The management of the wine bar directs the male femalers to the enclave and guides their other customers elsewhere (near exclusive male femaling world set within a loosely boundaried male/female world).

This group colonising of private, semi-private and public spaces and worlds will be variously exclusive, variously boundaried, variously extensive in space and place, and will be for varying periods at a time. It may range from an annual day-long river boat trip for male femalers, through occasional weekend 'private' functions for cross-dressers held at seaside hotels, to week-long 'Fantasia Fairs' held in a number of towns and cities in Europe and America. At these latter events, several hundred male femalers holiday in a welcoming male/female setting, and are enabled to cross-dress and go about their public male femaling with impunity. All such options may be open to Angie.

THEORY AND METHODOLOGY IN THE ANALYSIS OF SOCIAL WORLDS

Analysis of social worlds does, of course, presuppose a theoretical and methodological approach. My analysis is situated within three interrelated theoretical and methodological approaches: the sociology of knowledge as informed by symbolic interactionism; symbolic interactionist social world analysis; and grounded theory as a strategy for qualitative data collection and analysis (see Chapter 4).

G.H. Mead, symbolic interactionism and the sociology of knowledge

I began the research for this study in 1979, having just completed a study on the work of the American philosopher G.H. Mead (Ekins 1978). Although a philosopher by profession, Mead's major contribution to contemporary thought is as the founding father of symbolic interactionism, variously seen as a sociological social psychology and a methodology for doing sociology (Blumer 1969; Plummer 1991). In addition, there is contained within Mead's work an important incipient sociology of knowledge (McKinney 1955).

Symbolic interaction as a theoretical perspective on social life emphasises

> the meaningfulness of human life and action ... the pluralistic and conflictual nature of society, the relative openness of social life, the indeterminancy of social structure ... the cultural and social relativity of moral and social rules, and the socially constructed nature of the self.
> (Harré and Lamb 1986: 352)

As Blumer (1969) has detailed, symbolic interactionism rests on three basic premises. First, that human beings act towards things on the basis of the meanings the things have for them. Second, that the meaning of such things is derived from the social interaction that one has with one's fellows. And third, that these meanings are handled in, and modified through, an interpretive process used by the person dealing with the thing s/he encounters.

If the researcher is to take these assumptions and premises seriously, the task becomes not to uncover an intrinsic meaning in the social world. There is none. Rather the task is to trace the histories and consequences of the varieties of meanings that emerge from within social interaction. The researcher must account for a social world that is subjective symbolic reality, one that changes and is in process, and one that emerges within interaction. To do this any ethically justifiable research method will be used that enables the accessing of this emergence of meanings. This may include historical analysis which seeks to show how social constructions have emerged and changed within social interaction over time. It may also include analysis of the origins and consequences of particular meanings.

Specifically, the researcher asks a number of questions of the empirical world. How do informants define the situations in which they find themselves? How do they define their settings and themselves? What are the individual definitions? What are the group definitions? What is the process by which definitions develop and change? What is the relationship between the various definitions held by different informants? What is the relationship between informants' perspectives and their behaviour? (Bogdan and Taylor 1975: 84–5).

The initial phases of research entail what Blumer terms 'exploration'. Here the empirical social world is examined through a number of research procedures, particularly direct observation, field study, participant observation, case study, interviewing, use of life histories, use of letters and diaries, use of public documents, panel discussions and use of conversations. The researcher endeavours to develop as comprehensive and accurate a picture of the area of study as conditions allow. 'Exploration' is then followed by what Blumer terms 'inspection'. Here the researcher casts the problem in a theoretical form, unearths generic relations, sharpens the connative reference of his/her concepts and formulates theoretical propositions.

Obviously, researchers working within this framework do not approach the empirical social world as a *tabula rasa*, but if they are to avoid imposing their own particular version of reality on their subjects, they should enter the research setting with as few predetermined ideas as possible, and should be prepared to change those they already have, readily and frequently.

In addition to subscribing to the underlying premises and assumptions of the symbolic interactionist point of view, my entrance to the research arena was, of course, accompanied by the baggage of my personal and professional biography. My project grew out of previous studies in epistemology and sociology of knowledge. I was particularly sensitised to exploring the interrelations between what I had been calling 'member' knowledge, 'common-sense' knowledge and 'scientific' knowledge.

Unlike those perspectives which see the role of scientists as being to discover supposed 'truths' in a pre-ordained world, or which give primacy to 'scientific' knowledge over others, symbolic interactionists seek to uncover 'what counts as knowledge' to different individuals and groups, and to explore the complex interrelations between competing definitions, and their origins and consequences. They take very seriously the statement made by W.I. Thomas (1923: 14) that 'if men define situations as real they are real in their consequences'.

So viewed, symbolic interactionism is a perspective at the forefront of mainstream debates in contemporary social theory and methodology. In the late 1970s, Giddens identified the two major problems of social theory and methodology as being those of the double hermeneutic and of structuration. He argued that sociological research had to take on board the implications of these two fundamental problems if it was to follow what he called the 'new rules of sociological method' (Giddens 1976). I approached my own research arena, therefore, with an approach to symbolic interactionism which was set firmly within these two problems.

Symbolic interaction and the double hermeneutic

The double hermeneutic arises in social science because social science is concerned with pre-interpreted worlds, in which meaning frames are integral to their subject matter – what Giddens refers to as the inter-subjectivity of practical everyday life. The theories and provinces of meaning of social science (one hermeneutic) have to be linked to the pre-constituted worlds of its subject matter (another hermeneutic).

The linkage is highly complex in that it is multi-layered and multi-dimensional. The problems of social science emerge within social scientific perspectives which are themselves emergents from within pre-constituted worlds. But having emerged, they 'act back' on those pre-constituted worlds, so constituting new worlds, both of science and of practical social life. Furthermore, because social science cannot render problematic everything at the same time, there will always remain an unexplicated backdrop which subsequent investigators might make the object of their study, thus reconstituting the object of study and, hence, of social science and of the social world.

The problems that these issues create for the social sciences are immense. It is not just that there are alternative social scientific perspectives and alternative 'common-sense', 'taken for granted' worlds (Schutz 1967) which might become the object of study. If the knowledge claims and ethical responsibilities of social science are to be adequately considered we need to know which worlds are to be examined, and why. What is the effect of social scientific work carried out? What is the relationship between the alternative perspectives and their objects of study and the 'taken for granted' worlds within which all emerge and to which all must eventually return?

A simple example from the world of cross-dressing will illustrate.

In the early 1980s, Mr C. wrote to the advice page in the *TV* (television) *Times* thus:

> I am a single man of 25, and since my early teens I have found that I enjoy wearing women's clothes. I naturally feel confused and isolated, although I believe others share these feelings. I wonder if there is a support group or organisation that would understand my problem?

The advice given to Mr C. was as follows:

> You need neither be alone nor feel guilty. I receive tormented letters from both single and married men who feel this compulsion. A Clwyd reader wrote recently recommending the help he received from the Beaumont Society, Box 3084, London WC1N 3XX. There is also the Transvestite/Transsexual Support Group (UK), a charity which provides counselling, information, education, a journal, and social facilities for all members of the family. It also publishes a helpful booklet, 'Transvestism Within a Partnership of Marriage and Families' by

Yvonne Sinclair. For details, contact the group at 2 French Place, London E1 6JB, or telephone the helpline on 01–729–1466.

Here is a man who, finding himself feeling and acting in a manner deemed untoward within the provinces of meaning of his everyday life, feels his self and world to be under threat. Having a vague knowledge of others in his predicament, he seeks entry into a world where such untoward acts are understood.

Had this young man been a native of Samoa (Chapter 1; Haworth 1993), his feelings might well not have been perceived as untoward, which does, of course, indicate much about the construction of the everyday world of contemporary Britain.

Had this young man written the letter twenty-five years previously, he might well have been advised to see a psychiatrist to 'cure' him of his 'perversion'. Certainly, there would have been no support group to refer him to. Researchers sensitised to the workings of the double hermeneutic might take either of these 'facts' as points of departures for further investigation.

Let us, however, stay with Mr C. a little longer. Let us imagine he had first approached the Beaumont Society in the early 1980s. There he would have learned that if he said he was heterosexual, did not express a wish to engage in sexually explicit behaviour with other members, and was prepared to be discreet, then he would be made welcome. As likely as not, he would have been encouraged to express his 'femme self', to take on a 'femme name', to come to accept that he was a 'transvestite', that he had no need to feel guilty, and that there was no 'cure' available to him, nor need there be.

Secure in such advice he may no longer have felt confused or isolated and the matter may have rested there. He may, indeed, have come to feel superior to conventional men whom he viewed as being unable to express their feminine sides. In short, he would have been initiated into the meaning frames of a particular 'member' group. The meaning of his cross-dressing would have been reconstituted. He would have come to define himself as a 'transvestite'. As likely as not, he would have been further initiated into the arts and crafts of what Beaumont Society members considered to be 'feminine', and the appropriate thoughts, feelings and behaviour for a male 'transvestite'.

However, had our Mr C. contacted another group prominent in the 1980s – the TV/TS Support Group, London – a rather different set of meanings would have been available to him. There he would have learned that all 'transvestites', 'transsexuals', wives, girlfriends and boyfriends were welcomed (Sinclair 1984: 29). Also welcomed were those who were seeking transvestites and transsexuals as potential sexual partners. He might have found himself being chatted up and propositioned. He might have found himself enjoying the experience and embarking upon a very different course from a Beaumont Society member.

But where do these terms 'transvestite' and 'transsexual' come from? What is the effect of such 'namings'? The researcher sensitised to the ramifications of the double hermeneutic would be led to explore the origins and histories of such terminology. S/he would learn that their effect has been to demarcate conditions and types (King 1981). S/he would learn that there is controversy as to whether they mark conditions discovered or invented (King 1984); that their availability and adoption can have profound effects on individual identities and public perceptions and reactions; that whatever the view taken of the role of 'experts' – psychiatrists, sexologists and so on – the cross-dresser and sex-changer frequently exists in an umbilical relation with them (Ekins 1993). The researcher would learn that the availability of the terms can both constrain and enable (Plummer, 1981). Also, s/he would learn that in the period immediately prior to the rise of sexology in the late nineteenth century, cross-dressing was commonly understood as a harmless eccentricity, or as a source of innocent pleasure; that connotations of sexual perversion were not present (Farrer 1987); that at such times, there was no need for support groups to legitimise a stigmatised activity – it was not particularly stigmatised; that the possibility of an identity built around the activity did not arise (Weeks 1981) and so on.

These problems of the double hermeneutic are centrally concerned with problems of knowledge – of ontology, epistemology and methodology, but what of the problem of structuration?

Symbolic interaction and the problem of structuration

For Giddens, the problem of structuration refers to the fact that social structures and systems both reproduce and change over time. From the standpoint of both Giddens and symbolic interactionism, it is individuals who 'carry' social structures within social systems. All are emergents from within ongoing social interaction, all are ineluctably social, but it is individuals as the 'carriers' of social structures and social systems who are the agents of social reproduction and change.

The empirical task then becomes to plot these reproductions and changes. The researcher is sensitised to examining how particular theories and practices concerning cross-dressing and sex-changing participate in the structuration of society; to an examination of whether and how they reproduce or change the existing arrangements between the sexes.

The large portion of the subcultural literature which seeks to educate male cross-dressers and sex-changers in the art and technology of 'passing' – of appearing in public as a woman and being taken as one – is indicative of the way male femaling might be seen as reinforcing gender role stereotypes, thereby reproducing rather than changing the existing arrangements between the sexes.

Take, for instance, these selections from 'Your Attitude is Everything' (Fry 1993) which focus on private feelings and gendered presentations of self in public places. They can be seen as reinforcing particular stereotypes which correspondingly reproduce existing structures.

Those who want to go to public places and not be detected have to learn how to fit in. *Attitude* has to do with how comfortable you feel with yourself. It is very possible to spend hours selecting an outfit, dressing, doing make-up, and preening in general. When you are all done you are still not comfortable with yourself. There is always a reason . . .

There are many things that may cause this feeling. You might be wearing your favourite outfit, but you know in your heart it does not fit properly. . . The problem could be as small as you have the wrong type or color purse, shoes, jacket, or numerous other worrisome things. Your hair might not be just the way you like it. Whatever gives you the feeling that makes you uncomfortable should be searched out and dealt with . . .

At all times, you must be acutely aware of everything you do. Walking, sitting, gestures with your body, head and hands are all things which must be studied from females. Make sure the person you are studying acts feminine. Many ladies act like truck drivers: they are not good subjects for you to learn from. Thank goodness many women prefer to be ladies.

I sometimes dress and go to the mall just to study the women. I will sit and watch them and I get very comfortable. Many of the women do not take care of themselves; in fact it is a sin how they let themselves go. I select the ones I feel I should be watching and study them closely, and sometimes I will even follow the really feminine ladies for a while just to emulate them . . .

Learn to smile and nod your head gently . . . Act self-assured. Inspect whatever you are holding, check in your purse, look busy . . . When you walk take small steps. Keep your head up. Smile at people who look at you – don't ever look away. Never swing your arms close to your hips: ladies swing them out four to six inches. When you go to sit be very sure of how you will do it before you reach the chair. Always keep your legs or ankles crossed while sitting. Getting up properly from your chair is almost as important as sitting down . . .

I could go on and on about this subject, but if you just remember the word *attitude*; it can make you feel as good or better than most of the females around you.

Compare this with the phenomenon of 'gender fuck'. 'Some call it "Spit Drag", others call it "Half Drag", and still others call it a form of insanity. See what happens when the act of crossdressing becomes a personal, social or political statement' ('Genderfuck', *TV Times* 2: 18). Proponents of 'gender fuck' deliberately mix masculine and feminine gendered presentations of self in an attempt to subvert the present arrangement between the sexes.

Proponents of 'gender fuck' might walk down the street with a dress on, despite the fact that they may be wearing a beard and combat boots. Another type of 'gender fuck' involves the person wearing make-up along with his traditional male clothing. The combinations are endless. It is a way of stating 'I am both male and female, and there is no need for me to be only one or the other. I reject society's demand that I dress in a manner dictated by my genitals' (ibid.).

So much for the theoretical and methodological position underlying my entrance into the research arena. How did I actually enter that arena and gain access to its various sub-worlds?

ENTERING THE SOCIAL WORLDS OF MALE CROSS-DRESSING AND SEX-CHANGING

I penetrated the worlds of cross-dressing and sex-changing through three access points: I met individual cross-dressers and sex-changers; attended member support group meetings; and frequented drag bars and attended drag balls. Contacts made in these respectively private, semi-private and public settings rapidly snowballed until I was soon entering the full range of subcultural settings: private parties, wine bar socials, drag balls and 'transvestite' weekends held at various hotels. I was also concerned to follow cross-dressers and sex-changers in the full range of their private, semi-private and public interactions, both those related to cross-dressing and sex-changing, and those not.

Cross-dressers need female clothes and the paraphernalia of femininity. Many seek various medical, para-medical and cosmetic interventions. I accompanied selected informants when clothes shopping. Where possible I would directly observe sessions of electrolysis, speech therapy, deportment, wig fittings and so on.

Where factors of privacy predominated, such as in most psychiatric consultations or in major surgical operations, I would accompany selected informants to the treatment and re-join them for periods immediately after it. I obtained access to contact magazine and erotica networks, interviewed many participants in these networks and, as Director of the Trans-Gender Archive, had access to a large collection of the private correspondence of cross-dressers and sex-changers participating in these networks. I also accompanied cross-dressers and sex-changers in their interactions with their families and friends at home and at work.

The story began in January 1979 when I responded to an advertisement placed in the London magazine *Time Out* by someone who advertised herself as an intelligent, sensitive 'transsexual' who was seeking to meet people of both sexes.

I learned a lot from Julia, very quickly. She had just ended a relationship with a boyfriend and the windscreen of her large Audi car still had her and her boyfriend's name emblazoned on the sun visor, as was fashionable amongst young couples at that time. I had arranged to meet her in a pub car park. She was pre-operative and had just begun to go 'full time' – to dress and live as a woman all of the time – in order amongst other things, to fulfil 'the two year rule' that her gender identity clinic required before they would refer her for surgery. She had previously managed a restaurant, and in her androgynous state had been the butt of cruel words and playful pranks of the local boys who hung about the streets around her workplace.

Julia was frankly amazed by how she had been able to pass as a woman, once she began to dress as one. Shortly after making the transition she had attended an office party and was surprised to have been chatted up by a prospective male partner, who seemingly had no suspicions whatsoever of her 'transsexual' state. I, too, found her convincing as a woman. We got on well together. For the most part I related to her as a woman, and very soon she was introducing me to her friends. When she learned of my particular research interests she soon introduced me to her friend Carrie, who in a short while became my second key informant.

Carrie, at that time, was committee member, editor and librarian of the first and most well established support group for transsexuals in Great Britain, named SHAFT (The Self Help Association for Transsexuals). SHAFT had been established by Judy Cousins in 1980 and at the time of my meeting with Carrie had some 100 members. I soon gained access to the group, its workings and its literature. Indeed, my contact with Carrie and SHAFT eventually led to the establishment of the Trans-Gender Archive at the University of Ulster. It was initially established in conjunction with SHAFT who made a foundation deposit. For several years – after Carrie had retired from the support group scene, to live with her partner as man and wife in a community which knew nothing of her transsexuality – I took her place on the committee as the SHAFT librarian.

We remained good friends for many years, and I value the opportunity she gave to me to use her as a sounding board for my developing ideas in the early years of my research. I visited her in the period immediately following her sex-re-assignment surgery. We spent several evenings together out and about in London. There was no question of her being seen by casual observers and acquaintances as other than the woman she felt herself to be.

My entry to the social worlds of male femaling continued with attendance at drag pubs and clubs, soon making the acquaintance of Caroline, my third key informant. Caroline was a celebrated drag artist on the London drag circuit. Through her I was introduced to the major drag entertainers and to the off-stage scene of these female impersonators who cross-dress to entertain. She provided a striking contrast to both Julia and Carrie. While they were both educated middle-class professionals well versed in the literature of 'transsexualism' and happy to talk about it, the love of Caroline's life was stage dancing. She referred to herself as 'a change', occasionally, but for the most part liked to talk of her developing career as a female dancer. She worked as a chorus-girl well before her re-assignment surgery, a fact which bore striking testimony to her 'natural' femininity.

From time to time I would strike up a particular rapport with various frequenters of the drag scene, which led me to attend drag balls regularly, to participate in the preparations for the various 'Miss Drag Queen' contests, and the after hours activities of the various participants. In terms of numbers, this scene is undoubtedly predominantly homosexual. However, the scene has a major significance to many cross-dressers and sex-changers of all sexual orientations. It provides a semi-public focus where cross-dressers can learn their art, meet friends, and generally interact in a non-threatening setting. The tendency is for different groupings to attend the same functions, and interact in cliques, or for individuals to attend and remain, for the most part, alone. In particular, I attended the London Porchester Hall Balls during the period so vividly depicted in Kelly (1996). At such public events, I made it my business to remain a 'stranger' (Simmel 1908; Schutz 1944) to all individuals and groupings, being neither assimilated by any particular group or being seen to have any special alignment with any particular individual.

My next step was to contact the major 'transvestite' groupings. Here my collaboration with members of the Beaumont Society was particularly valuable.

Through the Beaumont Society I gained admittance to the wine bar circuit which was very active at the time. This led on to invitations to attend various other private functions held at various venues. A particular highlight was the annual Beaumont Society weekend, held in various seaside resorts. This provided the members of this very security conscious society with the opportunity to cross-dress for two full days and nights, in the company of other members, their wives and partners. It provided me with an invaluable opportunity to gain access to transvestites from all over the United Kingdom. I soon set up a network which enabled me to travel the length and breadth of the United Kingdom meeting, observing and interviewing Beaumont Society members in their various activities and settings. While for most, their cross-dressing was a well-kept secret from their families, I was nevertheless granted access to a number of family circles of members whose families knew of the cross-dressing and of the Beaumont Society and were prepared to tolerate it in varying degrees.

The Beaumont Society is but one national organisation in an international network stemming from Virginia Prince's Foundation for Full Personality Expression (King 1993: 145–8). Chapter 7 considers the Society in terms of its group functions. In the present context, however, it is noteworthy that because it is the most 'respectable' and security conscious of all the cross-dressing and sex-changing groupings, the feeling seems to be that anyone vetted by the Beaumont can be trusted in more or less any setting. This was a great help to me.

By 1985, I had earned enough respect in the cross-dressing and sex-changing community to be appointed as 'adviser' in various legal cases concerning transsexuals before the European Court of Human Rights (Ekins 1986; Burgess and Ekins 1986a; 1986b). My role was that of researcher for solicitors who needed assistance in uncovering legal precedents, expert opinions and so on. Such a role provided me with valuable opportunities to collect material on medical and legal formulations of cross-dressing and sex-changing, as well as opportunities to observe day-to-day interactions between members of the legal profession and cross-dressers and sex-changers. It also enabled me to consolidate my contacts with various medical and para-medical personnel.

As I worked on various different aspects of cross-dressing and sex-changing, I soon found that I had to set about getting the material more or less from scratch. So, for example, working on the *Mark Rees* case (Rees 1984), in Strasbourg, I had to obtain legal precedents and so forth, more or less one by one. Again, it seemed extraordinary that virtually no one in the transgender community was keeping any systematic recordings of even their own press or television coverage. Typically, many cross-dressers and sex-changers would destroy or keep very private their own material, while the academics and clinicians would restrict themselves to highly specialised material. There seemed to be a need for somebody to collect as much material as possible, and seek to make it available to all.

It was in this context that I established the Trans-Gender Archive, in 1986. The Archive received a steady stream of deposits from the outset. Several prominent transsexuals deposited their personal collections with the Archive early on, most notably Adèle Anderson of *Fascinating Aïda* and Terri (formerly Rachael) Webb. Invaluable life history material came in from all over the world. Worthy of special note, perhaps, is the collection of private correspondence between cross-dressers and sex-changers who became intimate following networking through the personal columns of contact magazines (see Chapter 8). Also, a number of male femaling telephone sex-line operators kindly gave me copying access to their many hundreds of pre-recorded tapes (see Chapter 6). Individuals and groups visit the Archive from time to time. Frequently, these visits have led to life-long informants. I would single out Bruce Laker/Phaedra Kelly (see Chapter 9) and Peter Farrer (Ekins 1992b), particularly. Several others, who use a variety of different pseudonyms in different contexts, will know who they are.

Although no satisfactory evidence is ever cited in the literature, it is generally estimated that 1–3 per cent of all males are cross-dressers (Ellis and Abarnel 1961). The well-researched *Just Like a Woman* (1992), puts the figure rather higher. This recent film concluded with the telling end title: 'It's estimated that one man in every twenty feels the need to dress up in women's clothes. You may be sitting next to him'.

We may suppose that the vast majority of these male femalers come to terms with their cross-dressing in their various ways without contact with medical men or support groups, and without revealing their male femaling to anyone. Of necessity, I have had to infer knowledge of the feelings, thoughts and activities of these totally private and isolated individuals. I have done so from information gleaned from those who retrospectively comment upon their time in the cross-dressing and sex-changing closet; from those who confide only in written form, or on telephone lines; and from the published reports of therapists who are privy to the private cross-dressing and sex-changing inclinations of their patients.

None the less, I am satisfied that I have accessed all the major types of male femaling worlds – both public and private – within what is increasingly referred to as the 'transgender community' (Roberts, 1995). It remains to detail the methodology I adopted to guide my access and sampling and order my 'findings', and it is to this I now turn.

4

MALE FEMALING, MASKED AWARENESS CONTEXTS AND THE METHODOLOGY OF GROUNDED THEORY

This final chapter of Part II outlines the particular use this study makes of the methodology of grounded theory and provides the framework for the more detailed grounded theory work that follows in Part III. It introduces the basic social process of 'male femaling' and its attendant sub-processes – those of 'displaying', 'disclosing', 'passing', 'reading' and 'pretending'. It introduces the social structural unit of the 'masked awareness context' and sets forth its importance as a 'near core' social structural process within which male femaling is played out. The sub-units of the masked awareness context – those of 'private', 'closed', 'open', 'suspicion' and 'pretence' masked awareness contexts – are explained with reference to a number of illustrative vignettes. Finally, the chapter returns to the basic social process of male femaling and delineates its major modes before introducing the phased ideal-typical male femaling career path which forms the organising principle of the subsequent 'mainly practice' chapters.

THE METHODOLOGY OF GROUNDED THEORY

Grounded theory is a methodology for the simultaneous collection, coding and analysis of data. It is a methodology widely written about, though rather less often used. The methodology was originally set forth in Glaser and Strauss (1967b), before being expanded in rather different directions, by Glaser (1978) and by Strauss (1987). Strauss and Corbin (1990) set forth detailed procedures to be followed by grounded theorists. Glaser (1992) detailed how far Strauss and Corbin (1990) had moved from the fundamental principles of traditional grounded theory. Glaser then published three compilations of previously unpublished and published material with the aim of setting grounded theorists back on the track of traditional grounded theory (Glaser 1993; 1994; 1995). In essence, his argument was that Strauss and Corbin had moved the method into the area of 'forced, full, conceptual description', as opposed to emergent grounded theory.

It is undoubtedly the case that many writers use the name of 'grounded theory' with the main purpose of legitimating their qualitative studies. Many make no attempt to seriously follow grounded theory procedures, either of the Strauss and Corbin variety, or of the Glaser variety. Other writers find it suits their purposes to use grounded theory for basic taxonomy development, focused conceptual development, and 'cycles of interpretation' (Henwood and Pidgeon 1995), or other abbreviated uses of the method. Rather few writers have written monographs – as opposed to short papers – using the methodology of grounded with the depth and rigour of Glaser and Strauss themselves.

Inevitably, perhaps, each researcher who adopts the approach is likely to develop his or her own variation of technique (Charmaz 1983). My own approach is most influenced by Glaser (1978). In that book, Glaser emphasises the fact that 'The goal of grounded theory is to generate a theory that accounts for a pattern of behaviour which is relevant and problematic for those involved. The goal is not voluminous description, nor clever verification' (Glaser 1978: 93).

Glaser delineates how the researcher generates substantive codes from the data which conceptualise the empirical substance of the research area; how s/he then generates theoretical codes in order to conceptualise how the substantive codes may relate to each other as hypotheses to be integrated into the theory (Glaser 1978: 55); and how both are then subsumed under a small number of core categories which have the greatest explanatory power.

Of particular importance to Glaser is the value of conceptualising codes and categories in terms of what he calls 'basic social processes' – a concept developed further in Bigus, Hadden and Glaser (1982). Basic social processes are those staged, patterned, pervasive and fundamental social processes in the research domain which enable maximum explanatory grip to be obtained on the data (Glaser 1978: 93–115). The basic social process in the research domain is the process that continually resolves the main concern of the subjects studied. To access it, the researcher asks the question: what is the chief concern or problem of the people in the substantive area, and what accounts for most of the variation in processing that problem?

MALE FEMALING AS A BASIC SOCIAL PROCESS

After a couple of years of simultaneous data collection, coding and analysis, I found it increasingly helpful to conceptualise male cross-dressing and sex-changing in terms of 'male femaling' viewed as a basic social process. Male cross-dressers and sex-changers are genetic males who 'female' in various ways, variously adopting what they take to be the thoughts, feelings, attitudes, behaviours, accoutrements and attributes of genetic females.

I found that the sub-processes of 'displaying', 'disclosing', 'passing', 'reading' and 'pretending' accounted for the variation in processing the main concern. Male femalers wish to 'display' their femaling. When they do so they are 'displaying' – a major 'near core' variable of male femaling. In doing so, they confront a range of problems which they will process in different ways depending on a wide variety of causes, conditions, contexts, contingencies and consequences. Those 'male femalers' who wish to 'display' full time and in all contexts as female and never wish their male identities to be revealed have particular problems. Others may wish to disclose aspects of their identities in certain settings and not in others. This 'disclosing' will have many properties – it may, for instance, be voluntary or involuntary. Where an interactant does not suspect that s/he is confronted with a male femaler, the sub-process is that of 'passing'. Where an interactant detects that s/he is confronted with a male femaler, the sub-process is that of 'reading'. On some occasions the male femaler is 'read' as such, but the interactant may pretend that a reading has not taken place – the sub-process is that of 'pretending'.

Focusing on male femaling as a social process rather than on individuals or types of male femalers has a number of advantages. It enables the proper respect to be paid to the processual and emergent nature of much cross-dressing and sex-changing phenomena. It facilitates the generation of categories which highlights facets of cross-dressing and sex-changing hitherto not studied. It enables existing categorisations in the arena to be studied as a 'topic' rather than utilised as a 'resource'. Finally, it enables the construction of a framework for a rigorous examination of the various shifting inter-relations between sex, sexuality and gender which feature so prominently in the arena.

Grounded theory can be used to generate substantive or formal theory. Substantive theory is developed for a substantive or empirical area of sociological enquiry. Formal theory is developed for a formal or conceptual area of sociological enquiry. This study focuses on substantive theory which is developed in the empirical area of male cross-dressing and sex-changing. It is, therefore, a contribution to the development of substantive grounded theory. While it would be possible to build upon its framework and 'findings' to generate substantive theories of 'femaling' or, indeed, 'maling', this study does not take that step. For this reason, the basic social process researched should be seen as 'male femaling', rather than 'femaling' in general.

MALE FEMALING, SOCIAL STRUCTURE AND MASKED AWARENESS CONTEXTS

A sociological study of male femaling cannot discount the fact that in contemporary Western societies cross-dressing and sex-changing are commonly viewed as deviant – that is, they fall outside the range of what most of us regard as 'normal' experience. They thus carry with them the prospect of stigma and social control; of guilt; and of negative reaction from others (King 1995). In consequence, the male femaler faces particular problems which arise from the fact of deviance: problems such as those surrounding legitimacy, secrecy, access and identity (Plummer 1984).

All these issues arise from the constraints of social structure. The grounded theorist working in the area of male cross-dressing and sex-changing soon finds how pervasive these issues are. It is possible to focus on social psychological process and assume social structural process – or simply treat social structural process as a changing set of structural conditions – without formulating it clearly as a process. Most sociological studies do this. However, grounded theory gives guidance for the generation of basic social structural processes, and for the combining of the appropriate mix of basic social psychological process and basic social structural process, having regard to the data confronted in any particular study.

I soon found that social structural issues could be considered with the maximum parsimony and bite by seeing them in terms of the analytic social structural category of 'awareness context'. An awareness context is a social structural unit (Glaser and Strauss 1967a: 54) within which social interaction takes place and within which social processes are played out. It has been developed in a number of works by Glaser and Strauss (Glaser and Strauss 1967a; 1967b; Strauss 1978) to facilitate analysis of similarities in interaction in many diverse areas, and to provide a means to incorporate the analysis of both social interaction and social structure in the research domain under consideration. It has been applied by Plummer (1975: 177–96) in the arena of male homosexuality. Specifically, as defined by Glaser and Strauss, it refers to 'the total combination of what each interactant knows about the identity of the other and his own identity in the eye of the other' (Glaser and Strauss 1967a: 670). More generally, it refers to 'the total combination of what specific people, organisations, communities or nations know about a specific issue' (Glaser and Strauss 1967a: 670, n. 1).

Glaser and Strauss focus on face to face interaction and single out four types of awareness contexts for special consideration. An 'open' awareness context results when each interactant is aware of the other's true identity and his/her own identity in the eyes of the other. A 'closed' awareness context results when one interactant does not know either the other's identity or the other's view of his/her identity. A 'suspicion' awareness context is a modification of the closed one: an interactant suspects the true identity of the other or the other's view of his/her own identity, or both. A 'pretence' awareness context is a modification of the open one: both interactants are fully aware but pretend not to to be.

I found that with a slight modification, the social structural unit of awareness context provided the 'near core' social structural process within which to set and analyse my emerging data on male femaling. Specifically, by considering the basic social process of male femaling within the analytic social structural category of the 'masked' awareness context (viewed as a social structure in process), I was able to order the mass of data having to do with the way structure impinged on process and the way process was utilised to alter structure in the particular substantive area under consideration. Thus, I viewed male femaling as taking place within a 'masked' awareness context which I then considered in terms of the sub-units of open, closed, suspicion and pretence, as in the formulation suggested by Glaser and Strauss (1967a).

Awareness contexts which involve male femalers are masked awareness contexts because male femaling entails 'masking' – a term which denotes the simultaneous display of core facets of identity with the hiding of others.

Arguably, human beings are constantly 'putting on fronts': adopting presentations of self which may have the simultaneous effect of expression and concealment (Goffman 1959; 1968) whether intentionally or unintentionally. In the area of male femaling, however, the masking is particularly fundamental. Male femalers seek to display as females while hiding aspects of their male identities.

Each incident of male femaling within a masked awareness context entails the display by the male femaler of the mask, and the simultaneous display of certain facets of identity and the concealment of other aspects. From the standpoint of those to whom he is displaying, his mask is either 'read' as a male femaling mask, in which case he is 'sussed', or it is not, in which case his mask 'passes' and the male femaler is thought to be female.

As already pointed out, the focus of this study is on male femaling from the standpoint of the male femalers themselves. And it is from this standpoint that I utilise Glaser and Strauss's sub-types of awareness contexts, each of which is now illustrated in turn. First, an additional awareness context – what I call a 'private' awareness context – is explained.

Mask display occurs whenever the person masking exhibits his mask to self or others. It may be more or less total or partial. Male femalers spend a great deal of time in self-display, before cameras and mirrors. Indeed, owing to the taboo nature of the activity and the possibilities for solitary male femaling activities, many male femalers never display in front of others. In this case a 'private awareness context' prevails throughout their lives.

Many male femalers do wish, however, to display in front of various others while variously masked. When they do, and their mask is not penetrated, a 'closed masked awareness context' prevails. This context prevails when the interactant with the male femaler does not know of his male femaling and the male femaler knows that s/he does not know. Two simple examples will illustrate – the first, of total display as female, where the femaling mask successfully conceals the male beneath it and where the male femaler is perceived as female; the second, entailing partial femaling where the femaling 'mask' is not detected as a femaling mask and the interactant perceives him/herself to be interacting with a male.

Mildred is a male dressed as a woman wishing to pass as a woman. A passer-by narrowly avoids bumping into her, and says 'excuse me, Madam', taking Mildred for a woman. The passer-by does not know Mildred is a male who is femaling and Mildred 'knows' that he does not know. A closed masked awareness context prevails.

Thomas wears female stockings under his male trousers but is otherwise attired as a male. When he sits down the stockings are visible to the person sitting opposite, between the tops of his shoes and the bottom of his trousers. The person does not notice they are female stockings. Again, a closed masked awareness context prevails.

The social process most closely associated with the closed masked awareness context is that of 'passing'. It is a term widely used by male femalers. Much time and trouble is spent on attempts to 'pass' as a woman in different settings and for greater lengths of time.

Sooner or later, however, the question of mask slippage, or mask penetration, will be likely to arise. Another interactant will suspect that s/he is confronted with a man who is merely masked as a woman. S/he may suspect the person's male personal identity; or s/he may suspect that the male is partially masking. In such cases a 'suspicion masked awareness context' prevails. I give one example (by Yvonne) from the male femaling subcultural magazine *Tranz*.

> In my early teens I often wore a suspender-belt and nylons under my male clothes, and I think my mother knew of my habits. My suspicions were confirmed when, on my 17th birthday, mother and I sat down after tea and she gave me a present. When I opened it I was very surprised. It was a white little X girdle, white nylon panties, and sheer nylon hose. My mother told me she had known my secret for some years and she had no objections.
>
> (*Tranz* 5: 35)

Here we see Yvonne's mother disclosing that she knows of Yvonne's male femaling. Yvonne's suspicions are confirmed. Her mother has transformed the awareness context from suspicion to open.

The social process most closely associated with that of the suspicion masked awareness context is best termed 'proto-reading'. I add the 'proto' prefix because while the suspicion masked awareness context prevails it is only suspicions that have been aroused. From the standpoint of the mask reader there is something about the mask that arouses his/her suspicion. The mask wearer may suspect that he has been 'read'. In terms of social process and awareness contexts, it is the proto-reading which provides the engine of transition from the closed masked awareness context to the suspicion masked awareness context.

The suspicion masked awareness context is likely to be fragile. Either suspicions fail to be reinforced and the closed masked awareness context is re-instituted, or they are confirmed, in which case there will be a transition to the 'open masked awareness context'. This context prevails when the person interacting with the male femaler penetrates the mask and knows s/he is interacting with a male who is femaling.

Jennifer wishes to pass as a woman and is dressed as such. She alights on a train and is 'read' by a passenger who fancies male femalers and is wise to tell-tale signs that indicate maleness (involuntary disclosure). The passenger takes her for a coffee, and indicates that he knows she is a male who is femaling. The passenger knows, and Jennifer knows that he knows. The social process most associated with the open masked awareness context is that of 'reading'.

Open awareness contexts may stay as open, but there is always the possibility that it will be in the interests of the parties to pretend that a closed masked awareness context prevails and that a reading has not taken place. This is the 'pretence masked awareness context' which prevails when the interactants know that the mask has been read but pretend that it has not been read. This is a common masked awareness context. To institute it may save embarrassment.

The social process most associated with pretence masked awareness is 'pretending' ('fake passing'). The interactants behave as if a reading has not taken place. This may take the form of studiously feigning a normality of interaction, a mode of interaction which inexperienced interactants may find difficult. Many male femalers spend much time 'fake passing' with intimates in the subculture. Everyone is likely to be wise to them, but nevertheless have a stake in pretending.

'Disclosing' may refer to either the mask wearer or the mask reader. In one sense, of course, displaying and disclosing always constitute a couple. Some information is always disclosed in any masked awareness interaction. However, particularly pertinent here is the disclosing of information relating to what lies behind the mask: information about the mask wearer which the mask normally hides. Disclosing may be voluntary or involuntary. It may be tiered. Mask wearers may adopt retraction devices. Disclosure stories may be prepared in advance. Thus the husband wishing to disclose his cross-dressing inclinations to his wife, but fearful that she might divorce him as a result, may joke about his enthusiasm for dressing up, and note the effect on his wife before more disclosure. If things seem to be going wrong, he may retract, claiming he was only joking anyway. In terms of social process and masked awareness context, the major feature of disclosing is that it may take place at any time and within any one of the contexts. It will normally lead to an immediate transition to an open awareness context, providing it is neither retracted, nor too partial.

Irene's disclosure plan is a good example of a planned tiered disclosure.

I am now only 29 and I got married three years ago and we have a baby now. I buy my wife all sorts of sexy undies and take great interest in her clothes. I haven't told her yet about my TV [transvestism] but she has made several remarks about what a girlish interest I take in undies and fashion and make-up.

Last week – just for a 'joke', and to see 'what it felt like' I suggested I tried on a pair of black nylon French knickers with pink lace edging

I had bought her. She said O.K. and was, I think, surprised at the erection I got from the feel of the knickers. I began to make love to her and she became a very satisfied young woman and has been teasing me about my 'love-pants' and I have worn them twice now as we made love.

I think it's only a matter of time before she will accept my passion for women's clothes. I hope so, as it is my dearest wish to be able to practice my hobby freely with her.

(*Tranz* 5: 46–7)

Despite the importance of the masked awareness context as a social structural process within which to consider male femaling, in terms of this study, it is only a 'near core' variable (Glaser 1978: 93–4) – that is to say, from the focus of this study's emphasis on male femaling, it is demoted and considered only in so far as it affects our consideration of male femaling as a basic social process.

In the remainder of the chapter, therefore, I return to male femaling and delineate its major modes. I then introduce the phased ideal-typical career path which emerged from my analysis of the staged male femalings of over 200 informants, and within which it became possible to order the mass of intimate detail observed. Each chapter that follows is constructed around the various phases in this ideal-typical career path that emerged.

BODY FEMALING, EROTIC FEMALING AND GENDER FEMALING

Male femaling takes place in three major modes: 'body femaling', 'erotic femaling' and 'gender femaling'. As these modes were emerging, I was trying to make sense of the many very different and confusing scientific, member and lay definitions of 'sex', 'sexuality' and 'gender' (Gould and Kern-Daniels 1977; Shively and De Cecco 1977). As introduced in Chapter 1, I found it useful for conceptual clarity, to restrict the term 'sex' to the biological and physiological aspects of the the division of humans into male and female; 'sexuality' to 'those matters pertaining to the potential arousability and engorgement of the genitals' (Plummer 1979: 53); and 'gender' to the socio-cultural correlates of the division of the sexes. A subsidiary theme of comparative analysis then emerged, namely, the exploration of the facets of 'body femaling', 'erotic femaling' and 'gender femaling', and their inter-relations in terms of the various facets of 'sex', 'sexuality' and 'gender' that emerged from the data.

In the interests of clarity and exposition it will be helpful to set forth the three modes of femaling in this chapter without reference to their inter-relations with each other or their precise inter-connectedness with the distinctions made between sex, sexuality and gender. These latter issues will form a focus of subsequent chapters. I emphasise that setting them out in isolation is no more than a focusing strategy. In particular, each illustrative example I give should be read specifically in terms of the respective mode of femaling under consideration. This is because the 'same' act, event, object or dimension, will almost certainly have alternative femaling potential. The simple act of cross-dressing, for example, will always be an instance of gender femaling. It may or may not be experienced in terms of erotic femaling. Much of the complexity in the area derives from the multi-faceted combinations of the three modes. The male femaler defining homosexual erotic encounters as heterosexual, or heterosexual encounters as lesbian, for instance, is frequently genderising his sexuality – he may be erotic femaling; as may the male femaler attempting to masturbate in what he perceives to be a female fashion. Both femalings may or may not involve body femaling.

Body femaling

Body femaling refers to the desires and practices of male femalers to 'female' their bodies. This might include desired, actual or simulated changes in both primary and secondary characteristics of 'sex'. Thus it would include chromosomal change (which is not presently possible), gonadal, hormonal, morphological and neural change, at one level (Money 1969); and change to facial hair, body hair, scalp hair, vocal chords, skeletal shape and musclature, at another level (Lukas 1978).

Body femaling has four major dimensions. The first is that of the degree of permanence. At one end would be the self-styled 'new woman', who has undergone treatment and surgery in such a manner that for all practical purposes she is now of her desired sex. Given a good surgeon and good fortune, the castration, penectomy and vaginoplasty she has undergone will not only convince her medically unqualified lover that she is a genetic female, but will also allow her to pass muster as such at a routine gynaecological examination. To date, it is impossible to reverse this operation. At the opposite end of the continuum would be body femaling of the most impermanent type, such as the addition of concealed padding to simulate the female body form. Such impermanent body femaling ranges from the practices of femalers who merely add bird seed fillings to their bras, to those who don elaborate body costumes such as artificial 'doll-like' bodies.

Overlapping with such practices would be the various procedures of depilation. This highlights a second dimension – degrees of visibility. Many femalers depilate all those parts of the body that cannot be seen by those observing them as males. Thus unconcealed parts of forearms are left hirsute. Siobhan shaves her arms in the autumn and winter, letting the hair grow in time for the cricket season when her arms will be exposed. Again, eye brows may be plucked with varying degrees of obviousness.

A third dimension is that of the degree of progression and accumulation versus oscillation. There are those femalers who follow a steady route to increasing feminisation of the body. Others oscillate, going on periodic sprees, in preparation for an important social function for instance, or for a lover.

A fourth dimension is the degree of premeditation. Suzie shaves her legs every Thursday and does 'everything else' every Friday. There are body femalers who execute their feminisation with protracted planning; others who do it frenetically and impulsively. Again, there are differing degrees of regret or celebration of the permanence or semi-permanence incurred.

Erotic femaling

Erotic femaling refers to femaling which is deliberately sexual, or has the effect of arousing sexual desire or excitement. Although the term might be stretched to include femaling intended to arouse, or which does arouse, sexual desire or excitement in others, the particular feature of erotic femaling in cross-dressers is that the desire, or excitement, is aroused in the femaler himself by his own femaling, and/or through the awareness of others of his own erotic femaling.

Erotic femaling is boundaried only by what the femaler finds erotic or potentially erotic, by his own ingenuity, and by what he and/or his culture deem to be associated with the female. Thus it may have to do with the behavioural, the emotional, the cognitive or the anatomical. In this sense, erotic femaling is the most embracive mode in that any facet of female 'sex' and the feminine 'gender', when it is adopted by the femaler, may be found erotic. At one extreme the femaler may experience what he perceives as a multiple female orgasm while experiencing himself as female during role-reversed love making. When Cyndi has intercourse with her wife she is the female, her wife becomes her male lover. Her wife has the penis, she the vagina. At the other extreme, the casual erotic thought may be evoked involuntarily by the sight of a women's magazine in a newsagency, and the fleeting imagining that the femaler is a female casually interested in this object of the world of women.

As regards sensations experienced, these might be placed on continua of focus/diffusion. The range of intensity continuum might be exampled, at one end, by the femaler experiencing intense orgasm following a dressing sequence, whilst at the other end, the femaler might find himself mildly enjoying the sensual feel of his bra strap against his shoulder as he makes the minor movements necessary to eat a meal or drink a cup of coffee. The focus/diffusion feature of erotic femaling may be more or less intense. The eroticism might be experienced over the entire body, inside and out, at one extreme (diffuse eroticism; more or less intense). At another extreme would be the highly focused sensations of pleasure as the femaler experienced a focused genital orgasm implicated in some femaling episode (focused eroticism; intense).

Erotic femaling may be more or less volitional, fantasied, scripted/ ritualised, visible, narcissistic, developmental/progressive and constant object-related. These properties may be illustrated by Suzanne, E. who on occasion chooses, in private, to initiate a protracted, ritualised erotic script which leads her to experience herself as her femme self, visually and tactually, and who reports the ability to do this as a 'break through'. Suzanne, E. is erotically femaling in a highly volitional, largely invisible, highly constant object-related (the script), highly scripted/ritualised, highly fantasied, highly narcissistic, highly developmental/progressive fashion. Jennifer, on the other hand, illustrates a less focused, and less keenly and carefully orchestrated episode of erotic femaling. Whilst masturbating she fantasies some facet of femaling ritualistically, finds other imagined objects/events emerging involuntarily, shifts from fantasied object/event to fantasied object/event, from one cross-dressing activity to another, until she eventually tires of the whole femaling episode, and moves on to some non-male femaling pursuit, which may or may not be related to the erotic.

Gender femaling

Gender femaling refers to the manifold ways in which femalers adopt the behaviours, emotions and cognitions socio-culturally associated with being female. Gender femaling need not be associated with erotic femaling.

At one somewhat stereotypical extreme would be Betty, a self-styled 'transgenderist' who is living 'full time' as a woman. Betty feels she has chosen a female gender identity that has developed from a more ambiguous self concept. She has no desire to 'cross over' physically. She avoids sexual relationships altogether. She does not masturbate. She deliberately chooses to work in a 'feminine' occupation. She spends her evenings in a stereotypically 'feminine' fashion – dress-making. She has the 'ordinary woman's interest in make-up and making the best of herself' and sees herself as passive, nurturant, compliant and emotional. At the other end of the continuum would be the gender femaler who ordinarily leads a contented life as a male 'in every sense', but periodically enjoys 'dressing up' as a woman, although he would feel foolish role-playing feminine mannerisms or voice intonation, preferring to act 'normally' while cross-dressed. Somewhere in the middle of the continuum would be those who enjoy stereotype role playing, such as Ginger (1980: 5) who reports:

I really get into feminine role-playing. I like to choose a typical feminine role and then dress and make-up for a stereotype of that kind of girl. I try to also suit my actions, manner and personality to the role. In the past I've experimented with these various female stereotypes: hooker; chic fashion model; dominatrix; French maid; little girl; slut.

Gender femalers, however, need not follow such obvious stereotypes. Many find them unreal, offensive or sexist. In so far as each and every 'RG' (real girl) provides a potential role model, it follows that the possibilities are boundless. Thus, many male femalers prefer to develop a middle-of-the-road femme personality they feel is suitable to their age, class, looks and background. Tracy models herself on a respected career woman acquaintance. In this vein, too, are femalers who are particularly complementary about the 'natural TV' (transvestite) who can 'pass' in 'straight' settings as an 'RG' whilst wearing 'little or no make-up, a skirt and top, and some flatties'.

Gender femaling may be seen in terms of the time spent doing it, its continuity and the degree of fine-tunedness to things feminine: some femalers quit gender femaling for years at a time before returning to it; many gender femalers make a study of 'beauty know-how'. A major dimension is the degree of development of a 'femme self' (or selves) with her own personality, tastes and preferences, and its relation to the male self of the femaler.

MALE FEMALING AND THE INTERRELATIONS BETWEEN SEX, SEXUALITY AND GENDER

In the process of male femaling, persons (bodies, selves and identities), actions, events and objects (clothes and the paraphernalia of femininity) are variously implicated. They are, or become over time, in varying degrees, and with varying degrees of interconnectedness, sexed, sexualised and/or gendered (SSG'd). Thus, for example, in body femaling the characteristics of the genetic female's (sexed) body are taken on by the genetic male's body which becomes correspondingly sexed as female. Whereas in erotic femaling the gendered object 'petticoat' may become eroticised (sexualised). Again, in gender femaling the gendered mannerism 'sitting down in "ladylike" fashion' may be adopted by the gender femaler as a facet of his gendered presentation of self (Goffman 1959; 1979). This is an exceedingly complex business, the components of which may be best illustrated with reference to the major phases in an ideal-typical career path of the male femaler that emerged from my analysis of the staged male femalings of over 200 informants. The five phases: 'beginning femaling', 'fantasying femaling' 'doing femaling', 'constituting femaling' and 'consolidating femaling', form the basis and organising principle of the chapters that follow.

Part III

MAINLY PRACTICE

5

BEGINNING MALE
FEMALING

From the symbolic interactionist perspective of this study, the starting point of any analysis of 'beginning male femaling' is, necessarily, somewhat arbitrary. Conception, personhood, intra-uterine and post-partum life are variously conceptualised in different times and places; as are babyhood, infancy, childhood, adolescence and adulthood. Throughout these various phases and stages, the particular mix of male and female, masculine and feminine, and their various interrelations, are subject to continually changing and differently phased and staged formulations and meanings to both self and other.

From the standpoint of contemporary everyday – particularly Western – life, it is 'clear enough', however, that there is a binary divide. What ethnomethodologists call the 'natural attitude' towards gender assumes that all human beings will belong to one of two discrete social categories permanently determined on the basis of biological ('naturally' given) characteristics. The latter is traditionally refered to as 'sex' and the former as 'gender' (Stoller 1968: 9). Congruence is expected both within and between a person's sex and gender. Congruence is also expected between sex and gender and a person's sexuality, with the 'default' assumption being probably, even in the 1990s, that this will be heterosexual. These are expectations in both cognitive (this is how things are) and normative (this is how things should be) senses.

When we speak of 'males' who 'female', therefore, it is 'clear enough' to what we are referring. We are speaking of males who in varous ways transgress the binary divide between the sexes. All such transgressions must have a beginning and it is the purpose of this chapter to consider those beginnings.

Beginnings refer to sources, origins, first parts. Beginnings of the end refer to the first clear signs of final results. From the standpoint of our phased ideal-typical career path, beginnings may be beginning of endings which end in the beginning phase, or beginnings which lead on to subsequent phases. Again, the beginnings may be more or less remarkable by self and other. Any observer of child's play may note male femaling behaviours. In so far as these are sporadic and forgotten by the child 'male femaler' and his audience, alike, we, too, may forget them for the purposes of this chapter. On the other hand, where male femalings persist, the initial beginnings may take on a retrospective importance, particularly from the standpoint of the transgressor of the binary divide.

The material in this chapter focuses on significant beginnings (whether in childhood or later) as reported upon retrospectively by the adult cross-dressers and sex-changers. In this retrospective reporting many male femalers refer to themselves in their female or 'femme' name, which has been adopted in a later phase of femaling. In what follows, I refer to male femalers in their male identities and names, following the male name with the femme name in brackets, as in John (Jenny), where a femme name has been adopted. This is to avoid the danger of imputing a 'naming' that was not present in the particular 'beginning femaling' phase. Typically, the male identity – though variously threatened by the 'beginning femaling' – remains more or less intact in this phase.

In the beginning phase of male femaling, the emphasis is upon initial femaling behaviours – what deviancy theorists would call primary deviance. Lemert (1951) first drew attention to the distinction between primary deviance and secondary deviance. The distinction emphasises the significance of social reaction. Primary deviance refers to an initial act of rule-breaking. Secondary deviance occurs when the rule-breaker is required to manage the response elicited by his transgression of the rule. It is only at this later stage that the possibility arises of new identities, selves and worlds emerging, as the rule-breaker attempts to make sense of his transgressions to himself or others by attributing labels and motives to his behaviour.

In beginning femaling the emphasis is upon the first incidents of cross-dressing. These may occur by chance, or by design. The femaling may begin alone or with others. It may be variously encouraged. It may be more or less charged with affect. The clothes may be those of the femaler's mother, sister, other family member, playmate or friend. The femaler might have access to clothes from another source. They might be acquired specially for him. The items of clothes vary, as do how many are worn during the beginning femaling phase.

The first incidents might take place in childhood, adolescence or adulthood. Precursors and incidents are variously remembered. The cross-dressing incident, which I take to include the context and accompanying feelings and cognitions, may evoke varying degrees of certainty about its meaning. It could be remembered, re-experienced or reconstructed as primarily erotic or sexual, especially when originally accompanied by perceived sexual excitement and arousal. It could be remembered, re-experienced or reconstructed in terms of variously defined pleasure, fascination, sensuousness, mystery or awe. Further, the experience may be conceptualised in terms of the tactile, the visual or the olfactory, or any combination of these, and with varying degrees of focus and precision.

Peter B. (Paula) provides an unusually clear picture of the precursors, the first incident, and its dramatic effect for him. Here the emphasis is upon the erotic result of the femaling. The description is taken from a letter written to *Tranz* (5: 6–7) a publication popular with erotic femalers, and regarded with distaste by many male femalers who emphasise their body femaling or gender femaling. It does, however, illustrate the erotic impact of initial gender femaling for many male femalers.

My first awareness of girls' clothes began when I was about 10. Maybe it was before that even, but I used to play a lot with the girl next door. She was two years older than me and wore regulation navy schoolgirl knickers. But at weekends she often wore pink or white bloomer style knickers and during our various games of Cowboys and Indians, or tree climbing, the sight of her firm smooth thighs and frequently exposed knickers produced a 'nice' feeling within me. This feeling was not a sexual one but a visual one and I found myself manoeuvring her into positions that would reveal her knickers during our games.

Whether she was aware of this I never knew. She certainly said nothing and was always co-operative and this went on for several years. As I grew older I began to have my first erections thinking of her knickers and this acted as an incentive to see even more of them. I grew bolder and invented all sorts of wrestling games during which I always finished up kneeling over her thighs, her frock up to her waist, her knickers fully exposed. This game quickly gave me an erection and she was soon aware of it and although we were great friends we were both too shy to say anything. We wrestled playfully for quite a while – in fact she was nearly 15 and I was 13 before she said we shouldn't do it.

I stole a pair of her knickers when I was 12 and rubbed them over my penis in bed in what was still quite childish masturbation, and then quite suddenly it dawned on me that *all* women wore knickers! I had two girl cousins, a sister of 19, two aunts and of course my own mother. Then there were her friends.

I became the most fanatical knickers observer you can imagine. I went to almost absurd lengths to gain glimpses up between any woman's legs and I was in a daze of pleasure to discover all the different styles! Briefs, panties, French, directoire, cami-knickers, schoolgirls'! The array was dazzling!

I was 13 when I stepped, quivering with excitement into a pair of French knickers belonging to my sister. I ejaculated almost immediately. . . The feeling was glorious and yet quite alarming and I felt as though I was leaking urine. The subsequent sight of this thick white liquid soaking and dripping from the knickers genuinely frightened me. I honestly felt I had injured myself in some way.

Some three days after this first 'event' I got home from school to find my mother out. I went upstairs to do my homework and through the half-opened door of my mother's bedroom I saw, hanging over a chair, a pair of her pink directoire knickers, obviously discarded in a hurry as she changed before going out.

That soft gleaming bundle turned my whole body and senses into a jelly-like state of desire and longing. I had to wear them, to try and see if I was all right. Would it happen again?

My answer was there almost immediately in my swift gathering erection as I struggled out of my clothes. Shivers of sheer lust wracked my body as I touched and fondled the knickers. I stepped into them drawing them up my legs. Being directoire knickers, and my mother a big woman, they hung on my body all baggy and loose, but I was beside myself with desire, dizzy with it, and yet my brain and senses already recognised this growing crescendo of feeling as the onset of climax.

As the feeling burst within me I was able to snatch the knickers down at the front and for the first time saw the heavy jets of my white semen leaping from me as I writhed and shook violently!

(*Tranz* 5: 6–7)

Whereas Peter B. (Paula) found himself taking the initiative in the events which led up to his beginning femaling, frequently the beginning femaler is variously seduced into it by a female. The extreme and rather rare case of this is where the boy child is deliberately and systematically brought up as a girl. Somewhat less rare are the cases where the boy is deliberately dressed as a girl and encouraged in female gender display, for greater or lesser periods of time. It might be for fun or punishment. It might be for display in front of selected people, but not others. Retrospective accounts of the cases which encouraged full cross-dressing and female gender display, provide excellent examples of beginning gender femaling. Here the erotic has no obvious place.

A particularly interesting example is that of Robert (Peggy), who was brought up to display as Peggy in the company of his mother, aunts and grandmother, but to remain Robert in front of his father. It took place in the late 1940s and early 1950s, well after the period when it was not uncommon to skirt young boys. Robert's mother had convinced herself that her life would be cheated without having a girl (Kendall 1993: 44–5).

Once my mother dressed me up as a girl and unveiled me to my aunts and grandmother, I was showered with affection, love and praise – all the very special way that only comes from a woman. The 'OHHHH, you look so cute'. 'Such a pretty dress'. 'Soooo dainty'. 'Such a pretty boy'. 'You should have been a girl' – comments and compliments helped me to feel that I was *like them*.

The change to wearing girl clothes was so quick and radical that it was puzzling. I was told that it was 'Mommys' who decide what a child wears. This explanation helped me to buffer my wonderings as to why I had to wear boys' clothes when my father was around. I was told things like 'Daddy doesn't want to know about that. That's just for you and Mommy'.

My father didn't really have a clear idea of the extent to which I was being effeminized, because the girlish mannerisms were easy to hide when I was wearing pants. He had no clue that I knew how to show off and model a dress, which my aunts loved to see me do. It would cause them to squeal with delight and made me feel so proud that I pleased them. He did not know that I knew how to take care of my skirts when I sat down.

Girlish behaviour was complimented and encouraged, but I could be and was more quick and boisterous when I was wearing pants. Docility and submissiveness was demanded and applauded when I wore dresses. I wanted to be just like my aunties, so I sat still like they wanted me to, like I saw them do and let them fuss with my hair. A curling iron styling, no problem, Barrettes, ribbons ... 'You're going to look so pretty today, Peggy. Let Aunty put a ribbon in your hair'. I did not resist. I wanted to be pretty. Then I would get more compliments.

These are particularly striking examples. Peter B.'s (Paula) account is written from the standpoint of a femaler who eventually came to accept the label 'transvestite'. Robert (Peggy) is now living as a woman.

More characteristically, in beginning femaling, the first incidents are not recalled as being so dramatic. Jack (Jean) was 7 or 8 years old when he remembers going into the family bathroom where his mother used to hang up her stockings to dry. He recalls touching them, smelling them, and on a sudden impulse tried one of them on. This became his little secret. It was pleasurable, but he was not very sure why. Afterwards he would dismiss the incident from his mind. Over a period of years, he began to experiment with other garments he found lying around. It was not until he was 16 that he tried on his first dress – one of his mother's. At about this time, he began to compile short lists of women's clothes, especially underwear: bra, panties and stockings. When alone in the house he would borrow the various items on his list, put them on and masturbate. Afterwards, he would carefully replace the items.

Trevor (Hilary) on the other hand, did not cross-dress until he was well into his 30s. He recalls the day his wife and family left him. He felt bereft. As he was going to bed that night his eyes alighted on his wife's nightdress. He picked it up and nestled it against his cheeks. He slept with it pressed against his cheek. The next night he wore it. He felt faintly ridiculous, but in a strange way found the experience to be comforting. Although he did not think too much more about the incident, he found himself sleeping in the nightdress occasionally, thereafter. Later, he found it comforting knowing of the various feminine things about the house. In due course, he began to spend evenings experimenting with make-up on his own face.

Despite the very different manifestations of beginning femaling, all beginning femalers are likely to be faced with the task of making sense of their experiences. In terms of the sociology of motivation (Mills 1940) this is because an untoward event will call forth the response to explain it. In terms of the sociology of deviance, it is because the male femaler is a rule-breaker who is required to manage the response elicited by his transgression of a rule. Put another way, it is because the untoward incident renders problematic the 'taken for granted', 'natural attitude' of everyday life that presupposes the congruity of sex, sexuality and gender.

From the standpoint of the beginning femaler, it is the untoward affect surrounding the incident that leads to his pondering it. Robert's (Peggy's) initial puzzlement led to his mother's response that it was Mommys who decide these things. This, he tells us, 'helped to buffer [his] wonderings'. It did not stop them. More usually, the beginning femaler is alone with his thoughts and feelings. He begins to ask himself questions. What is the meaning of this pleasure, mystery or awe that I experienced? What sort of person am I that could experience such a thing? In short, what does it all mean?

Robert's (Peggy's) circumstances led to his beginning femaling phase being very short. He was not allowed to cross-dress in the presence of his father, but as his father was at home rather infrequently, Peggy's male femaling rapidly developed beyond the initial phase. Peter B.'s (Paula's) feelings, on the other hand, were so intense that he felt in a sort of limbo for the next year. He felt 'torn apart' and that he must be 'slightly mental'.

Others, in this phase, dismiss the untoward incident. They do not take it seriously, or they see it as a temporary aberration. In these examples, for instance, Jack (Jean) partially cross-dressed for years, intermittently and infrequently, before his advancing years and his difficulties with girlfriends led to an increasing demand for self-explanation. Trevor (Hilary) was so preoccupied with the feelings about his broken marriage that his cross-dressing did not feature prominently in his thoughts for a number of years.

In terms of the interrelations between sex, sexuality and gender, what is particularly evident in cases like Jack's (Jean's) and Trevor's (Hilary's), is undifferentiation. The untoward incidents are dismissed or denied and this precludes the possibility of fine-tuned distinctions being made by the femaler. As Sandra B. puts it:

> I was always curious and vaguely excited by feminine things and I did sometimes 'borrow' the panties of female relatives and put them on. I loved the feeling of them, so soft and silky on my body. I found I enjoyed women's magazines and I took a great interest in make-up hints and fashion, but although I was aware of this desire to interest myself in such things I would not really admit to myself that it was true.

> (*Tranz* 5: 33)

Undifferentiation also occurs because the individual lacks the conceptual wherewithal, the sense of purpose, direction and volition and, indeed, the means to gain them through interaction with others or relevant literature.

The beginning femaler is likely to conceive the first incidents as 'something to do with sex'. Possibilities include variants of: 'I wish I was a girl/woman' (inchoate as regards fantasy body femaling versus fantasy/acted out gender femaling); 'I wish these clothes were part of my world'; 'I wish I could be part of this world' (inchoate as regards gender femaling emphasis). Where the erotic looms large, beginning femaling might be seen in terms of the sexual (the pre-history of erotic femaling), with the relations between the sexual on the one hand, and sex and gender on the other, obscure at this stage.

As regards the interrelations between the constitution of the self and world as SSG'd, typically, 'normality' reinstates itself after the incident. Nevertheless, from thenceforth the meaning of female objects – clothes, for example – may well be different. In some more or less undifferentiated way they may be seen as being, or capable of being, charged with affect, which may be built upon in a more or less cumulative fashion, pondered on and invested with new meaning. Likewise, will new self-concepts be rendered more or less negotiable; though, typically, in this phase, the re-involvement within the meaning frames of 'normal' everyday life, following the cross-dressing incident, are such as to leave 'normal' self-concept and world more or less intact.

BEGINNING FEMALING AND MASKED AWARENESS CONTEXTS

The beginning femaler is very soon confronted by problems having to do with the management of knowledge. He finds himself wishing to display as female, but he will not wish to disclose his femaling to others. Even Robert (Peggy) learned that he must not disclose his femaling to his father. This displaying/disclosing couple and its attendant issues of stigma, secrecy and information management is a major concern to male femalers in all phases of femaling. Here I introduce the problem with reference to vignettes taken from a number of incidents of beginning femaling.

Partial femaling in a private awareness context is most characteristic in the beginning femaling phase. Where the femaling is premeditated there will be the maximum of opportunity to plan techniques and strategies to maintain the private awareness context. Jack (Jean), referred to previously, had seen his mother's stockings hanging up in the bathroom on many occasions and had long been fascinated by them. On several occasions he had been seized by the impulse to try them on, but had resisted because of his feelings of guilt. As the impulse became stronger, fear of discovery became more overt. What if his mother wanted to know why he was in the bathroom so long? What if he could be seen through the bathroom window or the keyhole? What if he damaged the stockings? For a while the strength of these factors overcame his impulse to begin femaling. Slowly, however, he developed a strategy to maximise the possibility of his beginning femaling remaining undiscovered – of maintaining a private awareness context.

He would wait until a Tuesday afternoon when his mother went out shopping for several hours leaving him alone in the house. He would slip into the bathroom, lock the door, close the bathroom curtains, make a mental note of the precise fall of one pair of stockings over the drying rail where his mother had hung them, remove them and try them on. The next time his mother went on her weekly shopping trip he did precisely this. Once he had put the stockings on he spent several minutes in self-display – flexing his feet, but then an unpremeditated idea crossed his mind. He would angle the bathroom mirror down to his legs so that only his stockinged legs were visible. He did this, making a mental note to return the mirror to its original position for fear that his mother might suspect that he had been up to something. After a few minutes of self-display he could contain his sexual excitement no longer (erotic femaling) and decided to masturbate. He masturbated to ejaculation, ensuring that no semen could splash on to the stockings by carefully placing a folded handkerchief over his penis.

With the excitement of his erotic femaling over, Jack (Jean) was struck by an overwhelming fear of discovery. He removed the stockings – were they not larger in the toe now? He considered re-washing them, thinking this might return them to their previous shape, but dismissed this idea because he thought they could not possibly dry out in time. He replaced the stockings on the drying rail, but how could he be sure he had replaced them in precisely the same position? He remained apprehensive and determined never to female again. Eventually he dismissed the whole incident from his mind. He distanced himself from it. It was as though it was not he who had done it.

Unpremeditated, impulsive femaling is more likely to leave traces which may be more difficult to conceal. In these cases beginning femalers may have to develop different strategies. Larry (Lynette), alone in the house, was looking for a tennis racket in the wardrobe in the spare bedroom when he came across a party dress of his mother's. He was seized by the impulse to try it on himself. He removed it carefully off its hanger and took it to his bedroom. It was a dress that zipped up the back. He had no idea how to pull the zip up fully and as he contorted his body to effect this, 'disaster' struck: the delicate zip mechanism broke. He had no notion of how to repair it without a repair being evident. He returned it to the wardrobe and tried to replace the zip in such a fashion that it might appear as though his mother had broken it were she to take it off the hanger in the future. He then used his prayer time to seek divine intervention to maintain the private awareness context.

In these variously premeditated and unpremeditated incidents it is the props of femaling that have to be so managed as to avoid suspicions being aroused. Where suspicions have been involuntarily aroused, beginning male femalers may construct all manner of elaborate explanations to seek to avoid the institution of a suspicion awareness context.

Nigel (Jayne) waited until his parents had gone out with his sister one evening and then went into her bedroom, opened her wardrobe door, and was about to take out a frothy petticoat which he had long coveted. As he was doing this, he heard the sound of a car coming down the driveway. He quickly closed the wardrobe door, turned off the room light, returned downstairs and sat in front of the television. He realised with horror that the rest of the family had returned prematurely, and must have seen the bedroom light on and then off. He invented an excuse as to why he was in his sister's bedroom, but felt it to be somewhat weak and was acutely aware of the suspicious look that he felt his mother gave him. He vowed to himself to be more careful in future.

Thus far I have placed the emphasis upon partial male femaling which the male femaler wishes to keep secret because it is stigmatised. He does not want to be discredited and suffer the consequences and so seeks to conceal every aspect of his male femaling.

An interesting variation arises where the male femaler has the opportunity to male female in front of others in an unstigmatised context but is fearful that his subjective feelings about his male femaling, about which he feels guilty, will be revealed.

Henry, who had long been fascinated by female clothes and once or twice had worn them, was chosen to play a female role in the school play. He was terrified that if he appeared too interested or knowledgeable about the intricacies of female attire, his colleagues would 'know' that he had cross-dressed in the past. As the rehearsals progressed, he felt he had to make his female attire and make-up less authentic than it might have been, for fear of arousing suspicions. Once the play was over, his beginning femaling rapidly developed into more sustained femaling. He felt that being chosen for a female part had, more than any other single event, propelled him to a life of regular cross-dressing. Whereas most male femalers start with partial cross-dressing and 'graduate' to fuller dressing, Henry's appearance in the play launched his total cross-dressing more quickly than might otherwise have been the case.

In those rarer cases where beginning male femaling initially takes place in the presence of another, male femaling is, of course, taking place within an open awareness context. Likely to arise, then, is fear that the interactant in the know will 'spill the beans' to others. This can give the knowing interactant considerable leverage over the beginning femaler. Horace, fearful that the knowledge would leak out to others, would bend over backwards to please his sister, who in turn capitalised on her hold over him for many years. Later she would insist that he continue with their 'girlie games' when he feared to do so.

The first incident of male femaling is often very memorable to the male femaler, as is evident in many of the examples given in this chapter. Though its meaning may change over the years, particular 'firsts' are often recalled with great clarity. The time when the phase of 'beginning femaling' ceases and gives way to later phases, however, is more arbitrary. As the beginning male femaler reflects upon his femaling, his thoughts may turn to repeat performances of past femalings or elaborations which may be increasingly turned over in his mind. Inevitably, he will have far more opportunities to repeat or elaborate male femaling incidents in his thoughts, than he will have to enact them in reality. Whether such fantasies arise in tandem with masturbation, as pleasant day-dreams, or as plans for intended future actions, the ground will have been prepared for phase two in the career path – that of 'fantasying femaling' – and it is to this phase that I now turn my attention.

6

FANTASYING MALE FEMALING

Whatever the viewpoint taken on the interrelations between thought and action, it is evident that both will frequently arise in tandem. Again, it is the case that on certain occasions thought will precede action, whilst on other occasions action will precede thought. In the context of the male femaling career path, therefore, beginning male femaling will be variously accompanied, preceded or followed, by thoughts, memories and feelings pertaining to male femaling.

Whereas the initial male femaling *behaviours* mark the first phase in the male femaler's ideal-typical career path, it is in the second phase – where emphasis switches to thoughts and fantasies – that 'fantasying femaling' arises. Again, fantasying femaling will frequently arise in tandem with 'doing femaling' (phase three), but in phase two, as opposed to phase three, the emphasis is on the elaboration of fantasies involving femaling, rather than on any accompanying cross-dressing activities or on acting out aspects of fantasy body femaling.

The fantasies may be more or less elaborate, scripted, adapted from incidents in 'real' life, innovative and imaginative. They might entail nothing more than fantasying the feel and texture of an imagined petticoat as implicated within a femaling episode (cf. fetishism unrelated to male femaling). They might involve an elaborate script in which the boy child is taken shopping by his mother, who has chosen for him all sorts of 'feminine' finery, and he then lives 'happily ever after' as an accepted girl child in the family.

In terms of sex, sexuality and gender and their interrelations, a number of possibilities arise. There may be quite unambiguous fantasies of being a girl or woman (fantasy body femaling). A common boyhood variant is fantasying 'waking up in the morning as a girl'. Many femalers who later conceptualise themselves as transsexuals and who are conceptualised as primary transsexuals within the psychiatric-medical literature (Person and Ovesey 1974a) recall variations on this theme. For others, the fantasy femaling takes on a gender emphasis. Thoughts of male or female morphology do not arise. Rather, the emphasis is upon romantic fantasies relating to such things as

71

dreamy dresses, ribbons, doll play and the like. For still others, the emphasis is upon masturbatory fantasy cross-dressing in a range of situations.

There is a tendency in this phase for fantasies to initially cluster around certain themes, which develop only slowly. Such fantasies may have a body/sex, gender, or erotic/sexual core, which may then be fuelled by one or other mode.

As regards the interrelations between the constitution of self and world as being SSG'd, a number of points might be made. As with 'beginning femaling', there is a tendency for the meaning frames (Goffman 1974) of everyday life to reassert themselves when the incident of day-dreaming or masturbation is over. However, in the case of erotic fantasy femaling, gendered objects are increasingly invested with potential affect, to form material for future masturbatory scripts. *Pari passu*, the environment is gaining potential for being increasingly eroticised/sexualised. Alternatively, there may be an increasing fascination with 'the world of women' (the pre-history of gender femaling leading to a gender femaling emphasis), with varying degrees of volition. As regards self and world, body femalers may become so preoccupied with their fantasying that their self-concepts as males become increasingly under threat; gender femalers, likewise, in more dreamy a fashion. More typically, however, there will be merely – what might be termed – incipient 'dual worlding'. An embryonic world will be constituted within which a femaling self, and femaling related objects and practices are emerging; but which at this stage, the fantasying femaler keeps separate from his everyday world, thus keeping the latter more or less 'normal' and enabling its development as more or less boundaried from the incipient femaling world.

The focus in fantasying femaling is on femaling which does not entail manifest display and disclosure to others. In the nature of the case, fantasying femaling may take place in a private awareness context. Peter would become Penny, for instance, when watching television with his wife, who knew nothing of his male femaling. It was Penny who would identify with the female stars of the various soaps that he and his wife watched together. In her fantasying femaling, a special favourite of Penny's was Sue Ellen, JR's wife in *Dallas*. Like Sue Ellen, Penny could enjoy a wealthy life style, spend most of her time looking glamorous, and at the same time she could identify with a character who was married to a person who made no effort to understand her. Not only was Sue Ellen a beautiful woman; she was also a misunderstood and ill-treated woman. Penny felt the same way, particularly as she went to bed, a night's television viewing over, with only her fantasies for comfort. Peter had long since ceased having a sexual life with his wife, and would doze off to sleep as Penny, comforted by her identification with Sue Ellen. Penny did not perceive such day-dreams as sexual.

Such fantasy femaling may take place in complete privacy. Women's worlds are co-opted in the service of fantasy femaling. No one need know. We saw this in the case of Angie (in Chapter 3) who entered an entirely private male femaling social world whilst at work, in the company of her boss and a secretary. On other occasions, fantasy femaling requires the utilisation of minimal props from women's worlds. Penny (above) would surreptitiously acquire and read romantic novels of the Mills and Boon type. When she read such novels she became the heroine who so frequently ended up in the arms of the tall handsome man, the 'perfect' solution to her hopes and yearnings. Peter, however, was very wary of Penny's books being discovered. He frequently threw them away, and when he could not bring himself to do so, preoccupied himself with inventing plausible stories as to why he should have such books in his possession.

In principle, male femalers have the whole range of women's worlds to draw upon for their femaling fantasies. Such worlds may feed fairly stereotypical fantasies. Many male femalers enjoy fantasying themselves as attractive young women admired by other women for their dress sense, and desired by men for their allure. I can recall, for instance, travelling in a car with a number of 'transvestites' in the mid-1980s when ra-ra skirts were becoming fashionable. As we passed a bus stop, we saw a young woman waiting for a bus, 'dressed to kill', presumably for a night out on the town. She was wearing such a skirt. All my informants turned to each other with a similar wistful look, and in unison expressed their yearnings to be that woman wearing that ra-ra skirt, anticipating a fun night out. Other male femaling fantasies are more idiosyncratic. Donald enjoyed fantasying himself as an elderly Jewish woman taking tea with her elderly friends in high class tea rooms. Although only in his 30s at the time, Donald did not share the often expressed view that male femaling was more enjoyable for the young. Still others prefer being teenagers, pre-teen or even girl babies in their fantasies.

For the researcher interested in exploring the minutiae of male femaling fantasies, the extensive literature of 'transvestite' fiction provides a useful and accessible resource. 'Transvestite' fiction comes in many formats – straight prose, cartoon strips, photos, a combination of prose with cartoons, photostories and short poems (Beigel and Feldman 1963). All these formats feature widely in the subcultural literature. Many of the group magazines include 'transvestite' fiction alongside other male femaling material. *Fanfare*, the official journal of the South African Phoenix Society, for instance, had a regular 'fiction' slot until the magazine's demise in the early 1990s. Other groups separate out their 'transvestite fiction' and feature it in a special publication. The British Beaumont Society did this for many years, publishing the *Beaumag* – a collection of TV short stories and poetry – in addition to the *Beaumont Bulletin*, their official newsletter. Finally, there are the subcultural publishers who make a particular specialism of transvestite fiction, often featuring several scores of available titles at any one time. Sandy Thomas publications, for instance, has some forty titles in its 'TV Fiction

Classics' series; some twenty titles in its 'Contemporary Fiction' series; as well as many others in its 'TV Serials' series. *His First Dress, Vow of Femininity, My Sister's Shadow* are typical titles. Titles such as *Forced to be a Daughter, Learning to be a Daughter, Becoming a Daughter*, give the flavour of the serials.

This 'transvestite fantasy literature' has been examined by Beigel and Feldman (1963), Buhrich and McConaghy (1976), Stoller (1970), Brierley (1979) and Bullough and Bullough (1993).

Beigel and Feldman (1963) drew upon seventy-three published novels and on twenty pieces of unpublished fiction submitted for publication but unpublished. In their sample, it was the innocence of the male protagonist that stood out as the central theme:

> Only in 13 out of 93 stories does the male realize a desire to cross-dress before he has donned female attire. In 70 situations, the male, child or adolescent, at first puts on female clothing against his will; in 6 of the other instances he is forced and in 7 persuaded to continue wearing dresses.
>
> (p. 199)

Stoller (1970) details similar findings. He sees the fictional stories as 'transvestite pornography' and summarises the themes as 'a frightened, pathetic, defenceless boy-man, (who) finds himself, through no doing of his own, trapped by powerful, dangerously beautiful women, who bully and humiliate him' (p. 149) into wearing women's clothes.

Buhrich and McConaghy (1976) depict a more complicated picture. They identify such themes as 'the loneliness of the transvestite' in a quarter of their sample of twenty, and analyse various sub-themes in some detail, but again, the hero was almost always a male who was required to cross-dress because of some circumstance beyond his control. Bullough and Bullough's (1993) findings are congruent with the earlier studies, though they note that the scenarios in the 1980s and 1990s are 'less nice':

> The story lines continued to feature clothing, makeup, shopping and breasts. The fictional wives were still delighted with their husband's new clothing. However, the clothing was sometimes made of leather . . . and more of the heroes were homosexual. The line between transvestism and transsexualism was blurred, as some heroes talked about sex re-assignment surgery and a few actually had it performed. In 32 percent of the items analysed, pain was inflicted on the hero, usually by a dominating woman. Sometimes this pain was not severe (for example, it might be the pain caused by corsets or shoes that are too tight), but at other times it was the more severe pain of whipping.
>
> (p. 290)

There is no doubt that the so-called 'fem dom' theme is 'familiar and much loved' (source mislaid) in male femaling fantasy fiction. It would be misleading, however, to overemphasise its role in fantasy femaling.

I have examined the recently emerged telephone sex-lines which feature male femaling themes. When I focused on the many thousands of male femaling pre-recorded scripts it became evident that themes other than that of 'fem dom' can be equally important. In particular, what I term 'intimacy scripts' (Ekins 1996) have been neglected in the commentaries.

My study (ibid.) involved an analysis of over 200 male femaling telephone sex-line scripts collected between 1988 and 1994. The analysis of the scripts was supplemented with information obtained from unstructured interviews and correspondence with over thirty telephone sex-line producers and consumers. In these scripts the emphasis is upon erotic fantasy male femaling – all are intended to be masturbatory scripts – and they, therefore, provide an excellent and easily accessible source of material for a study of this type of fantasy femaling.

The male femaling scripts are mostly written *by* male femalers *for* male femalers. One informant, for instance, explained to me how he would draw on his own masturbatory fantasies and day-dreams to concoct his scripts. His intention was to provide the maximum erotic stimulation for 'transvestite' callers, over the maximum possible time span. In essence, this entailed so crafting his story that the caller's curiosity about the outcome would lead him to hold on until the end of the tape. He tried to so structure the story that sexual arousal would be maintained in waves of ever increasing pleasurable foreplay until the climax. He attempted to conclude the tape by providing an aesthetically and sexually satisfying climax for the caller's ejaculation.

By the early 1990s it became common practice for a phone-line operator to engage a number of specialist writers and script readers. The writers, often drawing upon their own favourite fantasies and those of their associates, would submit scripts which would become increasingly fine-tuned in response to user comment and popularity. Halcyon, for instance, runs *Apron Strings* for 'forced to feminise fans'; *Apron* for 'transvestites'; and *Pinafore Pages* for 'male maids'. These privately circulated magazines feature scores of phone-lines in each issue and invite suggestions for future lines: 'If you want any particular type of line write ... with all the sexy details. A free pair of knickers for the best suggestions'. Halcyon had so perfected its specialist lines for cross-dressed submissives that by 1993 it was receiving over 1,000 calls a day to its several hundred lines (Berry 1993). Callers frequently report an increasing addiction to the lines. As one user put it: 'I used to ring cheap rate times and be thinking "God! How much is this costing?" Now, I think, "What the hell" and ring whenever I'm feeling randy'.

The remainder of this chapter focuses on these pre-recorded scripts as a resource for accessing masturbatory fantasy. In particular, I place the emphasis upon what the scripts tell us about the interrelations between sex, sexuality and gender, and between self, identity and world when the caller enlists the aid of the script to 'fantasy body female' and 'fantasy gender female', in the service of 'fantasy erotic femaling'. I seek to demonstrate how the progression of the script traces shifting interrelations between the different modes of femaling and how different objects, events and actions are variously co-opted in the process. As we shall see, the male femaler's own person (body, self and identity) undergoes various alterations in the service of orgasm.

THE PARADOX OF EROTIC FANTASY FEMALING

It is the being, or becoming, female that provides the core of the erotic fantasy in all male femaling masturbatory scripts. What that being, or becoming, female is seen to entail – how the transition is effected, and how far; and what takes place when it is – constitutes the variations in the scripts.

For the male erotic fantasy femaler, to become, or to be, female, is erotic in itself. He has, to a greater or lesser extent, substituted the pleasures of identification with women for those of securing a female object choice. Whereas the conventional heterosexual male desires a female, the male femaler in varying degrees wishes to become one, or feels that he is one. Having become female, he may experience desire for an object, but the desire is female desire whether 'heterosexual' or 'lesbian'.

Erotic fantasy femaling rests on a paradox. Fantasy femaling for masturbatory purposes presupposes an erotic focus on the penis, which will become erect, and be a central source of pleasure, particularly as the channel of ejaculation. It might be supposed that this male source of pleasure would inhibit the identification with the female. However, this is not so, and it is the function of the masturbatory script to see that it is not. Fantasy femaling scripts frequently feature 'she males' – males who have become feminised with breasts and female curves but still retain their penises. They may be the source of both identification and object choice. 'She males' are, however, fantasied as phallic women. They are males who have become female in mind and body, whilst retaining their penises. In other scripts 'she males' never feature, enabling the male femaler to 'disavow' his maleness entirely, including his genitalia. Either it is 'as if' he has no genitalia, or his male genitalia become fantasied as female genitalia.

TEMPTRESS SCRIPTS, SADO-MASOCHISTIC SCRIPTS AND INTIMACY SCRIPTS

Male femaling masturbatory fantasy scripts fall into three major types. These I term 'temptress scripts', 'sado-masochistic scripts' and 'intimacy scripts'. All scripts within each sub-type feature female narrators. I shall not consider those overtly homosexual male femaling scripts which feature male narrators;

nor those scripts which feature male narrators seducing females with whom male femalers might be identifying.

The temptress scripts, whilst being widespread in conventional heterosexual scripts, are relatively rare in male femaling scripts. In these scripts the narrator affects the sexy, husky tones of the stereotypical, enticing seducer – the irresistable whore. In 'TV wedding belles' (Crimson 1993), for example, the caller is met with a 'Hello, my darling! Are you ready for your big day? I hope so, because there's no backing out now, you know. Today I am going to make you my wife. My gorgeous blushing bride dressed in silk panties . . .' Throughout the script the narrator maintains the sort of excitable, heavy tones most frequently associated with erotic scripts of a conventional heterosexual sort. Locations are not referred to. The caller and narrator remain encapsulated in the private space of a bedroom. The script ends with the caller kneeling on the bed, her wedding dress thrown up over her buttocks, her silk panties pulled down, submitting to the narrator as man, as her husband, enveloped in a torrent of sighs, squeals and the other accompaniments of sexual orgasm.

Temptress scripts are based on a limited role reversal in a stereotypically erotic situation. The female narrator assumes certain facets of the male role, in order to feminise the caller. She is active in his feminisation. She does, however, remain the stereotype of the alluring seductress, even as she may don a dildo to finalise the caller's feminisation.

Very much more common are the sado-masochistic scripts. These follow the basic patterns detailed in the accounts of 'transvestite fiction' (Beigel and Feldman 1963), and 'transvestite pornography' (Stoller 1970) introduced already. Buhrich and McConaghy (1976) give the flavour:

> The innocent male is coerced into wearing female clothes. The change is 'fantastically successful' . . . the protagonist decides to live permanently as a woman. Real women in the stories are 'feared and hated', often subjugating the transvestite to their every whim and even at times castrating him.

Accordingly, the tones adopted by the narrators of these scripts are dominant and bullying until the protagonist is feminised. At that point, the tones may become loving and protecting, although the subjugation must continue and the submissiveness be maintained. Frequently, third parties are involved. Thus in 'Maid for the dildo' (Halcyon 1993b), for example, Peter is prepared by Joan for her mistress Olga. After numerous attempts at feminisation to become the 'perfect' woman for Olga, Peter finally becomes Alice. Having been so prepared, he is left on a bed to be raped by Olga. The script leaves him heading towards the kitchen to spend the rest of his life as an obedient housewife.

Male femaling sado-masochistic scripts tend to overlap with sado-masochistic scripts more generally. In 'Transvestite spanking!' (Halcyon 1993c), Peter is forcibly cross-dressed. He is then spanked and humiliated by his own wife, in front of his mother-in-law, and 'maid (sic) to kneel and serve dominant women'. In 'Husband enslaved' (Halcyon 1993a), 'a fat, ugly bullying wife dominates a she-male husband'. The bizarre tends to take precedence over subtleties of femininity in these sado-masochistic scripts.

In intimacy scripts the emphasis is upon close familiarity with women, and upon participation as an equal in a shared women's world. The narrator's tones are sweet, friendly and confiding. Females are initiated into various biological, psychological and socio-cultural worlds from which males are largely excluded – worlds of menstruation, worlds of make-up and beauty routines, worlds of women's magazines and so forth. Intimacy scripts favour these matters in their content. In 'So you want to be a girl – like me?' (Eazee Come 1993b), for instance, Dave is dressed as Joanne, when the doorbell rings. She goes to the door as a woman and is met by Kate, who is a representative for a firm selling fashion clothes and accessories. The time flies by as they 'chat away, woman to woman', discussing the various items in the catalogue. In 'Girls must work' (Eazee Come 1993a), Suzanne (the male femaler) takes a job as a waitress. Jenny helps her in the selection of her uniform. Later, Suzanne is able to repay the friendship, by taking over the cash till, temporarily, whilst Jenny visits the Ladies, with the onset of her period. An intimate glance from Jenny is all that Suzanne needs to fully understand the situation and substitute for her new-found friend.

Intimacy scripts celebrate what is seen by fantasy femalers to be part and parcel of the everyday world of everyday (principally young) women. In these scripts, the male femalers become these women and variously feel and act like them.

THE CASE OF INTIMACY SCRIPTS

Male femaling intimacy scripts have been hitherto unexplored as a major source of masturbatory fantasy script. They are, however, particularly instructive in illustrating neglected subtleties in the interrelations between sex, sexuality and gender, and their interrelations with body, identity and world. In the first place, such scripts entail a disavowal of the male body in its entirety and the adoption of a fantasy female body, which is then sexualised. In the second place, they illustrate the importance of gender in the process of sexualisation. Finally, the scripts variously depict the role of identity changes in the service of the erotic.

There are two major variants of the intimacy script. In the first, the script details the male femaler's progressive initiation into a female world, from which there is no exit. These I term 'initiation identity scripts'. In the second, the oscillations between the male and female identities of the male femaler are detailed. These I term 'oscillating identity scripts'. I deal with an illustration of each in turn, adding a brief comment on the use made of each script by two informants who made extensive use of them in their fantasying femaling.

'TV DREAM LINE': AN INITIATION IDENTITY SCRIPT

In 'TV dream line' (CIC 1993b), the caller is speedily introduced into the all female world of the beauty salon. The caller's female identity is progressively reasserted and confirmed until, 'there is nothing more you can do about it. It's too late. You are a girl'. The caller's male identity is extinguished in the process of fantasy femaling leading to orgasm. There are various uses made of body femaling and gender femaling to procure this erotic femaling finale.

The emphasis upon erotic fantasy male femaling is made explicit at the outset, as the tape begins: 'Our TV wet dream line will guide you into *your* fantasy through the erotic feminine scenes that we've created for *you*. Femininity as you've not experienced it before, because you'll become part of each encounter'.

That an intimacy script is to follow is also made clear. The caller will be taken 'into a massage salon with other beautiful young girls. Your beautician is there waiting to probe your feminine body into sexual submission'.

'I'm Sarah, there now, don't be shy', begins the script.

> You're only with other young girls, and I'm here to relax you into femininity, working my hands into every inch of your body. You'll be in a room with other girls and you can keep your bra and panties on if you like. You might like to talk feminine talk with them while I gently rub over your body. And as I do that, either Ann or Joanne will be waxing your legs to get them nice and smooth right up to your bikini line. Feel the soft delicate skin of my hands, rub inside ... your legs. Right up to your crutch. Feel the motion of my body urging into every movement.

The 'bra and panties' are emphasised repeatedly throughout the script. As garments covering the female body – breasts and genitalia – they are associated, particularly, with body femaling. In the case of the male femaling intimacy script, their function is to simultaneously hide the male body and aid in the transition to, and maintenance of, the fantasy female body. As intimate and feminine undergarments, moreover, they are associated with both the erotic and the gendered. They therefore serve as a male femaling leitmotif which can utilise both body and gender femaling in the service of sexual arousal.

> When I move up to your breasts and gently work the oils into your cups, close your eyes as you think of being and feeling feminine ... your breasts ... your panties. They'll feel so silky soft and smooth to the touch. Permanently feminine. Isn't that what women like? Like yours ... shapely, in your bra and little white panties.

The movement up the body continues. 'I move into your neckline and caress your shoulders, with my firm arms forcing my feminine motion into every fibre of your body.'

Then, the other girls are introduced. Our caller is not merely one girl being treated by one other. He is placed firmly as a girl amongst many others in an exclusively female environment.

> Hear the sounds of the other girls around you talking, and laughing and chatting, in their soft, high, feminine voices. Be aware of their presence, here, with you. Girls, here, around you. Girls' talk ... sweet and feminine. And you feel the femaleness in you, as my body heaves into forcing you into feminine relaxation. Forcing you into our female way of life ... the bra ... the panties ... just give in. There's nothing more you can do about it. It's too late. You are a girl. Relax into that thought and just ... submit ... Our female way of life ... The bra ... the panties ... submit.

It is as if the repetitition is lulling our caller into a female world from which he is quite unable to escape.

Now the emphasis shifts from Sarah's hands and voice to her own body. 'Now be aware of my femininity. Open your eyes. See my breasts, perfectly formed. And hanging idly over your face, in the cups of my bra.'

No shift is intended, however, to Sarah as a heterosexual object choice. Her body is being made available to our caller as a mirror image of his own.

Female bodies are accentuated by female clothes, the wearing of which reaffirms the femininity of the wearer. Body femaling, gender femaling and erotic femaling coalesce as the script continues.

> Imagine yourself ... with girls ... like you ... wearing little gathered skirts tight at the waist and falling gently over the hips. The soft, delicate, feminine material wafting round their thighs, in the breeze ... to reveal long, shapely, smooth legs. You know ... the sort of thing you enjoy wearing when you want to go out and feel good.

The presence of onlookers further confirms the female identity. Furthermore, that identity is made retrospective.

> I bet you've accidentally bent over and people have caught a glimpse of your delicate panties. We've all done it. Haven't we? How embarrassing. And how your bottom sticks to the seat, on those hot days. Just like when you were a schoolgirl.

'Are you coming?' signifies the pending intended end-point of the script. The caller is now a 'woman', and able to indulge in the sort of fantasy gender femaling which appeals to many male femalers. 'Are you thinking of all those feminine things? That only you ... as a girl ... could experience ... The bra ... the panties ... little short, flared mini-skirts.'

Once again, the fact that the caller is a girl like the narrator is reiterated.

As you look down the length of my body, you become aware of my panties ... tight, on my hips ... Just like yours. Don't you want to be like that? The wonderful clothes ... The pretty underwear ... Come on ... Feel my hands probing your panties, as you submit to these feminine thoughts.

Climax is reached: 'Climax, with my fingers in your panties'. As the waves of pleasure increase to orgasm:

Now ... Our female way of life ... The bra ... the panties ... your breasts. Just give in. There's nothing more you can do about it . It's too late. You are ... a girl ... Our female way of life. There's nothing more you can do about it. It's too late. You are a girl. Relax into that thought. And just ... submit.

COMMENT

'TV dream line' is an erotic fantasy femaling script which is designed to have the caller enter as female, and remain so until orgasm. Erotic fantasy femalers who have consolidated (see Chapter 9) their male femaling around this mode of femaling will return to their male selves with the incidents of fantasy femaling over.

Graham, for instance, after a period of cross-dressing in public ('doing femaling' – see Chapter 7), settled down with a girlfriend. He did not want to lose her, was frightened to tell her of his interest in male femaling and stopped his cross-dressing. However, as Graham's sexual relationship with his partner deteriorated, he turned increasingly to telephone sex-lines as the focus for his sexual life. Graham told me how 'he could scarcely believe (his) ears' when he first heard 'TV dream line' – so uncannily did it fit his own 'perfect' masturbatory fantasy.

In the past, he had visited beauty salons dressed as a woman, and had received various beauty treatments. He did not experience these expeditions as erotic at the time. Rather he considered that he experienced the treaments in the same way as a woman might – as enjoyable, as relaxing, as pleasurably sensual. With the reality of the trip over, however, he would find himself incorporating incidents that had occurred in the salon into his own masturbatory scripts. He would recall the time, for instance, when the beautician unexpectedly slipped his bra straps over his shoulders, in order to make space for the unimpeded movement of her hands, as she cleansed and toned his face and neck. He would recall the conversations about boyfriends, Christmas presents, and so on, he had shared with the 'other girls' in the salon. 'TV dream line' revived his own experiences and provided embellishments upon them. He incorporated the script into his preferred masturbatory fantasy, telephoned the line regularly and eventually made a tape recording of it.

GIRLS' CHANGING ROOM: AN OSCILLATING IDENTITY SCRIPT

Oscillation between male and female identities is well illustrated by 'Girls' changing room' (CIC 1993a).

In 'Girls' changing room', the female identity Amy, takes over from the male identity David, and it is Amy who goes shopping. Amy finds herself in a communal girls' changing room confronted by a near-naked 'attractive' girl. As sexual attraction emerges in David, Amy disappears and David begins to return. The script provides an excellent example of the inverse relationship between heterosexual object choice and identification that is reported by many male femalers.

The script starts with an involuntary identity transition:

> Yes, something inside was pushing him into changing. The transition, transformation, call it what you like, it made no difference. Amy, beautiful Amy, was about to appear as a fully fledged attractive female, and there was nothing Dave could do about it. Nothing got in Amy's way. Soon, Dave would be gone. And Amy would take over completely.

Soon Amy is admiring herself in the mirror (reinforcement of the identity shift), her body 'filled with feminine warmth and charm' (body femaling emphasis).

The gender femaling that follows is emphasised both to reaffirm the identity transition and to provide erotic focus. Amy has momentarily forgotten her earrings. 'Oh!' she muttered, 'forgotten your earrings, again. Darling, this will never do'.

'But soon, Amy had flittered out of the house with breezy air, to join the rest of her society, in her rightful place (as a woman).' The caller is left with the suggestion that the script is going to be an 'all girls together' intimacy script.

'Of course, to Amy that meant shopping, as it does to most girls.' Further gender femaling is then elaborated. Amy enters a 'lovely' boutique. Great emphasis is placed on the 'glamorous and gorgeous outfits' inside, on the feminine materials – the chiffons and the satins and so on. Amy's natural place is seen to be within this gendered female world.

Just as 'TV dream line' introduces the beautician to reaffirm the caller's female identity, so in 'Girls' changing room' a boutique assistant is introduced to serve the same function.

'Goodness me! Yes!' says the assistant, 'That's just you'. 'It's not too short, do you think?' enquires Amy. 'Oh, no Madam! It's got verve and life in it. And the little short flared skirt will simply swish around your thighs, causing the greatest attention to your legs' (continued emphasis upon fantasy gender femaling, to accentuate fantasy body femaling).

Amy makes her way towards the communal changing room. As she enters it, she is in her element. She can now become part of an intimate female world, try on clothes to her heart's content, exhibit herself in front of the mirror, and so on. The fantasy male femaling caller will be identifying with Amy in these various confirmations of her identity. It is the identification with Amy that is erotic for him.

As a woman, the caller will not find the other women in the changing room potentially sexually desirable. As a heterosexual man, he might be expected to. It is this dilemma which the oscillating identity script exploits. Appropriately, a transitional passage follows which introduces TVs (transvestites), in order to presage the female to male identity shift which is to follow.

> The sight that beheld Amy's eyes could have started any TVs' (transvestites') eyes streaming. There were boobs, and buttocks, distributed all over the changing room. With panties and tights ... bras ... strewn in all manner of haphazard ways on the floor.

Initially, Amy maintains a distance from all this.

> Amy was Amy. She loved the attention. The feminine atmosphere. The feeling of being female. Amy was high. Drugged to the eyeballs with her own infatuation of simply being a woman. And now she was ... She was here ... Bare bottoms and breasts ... Femininity, females ... She was here.

However, a girl (Estelle) next to Amy smiles at her. She is 'wearing only panties'. As she steps into her skirt, 'her breasts idly swing down in movement to her hips'. This is all too much for the heterosexual Dave. Dave's identity begins to reassert itself.

The script 'explains':

> But I suppose that's what started it. You know. That deep down urge that something is no longer right. The drug was waning. The heart was not so much pumping in anticipation as in fear of what she was really doing here. With all these near-naked women around her, close to her. Amy should have been as high as a kite. She had made it. She had passed, successfully. But something else was beginning to happen. Dave was beginning to make himself apparent. What the hell was he going to do now? By now (Estelle) was standing in front of Dave, wearing only a skirt. He became aware ... of her breasts ... idly hanging down ... forming a perfect cleavage. Her hand, gracefully rested on her hip. And she was looking straight at him. Girl to girl. Dave swallowed. Err ... err ... erm ... my name is – Amy, she croaked in his best feminine voice. The girl relaxed. The atmosphere so tense, up to now, calmed a little.

Will Amy vanish without trace? If she does, how will Dave escape his predicament? Or will Amy return?

Amy's eventual reappearance is enabled by what the script refers to as 'an unusual show of high feminine behaviour'. Exclaiming that the dress is 'quite awful', she adds that Dave wouldn't like it, either. She is now free to leave the changing room with her new-found friend. They look through the racks of clothes and eventually make their purchases as 'girls together'. With the intimacy of the 'girl to girl' interactions, a female order is reimposed. Intimate gender femaling reaffirms and maintains Amy's identity.

The 'girls' chat. Amy shows Estelle a particular dress she likes and they both make their way to the cashier to pay for the items they have chosen. 'After you!' said Estelle. 'Oh thank you, darling' (intimacy affirmed, again). 'Amy placed the dress on the counter, and the young cashier totted up the bill on the computer.'

So relaxed is Amy in her identity, now, that she can joke with the female cashier (more girls together): '"How would Madam like to pay for all this?" She asked. "Not at all", replied Amy, whimsically. She took out a credit card and passed it to the cashier'. However, at that moment disaster struck, for the cashier calls the manageress to check the discrepancy between the male name on the credit card and the female Amy before her.

Confronted with an abrupt questioning of her identity, Amy's fragility is revealed, and Dave returns. Just as he is wishing he wasn't there, his wish is granted. The entire sequence is now revealed to have been a dream.

Amy has gone and it is now Dave who awakes in a sweat. He clasps his hands over his face. He gets out of bed and looks around for reassurance. He sinks down in relief. 'Dreams', he sighs, 'Goodness! If I ever try that one . . . I'll be absolutely mad. Fantasising's fine but that was murder. And as for Amy. . . I think he'd got a point. Don't you?'

COMMENT

It does, perhaps, stretch the limits of credibility to suppose that a male femaler would enact such a fantasy, and use a credit card with a male name. Maybe the device was used simply to secure the ending of the script, or to provide a particular twist to the story line. Many male femalers, however, do acquire credit cards in their female identities. This strategy frequently enables a more satisfactory outcome for the male femaler.

Jeremy, for instance, used his credit card made out in his female identity at every available opportunity when he went out shopping as a female. Like David/Amy, in the script, he took particular enjoyment from being a woman in a woman's world. He savoured the moments as he would go through the racks of women's clothes. Like David/Amy, he was never bold enough to try on a dress in a communal changing room. He thought that too risky. Rather, he tried on skirts. As he put it: 'With my handbag over one arm and a selection of skirts over the other, I feel exactly like all the other girls as I approach the changing room'.

Jeremy would feel a mounting sense of excitement as he entered the changing room. What would happen if his male identity was detected? He was never quite sure he would not be detected, but, as yet, he had never been knowingly suspected. In particular, he would recall the tremendous feeling of well-being he experienced on his arrival home with his purchases. As he reflected upon the various male femaling activities of the day, his thoughts would ponder the 'highlights'. Invariably, it was what he took to be the affirmations of being a woman that provided him with the most pleasure: the waiting in the queue of girls and women making their purchases, whilst some of their boyfriends and husbands waited for them, at a distance, at the side of the queue; the appraisal of himself and his clothes in the mirror and the like. Paying for his purchases with his credit card made out in his female name was very important to him. Here was a (preferably) female cashier accepting him as another female, as he made his female purchases in his female name.

Just as with Graham's visits to the beauty salon, Jeremy did not find his shopping trips sexually arousing at the time. It was only when they were over that their erotic potential arose. Alone, at home, as he thought about his exploits, he would find himself becoming sexually aroused and wanting to masturbate. As he masturbated, his thoughts would oscillate. For the most part, he would be thinking of himself as female in the all female world of the boutique and changing room. In these thoughts he was just one woman amongst others. But then, and most usually involuntarily, he would find himself thinking of the glimpses of the women he had observed trying on their own potential purchases. While it was sexually arousing to *be* one of the women, he also lingered on his thoughts of the women in the changing room as they looked at themselves in the changing room, unaware of his gaze. As with David/Amy, it was at these moments that Jeremy's male identity re-emerged. Little wonder, then, that 'Girls' changing room' was one of Jeremy's favourite masturbatory scripts. For him, the oscillating identities featured in the script enabled him to enjoy the best of all possible worlds. They reminded him of his own experiences. Furthermore, he could enjoy the pleasures of identification with both David and Amy as he revelled in the oscillations of identity and their various concomitants.

Graham and Jeremy's enjoyment of their respective masturbatory scripts was heightened by the fact that they had previously engaged in similar 'doings' on previous occasions. Memories of past actions infused the present fantasies. Many male femalers, on the other hand, remain at the fantasy femaling stage and never move on to the phase of 'doing femaling'. Those that do, however, are considered in the following chapter.

7

DOING MALE FEMALING

The fact that male femaling is commonly viewed as deviant in contemporary Western societies ensures that many male femalings will not 'progress' beyond the beginning and fantasying phases. The force of potential or actual societal reaction is such that either 'beginnings' are nipped in the bud and male femalings cease entirely, or the male femaler learns to keep such strivings to himself. He tells no one, and restricts his femaling to fantasying. No one need ever know.

Where, however, the move is made to 'doing femaling', the male femaler is likely to be immediately assailed by fears that his femaling will lead to his being variously humiliated, derided, rejected, ostracised, even criminally sanctioned. It is in this phase, therefore, that the sub-processes of male femaling introduced in Chapter 4 – those of 'displaying', 'disclosing', 'passing', 'reading' and 'pretending' – become particularly germane. Moreover, it is in this phase that social process must be set firmly within the constraints of social structure if we are to understand and explain the manifold ways male femalers process the problems attendant upon their engaging in a stigmatised activity.

As outlined in Chapter 4, the manifold ways that structure impinges on process can best be dealt with by setting the social process of male femaling within the analytic social structural category of the 'masked awareness context'. Focusing on 'doing femaling', this chapter develops the various ways in which process and sub-process are played out within structure, in terms of the masked awareness context and its sub-units – those of private, open, closed, suspicion and pretence.

'Doing femaling' might be said to take place whenever male femalers adopt what they take to be the thoughts, feelings, attitudes, behaviours, accoutrements and attributes of genetic females. From the standpoint of our ideal-typical career path, however, 'doing femaling' refers to the more 'serious' cross-dressing and acting out aspects of fantasy femaling that develop from activities found in the 'beginning' and 'fantasying femaling' phases. The body femaler may, for instance, depilate parts of his body periodically. He may experiment with hiding his male genitalia ('tucking'), and producing a simulated vulva. With, or just as likely without, body femaling variants, the gender femaler may well build up private collections of clothes and may experiment with more complete dressing using make-up, jewellery and accessories. All of these may, or may not, be built into masturbatory routines (erotic femaling), which may become more protracted.

It is instructive to divide 'doing femaling' into two phases. These, I term primary and secondary. In the primary phase the male femaler develops along clustered lines, as regards sex, sexuality and gender, and their interrelations, without really quite knowing what he is doing. Cross-dressing is likely to play a major part in this phase whether the clusters follow sex, sexuality or gender patterns, but in this phase of doing femaling the male femaler is not sure of the differences or where precisely he stands with regard to them. Gender femalers make a start in becoming knowledgeable about the gendered world of girls and women, about what dresses they like, about styles and so forth. This, in itself, gives pleasure. Others may place more emphasis upon increasingly elaborated masturbatory routines. Others may become more preoccupied with aspects of their morphology.

As regards the interrelations between the constitution of self and world as being SSG'd, the initial phase of doing is likely to be a period of particular personal confusion and of vacillation. Not only is the femaler 'betwixt and between' two worlds, but he has no clear notion of what he is doing or its likely outcome. His 'everyday' meanings in respect of self and world are increasingly threatened by his developing 'doing femaling', but he is still not advanced in his conceptualisation of what he is doing or what it means. The femaler may vacillate, for instance, between cross-dressing episodes, confusion about their meaning and, in many instances, repeated attempts to stop what he is doing, marked symbolically by frequent 'purges' – the periodic throwing away of offending collections of clothes, cosmetics, jewellery and so on.

In this initial primary phase, the male femaler has not yet constituted a meaning for his activities. As his 'doing femaling' becomes more frequent, the tendency to seek to 'explain' it may well become more pressing. The search for meaning is incipient. But unless the femaler chances upon, for example, media coverage of 'people like me', or comes across 'explanations' by others in scientific texts, he may well continue to think that 'I am the only one in the world' to do these things; 'I am a freak'; 'I don't know why I do this'; 'where will it all end?'

The secondary phase of doing femaling, however, embraces the femaler who has come to some *modus vivendi* and *modus operandi* for what he is doing and is freer to develop his personal doing style. For some, the mere knowledge that there is a term 'transvestite' to describe their activities is sufficient for them to continue to 'do femaling' with less guilt or agonising about the meaning of their activities. For others, reflection upon the meaning of their activities never really ends. In terms of our ideal-typical career path, we might say that actual career paths of concrete lives evidence different interrelations between 'doing femaling' and 'constituting femaling' (Chapter 8) and, indeed, between 'doing femaling' and 'consolidating' femaling' (Chapter 9). For the purposes of this chapter, however, we largely ignore questions of meanings and focus upon detailing doings.

Doing femaling is best seen in terms of four major doing styles. These I term 'solitary doing', 'solo doing', 'dyadic doing' and 'group doing'. I detail each with particular reference to the sub-processes of male femaling and the sub-units of masked awareness context pertaining to each style. This treatment places due emphasis upon the 'with whom?' and 'to whom?' of male femaling which are so important from the standpoint of awareness contexts. Questions of the where? when? and how? of male femaling are considered as subsidiary themes within each doing style.

SOLITARY DOING

Solitary doing refers to the doing style in which the male femaler females alone, in solitude. We might say he does his femaling in solitary confinement. His displaying while male femaling is private or self-displaying. His intention while 'doing' is to maintain a private awareness context and to ensure that other sub-processes and sub-units do not pertain. The problem of disclosure is likely to loom large and is considered in the section which follows this. Other sub-processes – those of passing, reading and so on are inapplicable as long as solitary doing pertains. Similarly, the sub-units of open, closed, suspicion and pretence awareness contexts are inapplicable while the solitary male femaler successfully maintains his private awareness context.

Solitary doing may take place in variously private and public spaces and places – in the privacy of home, in a rented space such as a hotel room, in a private public place such as a cubicle in a public convenience, or, indeed, in a secluded spot outdoors. Wherever the space or place, however, the feature of solitary doing is that the femaler seeks to privatise the space for the duration of his doing femaling.

Doing femaling may entail no props, as with the femaler who body females by hiding (or 'tucking') his genitalia. It may involve improvised props – a towel might be used to make a skirt, for instance. Such cases minimise the risk of discovery. However, once female props are used, problems arise as to how and where they are to be obtained, used, stored or disposed of. Solitary male femalers often go to great lengths to maximise the chances of maintaining a private awareness context, as illustrated by Joshua's male femaling pattern. Joshua lives with his parents in a suburb of Manchester.

Too frightened to 'borrow' his mother's clothes, buy female clothes locally, or store female clothes at home, Joshua would drive to a town many miles from his home in order to buy various items of female clothing. He would then cruise around in his car until he had found what seemed like a secluded spot. He would not cross-dress in his car for fear of suspicions being aroused and his identification being traced through his car registration number. Rather, several hours would be spent tramping through undergrowth and woodland until he found a spot so isolated that he dare risk cross-dressing. Joshua never dared to put on make-up: he would not be able to remove it quickly enough, should he be disturbed. Rather, ever vigilant for intruders, he would cross-dress as quickly as he could and masturbate. He was then faced with the problem of disposing of his items of female clothing as he felt it to be too risky to keep them. He would then drive to yet another town, scour the streets for a secluded litter bin, and drop the 'offending' articles into a bin after wrapping them up in insignificant looking brown paper.

Joshua's male femaling is exceedingly restricted. It is solitary, brief, highly episodic, in a highly restricted setting, and it uses minimal props. It demands only a tiny fraction of his everyday life as a man.

At the other end of the continuum would be Elena. Elena is a professional photographer in her 30s who lives alone and has converted an upstairs attic into a room which can only be accessed via a 'secret' door that appears to be a cupboard door which she keeps locked. The door provides access to a stairway, at the top of which is another door which opens on to what she calls her 'grotto'. The grotto has wall-to-wall mirrored wardrobes. The wardrobes are brimful with female clothes, shoes, accessories, make-up and so on. Elena spends upwards of ten hours at a time 'doing femaling' in any one session. She tries on outfit after outfit. She poses in front of the mirrors in continual self-display. She takes scores of photographs of herself in various states of feminine dress and undress. She experiments with several alternative make-ups in any one session and frequently video-records her entire sessions of doing femaling.

When I visited Elena in her grotto, she told me that I was the only person, apart from herself, who knew of the room's existence. She felt it to be an entirely private and secret hideaway. Her only fears were what would happen if she died, or was suddenly incapacitated and her executors or heirs discovered her 'shrine' to male femaling.

The extremes of Joshua and Elena are somewhat uncommon. The vast majority of solitary male femalers 'do' their femaling at some point in between such extremes and develop different strategies to facilitate it. Many femalers 'borrow' their props from mothers, sisters or partners. This solves the problem of acquiring them but, as we have seen (Chapter 4), raises dilemmas of how to return them undisturbed and undamaged. Others acquire clothes and acessories via mail order using a post office box number and/or assumed name. Many buy clothes and accessories from retail outlets, saying they are buying them for their girlfriends or wives.

Similarly, the problem of storing the paraphernalia of male femaling is dealt with in different ways. A commonly discernible pattern is where collections are gradually built up and then periodically 'purged': offending articles are burnt or otherwise disposed of. This assuages the male femaler's guilt and fear of discovery until, that is, he finds himself building up a replacement collection. Jane kept her female clothes in carrier bags in the spare wheel compartment of her car. Juliette kept hers in a locked suitcase in the garage amongst assorted bric-à-brac. Jane and Juliette had similar doing femaling styles. When the opportunity arose, each would drive off to a distant town and change into their female clothes in a tiered fashion. They would put on their female underwear and tights in a public toilet and leave the toilet with their male clothes over the top so as to avoid any suspicion. Then they would find a secluded spot, make-up, slip on a skirt, blouse, jacket and shoes. They would spend a couple of hours in the car, cross-dressed, before changing back into their male attire and carefully removing all traces of make-up before driving back home.

Solitary doing may include the gamut of partial and complete male femaling of various types. A variant that lends itself particularly well to solitary femaling is where the male femaler indulges his preferences for a style of dressing that would be inappropriate in most public settings. Sado-masochistic styles with the focus on leather or rubber are obvious examples. More idiosyncratic are the adoption of styles from a past era, or a focus exclusively on one particular material, such as satin, lace or taffeta.

Nikki's interests dwell on late 1950s and early 1960s glamour outfits.

> Although present-day fashion trends are very pleasing I love to wear those of the late 1950s and early 1960s. I adore the hats and veils, the earrings and pearls and of course, the seamed stockings and court shoes. Women appeared more fragile and feminine in neat little suits, dramatically simple cocktail dresses and devastating evening gowns. Epitomizing the era was the classic 'Little Black Dress'. Worn with a string of pearls and ravishing long black gloves it provided a simple, cheap way to look absolutely stunning. The long gloves were exquisitely feminine, luxurious and sexually stimulating accessories rivalled only by stockings and high heels. They were part of any smart woman's wardrobe but now, alas, they are a rare sight indeed.
>
> (Nikki undated: 15)

Accompanying her letter is 'Nikki's Fashion Show' which features twenty-five photographs of Nikki in various outfits. Hats, gloves, stockings and high heels feature prominently, accessorising a variety of little black dresses, suits and skirts of the late 1950s and early 1960s.

Cyndi (1993), on the other hand, indulges her interest in taffeta.

> I have always had a passion for taffeta which has now become a very powerful fetish. Acetate or polyester taffeta and smooth woven nylon are the particular fabrics I find to be sexually stimulating. I just love the feel of these fabrics especially when they are worn against the skin. So

cool and highly sensual. I get excited at the rustle of crisp taffeta and the sound when caught by fingernails and objects. Taffeta bridal wear is top of my fetish list. Brides and bridesmaid's dresses of this fabric absolutely drive me wild! I am extremely in love with bridal wear. Bridesmaid's dresses in particular are in my opinion the prettiest and most feminine of all female attire.

At the time of writing Cyndi is living at home with her parents. She is fearful, however, that her preoccupation with taffeta will be discovered. She is determined to acquire a private space where she can develop her solitary femaling in safety. She concludes: 'I am hoping to buy myself a static mobile-home in a nice part of the country. Hopefully this independence should allow me to enjoy my cross-dressing to the full'.

SOLITARY DOING AND THE PROBLEM OF DISCLOSURE

It is implicit in the above accounts that it is the problem of disclosure which is paramount for the solitary male femaler. Solitary doers always seek to female in private and in isolation, and usually wish their activities to remain totally undisclosed. In some cases, however, they may disclose the fact that they female to others whilst still maintaining a solitary doing style. We saw above that Elena feared that her grotto would be discovered after her death. In such cases femalers may make provision for keeping their femaling undisclosed to all but a carefully chosen confidante. The confidante never sees them female, but is told that they do so and is given instructions to dispose of incriminating femaling paraphernalia should they die.

Tony was a successful accountant who, as he grew older, developed a particular mixture of cross-dressing and bondage. He would dress up as a 'leather whore' and tie himself up, often remaining in this state for weekends at a time. He told a solicitor friend about his solitary activities and the solicitor agreed to remove any incriminating evidence from Tony's home in the event of his death. One night Tony died tragically in a fire caused by a faulty electrical appliance. When his solicitor friend came round to his house he found police officers sorting through whips, chains, leather boots and coats and so on. According to the solicitor 'the police were very good about it' and allowed him to remove the offending articles. Nothing more was said about the incident.

Another common variant of 'disclosing' is for the solitary male femaler to female in private but to write to the problem pages of women's magazines disclosing his male femaling and seeking advice about what he should do. Many find this relieves their loneliness to some degree. Another possibility is for the solitary male femaler to write to contact magazines such as *Tranz* and describe his 'doing' (see Nikki's story above). Anonymity can be maintained through the use of pen names, post office box numbers and so on.

Whatever the variations, however, the solitary femaler will be vigilant to secure a private space for the duration of his male femaling, and will take particular care to remove all traces of male femaling from his person, in addition to hiding any male femaling props when the incident of male femaling is over. Many solitary femalers relate 'near misses' when their cover was nearly blown (near involuntary disclosure).

James was too frightened to secure his own female clothes while living with his wife. Instead, he would wait for the time his wife visited her parents on an overnight trip. He would dress in her bra and pants at night, masturbate and fall asleep while still wearing them. Early one morning, he was disturbed by the sound of banging on the front door. It was his wife who had returned unexpectedly early. He had latched the door as a precautionary measure. With his heart pounding he hastily removed the bra and pants before returning them to their rightful place. He feigned sleepiness, grunted a welcome to his wife and went back to sleep and the matter was never mentioned again.

Jane (mentioned earlier), who stored her clothes in the boot of her car also spoke of a 'near miss'. She had driven to a motel and spent the day cross-dressed in her motel room, when her partner thought she was at work. She was careful to return home at her usual time and poked her head round the sitting-room door as usual, to say 'Hi'. A couple of minutes later whilst making a pot of tea in the kitchen she was horrified to realise she was still wearing her bright orange clip-on earrings. Her partner never said anything and she assumed, relieved, that the earrings had gone unnoticed.

On other occasions more complicated strategies for avoiding involuntary disclosure have to be engineered. Tight bra straps make marks on the flesh that take time to disappear. Carole would plan her male femaling and bedtime to ensure that when she went to bed with her wife the marks would have disappeared. When it is impossible to remove tell-tale signs, 'cover stories' have to be concocted. Celia had large feet and on one occasion squeezing them into women's shoes for too long caused her big toe nail to bleed heavily under the nail. It was an injury which took several months to heal. She exlained to her wife and doctor that she had accidentally stubbed her toe. Pauline's cover had to be more elaborate. Pauline favoured a particular pink shade of lipstick which she wore to bed one night. She discovered, too late, that it stained her lips. Rather than delay joining her mother at the breakfast table, she deliberately cut her lip with her electric razor in an attempt to cover up her lipstick-stained lip.

SOLO DOING

The distinction between a solitary and a solo femaling style might not be immediately clear. The Concise Oxford English Dictionary (1975) defines 'solitary' as 'living alone, not gregarious, without companions, secluded, single, lonely, sole'. It defines 'solo' as 'unaccompanied, alone'. However, 'solo' may also refer to 'a vocal or instrumental piece or passage, or dance, performed by one person with or without subordinate accompaniment' (ibid.). Herein lies the key to understanding the meaning of 'solo doing'. There is a marked difference between the isolated musician who practises alone and never plays in the company of others, and the soloist who may practise alone and in private – but whose *raison d'être* is the public performance, whether accompanied or not. Thus, whereas solitary doing takes place alone with nobody and to nobody, the solo style of doing takes place in a 'lone' fashion, but *in the company of others* and (very often) with a sense of performance in front of others. These others are not participating in the male femaling but they are vital accompaniments from the standpoint of the male femaler 'going solo'.

Whilst there are femalers who 'go solo' from the outset, most solo femalers do so after varying periods of doing solitary femaling. These femalers may then develop a taste for a solo style of doing that becomes the focus of their subsequent male femaling.

Generally speaking, there are male femalers who display as female in public and do not much care how others react to them. Some gain pleasure from presenting an androgynous appearance and being taken as either gender. Others get a kick out of being thought eccentric or outrageous. Most solo doers, however, do not want to face the ridicule that is likely to accompany public doing if their femaling mask is 'read' as such. They wish to pass as women, and gain great pleasure from the fact of passing. They therefore spend considerable time and trouble perfecting their doing to maximise the chance of 'passing' in public.

With time, attention and experience, many male femalers are able to 'pass' in most public settings. While 'pretty' young male femalers and middle-aged or elderly femalers may be able to capitalise on their androgynous physiques, other male femalers may achieve the desired effect by taking female hormones and undergoing facial electrolysis. Without recourse to such body femaling, however, most males find it difficult to hide their masculinity. Height, bone structure, beard shadow, the wearing of a wig and general masculine demeanour all indicate a male behind the mask of femininity. The most that such male femalers can realistically hope for is that they so engineer their interactions that they avoid close scrutiny. They may then pass in a crowd or in a brief encounter, particularly if they do not speak.

The male femaling subcultural literature is replete with accounts which detail that 'first walk (*en femme*) to post a letter', or that 'first walk around the block'. Many femalers get progressively bolder as the pleasure they obtain from public male femaling takes an increasing hold on them. With these male femalers, the more they display in public, the more they want to. The solo style of display is generally very prevalent amongst male femalers. Jacqui, for example, would talk of her 'Jacquescapades'. She took particular delight from the time she attended an academic conference dressed as a woman, spending her time there wandering around the university campus on her own. She felt certain she was never read, and took great pleasure from writing up an account of her experiences and circulating it to selected male femaling friends. Susan would male female in her car and let her skirt ride up her legs at traffic lights so that lorry drivers could see her legs and undergarments. Frequently, the drivers would give chase to her car in order to get further glimpses of her. Susan preferred partial display on these occasions, in order to maximise the chance of maintaining a closed awareness context. Consequently, she strove to position herself and her car so that her face could not be seen by the lorry drivers from their cabs.

Those unfamiliar with the subjectively felt pleasures to be obtained from male femaling often fail to see the point of such solo femaling. What needs to be stressed is the great pleasure the male femaler obtains from this part-time 'escapading'. This need not be overtly sexual. There is apprehension and fear of involuntary disclosure, but the 'high' to be gained from it more than compensates for these fears for those who enjoy this style of doing.

Michelle P. is an excellent example of the 'doing femaler' who, having built up a collection of clothes, feels the need to display outside of the house. She fears disclosure, so she goes out at a time which minimises the possibility of interaction with others. When she meets a male who seems to be treating her as an attractive female, she is ecstatic but terrified. Fearful that she will be 'read' (involuntary disclosure leading from closed to open awareness context), she beats a hasty retreat.

> I graduated from wearing only female underwear to wearing skirts, petticoats, blouses, make-up, outdoor coats, headscarfs, and to carrying a handbag. Later, having bought my own pair of second hand high-heeled shoes I decided that I would try going outside of the house dressed. It had to be early morning before anyone else was awake and while it was still quite dark. This was due to my lack of confidence in my girl-self appearance I suppose.
>
> On one memorable occasion I was sitting on a bench in the park near my home fully dressed in female clothing, when I saw a man coming towards where I was sitting. He was about 30'ish and I was 18 or 19 at this time. As he walked past me I cast my eyes to the ground so as not to encourage him to stop. However, as I glanced up he stopped about ten yards away from me and started to stare at me. This was during the days of the mini skirt and, of course, wanting to feel feminine and 'with it', I was wearing one, thereby showing quite a lot of my legs. My heart was beating like mad as I tried to appear as demure and feminine as I could. I wanted this man to think I was a girl but at the same time I was scared stiff in case my girl-self was not convincing enough. He came over and sat down next to me, eyeing my uncovered legs as he did so. He had obviously decided to 'chat me up'.

I felt very feminine at this point, just like an ordinary girl would, I suppose. I made a pretence of pulling my mini skirt down to try and cover my legs but it was too short. I was still showing plenty of my thighs. He asked me what I was doing out so early in the morning (5.30 a.m. I think). I decided that I had better not speak so I pretended that I was dumb. He just kept smiling at me and looking at my bust and legs. I felt every inch a female right then.

With regret I decided that I had better leave before the situation got out of hand. I rose from the bench, smoothed my coat down and walked away as fast as my high-heels would carry me. He did not follow me fortunately. I often wonder now what would have happened had I stayed and let him discover my secret. The only regret I have over the incident is that feeling very feminine at the time I could not carry on in the way an ordinary girl might have. I am not homosexually inclined in any way so I would not have let anything untoward happen. It is a fond memory to look back on though and one of the rare occasions when I have been treated as a female by a male person.

(*Tranz* 17: 40–4)

Michelle P. remained content to solo female for occasional sorties. These expeditions apart, she always displays to others in her male identity. At the other end of the continuum, however, is the male femaler who decides to kill off his male identity entirely and reappear in another setting as a woman. If successful, he comes to be known only as the woman he displays as.

On the day Brian decided to live full time as Joan, he wrote a note to his wife and family saying that he had left the country and was going to commit suicide. Joan then moved to a distant town and began to live openly as a woman with a new identity. Joan was a post-operative transsexual who had changed all her personal documents into her new female name. She 'passed' well and succeeded in her plan for several years. As it happened, in Joan's case, her inner turmoil and guilt led her to re-contacting her family. However, it is by no means impossible for this 'solution' of living a completely new life to be taken, undisclosed by the male femaler, to her grave.

Michelle P. sought to pass as a woman occasionally in selected public settings. Joan sought to pass as a woman in all settings, at all times. Both, however, wished to maintain a closed masked awareness context while they were male femaling. Both had to live with the possibility that at any time their masks might be read.

SOLO DOING, READING AND THE PROBLEM OF DISCLOSURE

Just as the subcultural literature is replete with 'passing' stories by solo male femalers, so it is with 'involuntary disclosure' ('reading') stories. Indeed, much male femaling within the solo doing style revolves around the management of the tension that arises between the pleasures of passing and the fear of being read, with its attendant disappointments and feared or actual consequences. These disappointments and consequences may lead to a modifying, or, indeed, abandoning of the solo style.

Penny's male femaling, for instance, despite all her efforts to improve her mask, was frequently detected by youths who would make comments to each other indicating that they had read her mask. 'Ooh look! There's David Bowie', said one youth to his mates, on one occasion. Penny could live with this, even finding it slightly amusing. When, on another occasion, however, a youth yelled out: 'It's a transvestite. Bloody cock fucker!' she was so hurt and frightened that she thenceforth restricted her sorties to settings that would minimise the possibility of ever displaying in front of groups of youths. She developed a solo style that restricted itself to male femaling in female settings such as boutiques, or in the relative privacy of hotels. Her sorties in more public settings were restricted to short walks, never far from her car.

Many male femalers, however, just abandon the solo style following unsuccessful passing. It is simply too fraught. Others may, for instance, body female with renewed vigour in the (often successful) hope that with more feminine display they will be able to pass more successfully in the future. An interesting variant arises when the male femaler is not intending to present as female, but is taken as such. Gail's case provides an interesting twist in this regard.

Gail (see Chapter 9) is male femaling with the intention of living 'full time' in the future when she feels she can pass successfully. She has been taking female hormones for some time and is dressing androgynously in unisex clothes, but in her own eyes is presenting herself as male on the occasion she describes. She is with her young son, Joe, at a supermarket cash desk:

> And I remember the changes being very imperceptible to me, but I think to other people, less so. At this stage I'd got dual credit cards, and so on. I remember one occasion. My hair was quite long. I was having voice therapy as well. I remember we were in Tesco's one day and I gave a credit card to the girl at the cash desk. She said, 'I'm sorry, you've given me the wrong card'. I was in an utter panic, because, I thought 'My God, I've given her *Gail's* card, instead of my other card'. 'Ooh, I'm sorry', I said. As it happened I didn't have any other cards with my male name and I thought 'What am I going to do?' And then she said, 'You've given me your husband's card'. I said 'Pardon'. I'd actually given her my card with my male name, but she assumed that I was Joe's mum and that the card was my husband's. I went bright red, and said, 'No, actually, that is my card'. Then SHE went bright red. We looked like a couple of tomatoes! To put her out of her misery, I said, 'Actually, you are not too far from the truth', and we left it at that. It made me realise

that I was changing, and the way I was interacting with Joe and other people must be changing as well.

(Research interview)

Shortly afterwards, Gail began to live full time as a woman and has been doing so ever since. In her case, involuntary acceptance as a woman led her to full-time femaling before she had originally intended.

Even the most 'passable' of full-time male femalers, however, can never be sure their past will not catch up with them and lay them open to the possibility of involuntary disclosure. Adèle Anderson, for instance, was a post-operative male-to-female transsexual who had made a successful career for herself singing with the celebrated all girl trio *Fascinating Aïda*, when her male femaling was disclosed by the press in the early 1980s. Many less celebrated male femalers have suffered the same fate. As Terri Webb tellingly puts it in her 'Autobiographical fragments from a transsexual activist' (Webb 1996: 194): 'I am able to say that those who do not know my history assume I am a woman, born as such'. Nevertheless, 'I do – as we all do – suffer from the fear that someone will say "You're a man aren't you?"'

Little wonder, then, that many male femalers opt for a doing style which is less fraught than solo doing.

DYADIC DOING

While solo doing may take place within any of the four sub-types of masked awareness contexts, dyadic doing, however, always takes place within either an open or pretence awareness context. This is because the feature of the dyadic doing style is that the male femaler male females with another person who is fully aware of, and assists his male femaling by variously participating in it. Dyadic doers may prefer either doing with another male femaler, doing with a non-femaling male or doing with a female. Many male femalers dyadically do with their wives or partners in the privacy of their home. Others prefer those privatised spaces in public places such as hairdressing and beauty salons, where they can dyadically do with the hairdresser or the beautician in relative privacy. Still others dyadically do in pairs in public places. Whatever the preference, the rewards come not from the pleasures of passing within the dyad, but from the pleasures of doing with another person – of variously sharing in the intimacies of male femaling within the intimacy of a one-to-one relationship.

Male femalers who favour dyadic doing often see no point in solitary or solo male femaling, once the initial doing of these phases has lost its appeal. Tom, whom we shall meet again in Chapter 9, is typical. Even though his image as a male femaler is a very presentable one, he would seldom cross-dress on his own and never go on jaunts on his own, not least because he would

97

have been terrified of being picked up by the police and being forced to furnish his male identity. As he puts it:

> I've never been interested in trying to pass. I'm 5' 10". I'm slim build, but with heels on I'm going to be about 6' 1". To me it just seems absolutely ludicrous to consider that I could pass. People would be nudging one another and saying – ooh, what's he doing?

Rather, Tom used the columns of contact magazines to try to forge an introduction to a girl who was sympathetic to cross-dressers, with whom he could meet and be 'girls together': 'I wanted to meet a girl who was interested in transvestites and would help someone to dress and go out shopping'. His first successful such contact made it clear that she was not interested in a sexual relationship with a transvestite but that she enjoyed 'unusual' types of dressing. 'She was mildly interested in fetishism and liked the idea of boys dressed as girls and going out'. He continues:

> I had mentioned in my letter to her that I went to drag balls. She said she'd never been to one but perhaps we could go together. I went to London to meet her. She was a very nice girl. She helped me to organise some clothes. We went out that day and bought a wig, some shoes and some clothes. We went together to the drag ball. She did my make-up. She helped with the wig and made me look very nice. We met one or two people and it was interesting being dressed as a girl and being with a girl at a place like that.

On an earlier occasion, Tom met another male femaler. We see something of the same yearning for a sensitive and easy intimacy in his account of this incident:

> When I lived in London I contacted a Beaumont Society member and said, 'Look, you know I've never actually managed to dress up properly. Would it be possible? I haven't got any of my own clothes and I really don't know about going out buying them. Would it be possible to to to come along to your place and dress?' And this was a young person – probably in their early 20s. He said, 'Yes, no problem'. It wasn't too far out of London, where I was living. I went along. She lent me some clothes, did my make-up. Sorry, he did my clothes, helped me with my make-up and took some pictures. I thought we both looked extremely nice. I was quite startled to see myself in the mirror. I thought I looked just like my sister. I think I took one or two photographs. Then I started to get quite attracted to this man – when he was dressed. He was quite a nice person. He had been extremely kind and helpful. And I think possibly he may have realised what was happening with me sort of complimenting him about the way he looked, although, I was also dressed as a girl at the same time, so it might have seemed a bit ludicrous. So we took our things off and I went home. But I was quite surprised

to be there with somebody and to be chatting him up. Because when he was not dressed as a girl, I wasn't attracted to him one bit. But when he was, then I was attracted to him.

It is important to Tom that he is taken as a male who is femaling, and this remains the case whether his partner in the dyad is male or female. The awareness context must be open and he finds absurd any pretence that he is female. For many femalers, however, male femaling within a pretence awareness context is of the utmost significance. Such awareness contexts make particularly striking case studies in role-play situations. Male femalers who enjoy enacting elaborate rituals, however, find it difficult or impossible to meet compatible partners due to the specificity of their demands and this leads many to prostitutes.

Conscientious prostitutes who specialise in these services become conversant with major male femaling rituals and make it their business to find out the particular idiosyncracies of their clients. With a certain amount of good will on either side, many male femalers can be accommodated in this way. Many potential clients, however, are so specific about their favoured ritual that they eventually abandon any hope that prostitutes will be able to meet their requirements. A particularly striking example of this is that of Millie.

Millie is a male femaling 'sissy maid' who has abandoned the search for the conventional prostitute and seeks out Mistresses with whom she enacts a favoured dyadic role play that is so important to her. She has worked for five different Mistresses in five years. Currently, she has three, one of whom is Mrs Silk. I asked Millie to tell me about 'becoming' and 'being' a maid. She replied as follows:

Becoming a sissy maid: Experiences with prostitutes who claimed to offer a maid training were costly and disappointing. Their uniforms were torn and tatty. They did not have the least idea how to behave as a Mistress with a maid in service or how to train her.

The ideal would be to find someone who had some idea of how things were done in the old days and who would be prepared to accept a middle-aged man dressed as a maid into her household.

The first step was to acquire a proper outfit. I went to an overall/ workwear shop and explained to the young assistant what I wanted. She did not bat an eyelid. She gave me several maid type dresses to try on. When we found one that fitted I bought an apron and a coverall cap. I had a proper outfit that any woman might find acceptable in a domestic.

The next step was to pay several visits to a cross-dressing centre where I was made-up and dressed. This gave me the opportunity to learn about make-up and get some hints on dressing.

Meanwhile I was answering advertisements in a contact magazine. Some ladies advertised directly for TV maids. At first all my letters were returned with 'No Thanks'.

I eventually found a lady who took me on. She was a business woman who struggled through the recession by getting extra cash through advertising corrective services for gentlemen. By the time I went to her she was stopping this. At first I paid her as if I was a client, but she soon took me on and I have been there for five years. That was the start.

I first came across an advertisement from Mrs Silk over two years ago. Once again, after several visits she accepted me without any payment to work as a maid servant cleaning her house.

There have been other positions in between. It has been my experience that it is possible to find households where you will be accepted as a maid and given a real 'in service' experience.

Being a sissy maid: The effect of dressing as a maid is very powerful and releases in me strong feelings of submissiveness and a desire to win the approval of a Mistress.

There are a number of elements to this:

I always wear a panty girdle which holds my male genitalia tightly against the belly. This has a very powerful effect of depriving me of feelings of masculinity. I have no desire to become transsexual. I only dress as a maid for purposes of recreation and relaxation.

Once I am wearing the panty girdle and start to put on the underwear feelings of submissiveness come over me. These feelings are strong and are not very present in the rest of my life. It is important to point out that I do not choose what I wear as a maid. Mrs Silk always leaves out a list of chores to be done during the day and what uniform she wants worn. This sort of token 'enforced dressing' adds to the feelings of submissiveness.

Whenever I arrive at Mrs Silk's I let myself into the house and go straight upstairs to the attic room. There I find my list. From this moment on I have no say at all in what happens to me for the rest of the stay.

I have to begin with a bath and a shave. Then into the uniform chosen by the Mistress. I have to make sure it is clean and pressed.

I then go downstairs and start my chores. When Mrs Silk meets me she often checks the uniform and especially the underwear. I am not allowed to wear anything frilly or very feminine. In fact she has had a set of unbleached calico slip and bloomers made for me.

All this serves to deepen the submissiveness. I have lost all contact with my masculine arrogance. I really am a little maid servant.

Mrs Silk expects me to curtsey and behave meekly and politely to her. I speak only when spoken to. She expects me to get on with my work unsupervised. Sometimes the contact between Mistress and maid is minimal during the day.

Usually the heavy cleaning jobs are first thing in the day. I have to wear a plastic apron for washing floors, windows and toilets. When the lighter jobs like dusting and hoovering come along I usually wear a different dress and a frilly apron. Mrs Silk is quite keen on at least two uniform changes in a long day. This keeps me feeling submissive.

The work is routine domestic work. The Mistress expects it to be done properly. She always indicates whether she wants a room tidied, cleaned or spring cleaned. I then know what she wants.

I am allowed breaks during the day. Then I go up to my room to rest and eat. I am not allowed about the house without being in a proper uniform.

These rules and regulations serve to enforce the maid servant status. Mrs Silk is a natural Mistress. She doesn't really have to act it out. She just behaves as the Mistress of the house. I must always refer to her as 'Mistress' and not call her 'Madam'.

I hope this gives you an initial idea of what it feels like. I am a maid servant. There are other men in the house who always call me Millie (a name chosen by the Mistress) and they treat me as the maid.

When I leave, I am dismissed by the Mistress. I can change and leave the house without seeing her again. I am also present when she has parties or houseguests over a weekend.

When I leave, as I drive home I gradually revert to my masculinity.

GROUP DOING

Male femalers who are inhibited about sharing the intimacies of their male femaling with others in a dyadic situation may adopt (or revert to) a solitary or solo style of doing for their entire male femaling lives. Other male femalers rest content with doing within the intimacy of the dyad. As Millie puts it, in relation to the particular dyad of Mistress and maid: 'The Mistress/maid relationship is quite special and quite unique ... A real bond grows up which I don't think you could establish in any other way'. Other male femalers, however, seek others with similar interests in male femaling with whom they can pursue their various male femaling activities in a group situation. This I refer to as group doing.

Of necessity, group doing takes place in either an open or a pretence awareness context as regards the group male femalers themselves. Each participant knows that the others are males femaling. There is no question of 'passing'. Group doing does, however, provide maximum opportunity for the preparation and displaying of the femaling mask, the sharing of the intimacies of male femaling and, if desired, the disclosing of aspects of the male behind the mask in a non-threatening situation.

Group doing styles emerge within the interrelations between what I term 'spaces and places', 'group size and organisation' and 'group belief systems and ideology'. Drag balls, for instance, are usually public events held at regular intervals in the same venue. Anybody who pays the admission can attend in whatever dress they like. The London Porchester Hall balls, held throughout the 1980s, for instance, used to attract upwards of 700 participants at each ball. Whereas in earlier times they were patronised by the drag queens and their escorts, by the 1980s the balls were attracting 'drag queens, TVs, TSs, androgynes, teenagers, pensioners, straights, gays, even the men who fancy men in frocks' (Kirk and Heath 1984: 56). The atmosphere was free and easy. Gay drags camped it up, while cliques of transsexuals discussed the latest techniques in breast augmentation. Groups of out-of-town transvestites could meet up with local Londoners. Above all, male femalers of all hues could 'let their hair down', enjoy themselves and have a fun time.

How very different were the small one-off events organised around a particular dressing theme for carefully vetted members of transvestite support groups in hotels hired for the occasion. Note the air of respectability in the following (Peel 1992: 30):

> Last Spring Bank Holiday, seven potential brides arrived at a discreet hotel in Torquay, with all their finery for a traditional wedding.
>
> They were accompanied by various wives, photographers, helpers and advisers. There was a pre-wedding meal on the Saturday evening with all the signs of a hen party.
>
> On Sunday at noon, the brides assembled in their wedding dresses, resplendent with head dresses, veils, petticoats, ribbons, gloves, bouquets and, probably, frilly garters.
>
> Not a sign of a groom, but the brides were not in the least crestfallen. Instead, they spent the entire afternoon being photographed in the gardens and on the hotel patio.
>
> At 5pm they changed into going away outfits for the reception. This was a traditional wedding buffet with a magnificent wedding cake.
>
> All this was organised by Christina Peel, who has agreed to arrange another event for the May Bank Holiday next year. Dates are 1st to 3rd May inclusive and the theme will be 'Spring Fashion Fun Weekend'.

Male femaling groups are variously organised around body, gender and erotic femaling. 'Transsexual' groups, for instance, are organised primarily around body femaling. Here the emphasis tends to be upon the exchange of information about sex re-assignment procedures and experiences, referral networks and so on. Mutual support is secured principally through newsletters and correspondence and members may meet, if at all, only occasionally and in twos or threes. On the other hand, the many 'transvestite' groups place the focus on gender femaling. These groups seek to provide spaces and places where cross-dressers can gender female without ridicule or harrassment. Also embedded within the social worlds of cross-dressers and sex-changers are a number of sometimes overlapping and interrelating social circles (Simmel 1955; Kadushin 1966) of erotic male femalers. Erotic femalers may meet through personal advertisements placed in contact magazines (see Chapter 8), or through group meetings designed principally for social gender femaling, but used by erotic femalers to secure partners for subsequent small group erotic femaling. One such group, for instance, used to meet regularly after the London Porchester Hall balls for 'a discrete after-hours private orgy', as one informant put it.

Groups vary to the extent to which they are more or less consciously engineered in relation to the terms supplied by modern medicine. From the emergence of such groups in the 1960s through to the 1990s, the majority have deliberately adopted the medical categorisations 'transsexual' (TS) or 'transvestite' (TV) in their titles and Constitutions. Relatedly, they have they been centrally concerned with a distinctive individual 'transsexual' or 'transvestite' identity, distinguishable from others popularly and (to them) erroneously equated with them, such as 'homosexual' or 'pervert'. They have expended much effort promulgating their point of view to the general public and relevant professional bodies.

More recently, however, it is possible to discern a shift in focus. Groups previously happy with the term 'transvestite' are increasingly using the term 'cross-dresser' (Rose 1993). They see it as a less perjorative and less clinical term. More fundamentally, in many quarters, there is less concern with rigid demarcations between categories and more with 'mixing, merging and matching', even 'transcending, transgressing and threatening' the divide between the genders, the sexes and the sexualities (Ekins and King 1996b). This shift is well illustrated by comparing the 'group doings' of the most established group for 'transvestites' in the United Kingdom: the Beaumont Society, with the first British club for 'Boys, Girls and Inbetweenies' established in 1993 and currently riding on the crest of a wave. The comparison illustrates something of the way very different 'group doing' styles emerge from within the interrelations of 'space and place', 'group size and organisation' and 'group belief systems and ideology'.

The Beaumont Society is the largest and most well established self-help and social group for transvestites in the United Kingdom. According to its current 1992 Constitution, its purposes are

> to form an association of those who cross-dress and for transsexuals and, through this association, to provide a means of help and communication between members, in order to reduce the emotional stress, eliminate the sense of guilt and so aid better understanding by them and their families and friends.

In fact, some 90 per cent of its membership (around 800 at any one time) are 'TV' (Scott, 1992: 7) and are overwhelmingly heterosexual.

In its texts, the Society conceptualises transvestism in terms of love of the feminine; and the transvestite self in terms of 'full personality expression'. Moreover, the Society, through its various activities in promulgating its ideas and in holding 'respectable' gender orientated meetings at 'respectable',

103

'straight' venues, provides those identifying with it opportunities for managing the sexual stigma often attached to cross-dressing activities, both by cross-dressers themselves and the general public. Many of my Beaumont Society informants constituted their femaling selves and world in terms of 'the Beaumont' and would state publicly that their cross-dressing had nothing whatsoever to do with sex or sexuality.

The Beaumont Society is the only truly national 'transvestite' group in the United Kingdom. It does not have a base or central office, rather, the contact address for the Society is just a forwarding address. All the officers – the volunteers who run the Society – are scattered around the country and only actually get together three times a year for committee meetings.

From the standpoint of its membership, however, the Society provides a means to developing a transvestite identity, and, when desired, the opportunity to meet others in private settings. Regular meetings in the private houses of 'regional organisers' are favoured by those who have most to lose from disclosure. The more adventurous take the opportunity to attend weekends held at seaside hotels in such resorts as Weston-Super-Mare or Scarborough. Only sponsored members can attend such events, it being the job of the regional organisers to sponsor only those members whom they feel sure can uphold the respectable image of the Society. While it is recognised that not all members can present an equally convincing feminine appearance, far less 'pass' in public, all are expected to be as 'ladylike' as possible. 'The Laura Ashley/Stepford Wives look is in', as one informant put it. 'This *is* "ladylike"'.[1] Conversely, those unwilling to conform to the Society's version of TV identity and behaviour will be made to feel uncomfortable and may, indeed, have their sponsorship withdrawn. Thus, at one hotel weekend event, when a member arrived wearing a beard and a dress, and was observed dancing with his girlfriend in this state, considerable consternation resulted. It constituted an impropriety on no account to be repeated.

Up until 1987, the Society officially excluded gays from its membership. That rule was then relaxed after a lengthy and sometimes acrimonious debate, but an ethos which discourages overt displays of sexuality of any sort is still firmly in place. The focus is on providing the space and place to gender female ever more presentably. To this end, many organisers of meetings arrange for various servicers, such as wig-fitters and beauticians, to attend meetings and give demonstrations. Wives and partners are encouraged to attend Beaumont events and it would be in the worst possible taste to alienate any of them by engaging in any behaviour that might be regarded as unsavoury. In particular, wives are said to fear that their husbands may be (or become) homosexual or transsexual, and a sharp distinction is made between these two 'conditions' and that of the heterosexual transvestite.

The Way Out Club could hardly be more different. Prior to the 1990s, there were no *overtly* public venues in the United Kingdom where cross-dressers and sex-changers could socialise in settings created specifically for them and their friends. There were the support group meetings, and the meetings in private houses and variously privatised public places, or there were the niches carved out in various gay worlds. The Way Out Club changed all that. It provides twice-weekly night-time venues (permanent spaces and places) where cross-dressers and their friends can meet. There are limited changing facilities for those who wish to change when they get there, but most arrive cross-dressed.

On one occasion, a regular visitor took to exposing his male genitalia. In another incident, a group of self-assured S/M (sado-masochist) scene members arrived, intent upon creating maximum impact – the women exposing their pierced nipples and so forth. On both occasions, organiser Vicky Lee's bubbly charm and firmness ensured that the 'offenders' left the club, until appropriately dressed. Such 'extremes' apart, however, anything goes at the Way Out Club. Body, gender and erotic femaling are embraced with equal enthusiasm. Classifications such as 'transsexual' and 'transvestite' are tolerated, but not dwelled upon. Rather, the Way Out philosophy is to

Figure 7.1 Vicky Lee 1995
Source: © Debbie Humphry 1995

105

work to break down barriers between categories. A favourite catch phrase at the Club is 'Welcome, Boys, Girls and Inbetweenies' and each of Way Out's three organisers are committed to this approach in their different ways. Steffan, the Club's Marilyn Monroe look-a-like, identified himself as gay for many years. Now he identifies as an 'inbetweenie' who revels in the attention guaranteed by his glamorous outfits. His only female clothes are his various stage outfits, which he wears only for clubbing and performing in cabaret. Caroline Eggerton favours a mix of fetish and office wear – thigh length leather boots with smart two piece executive skirt suits. Vicky Lee never wears male clothes but selects her attire as she feels a woman does, wearing outfits appropriate to the occasion. 'Some think I'm a drag queen, some think I'm a transsexual, most assume I'm gay. If they ask, I explain proudly that I'm an inbetweenie. In every possible way'. She continues:

> For over two years now we've attracted 150–200 people at each of our weekly Saturday meetings. About a third to a half of those that now come, 'dress'. Many more are trannies that don't go out dressed, but like to see those that do. Some, fondly refered to as 'trannie fuckers' or 'TF's', are looking for trannie girlfriends, but many come just for the atmosphere. Some regulars come from miles away. Every week is an international mix, and everyone is amazed by the relaxed atmosphere, where gender and sexuality are never an issue and often an illusion.
>
> (Lee 1995: 19)

Since its inception in 1993, The Way Out Club has run a number of other ventures – Caroline's dressing service, TV/TS Magazine distribution, dinner parties for professional cross-dressers, a 'Paris Coach Trip for 50 Way Out Trannies' and so on. Most recently Way Out has gone 'on the Web' and in its first week on the internet had over 6,000 people cruise its pages from all over the world.

Doing male femaling, then, has many variant styles. In its execution, private spaces and places are variously made available, and public spaces and places are variously colonised for greater or lesser periods of time. Whether the focus is on solitary, solo, dyadic or group doing styles, however, the focus on 'doing femaling' is always on the *activities* of male femaling. Questions of the *meanings* of these various activities are either of no particular interest or (as with much group femaling) provide a backdrop against which the manifold male femaling activities take place. Once the issue of meaning does become paramount, however, we are entering another phase of the male femaling career path – that of 'constituting male femaling' – and it is to this phase that we may now turn our attention.

8

CONSTITUTING MALE FEMALING

The symbolic interactionist focus on the constitution of meanings within interaction makes it a perspective particularly well suited to unpacking the phase of 'constituting male femaling'. 'Constituting male femaling' marks the period where the femaler begins to constitute the meaning of his activities in a serious and sustained way. As femaling experiences and activities increase, many femalers are increasingly drawn to 'explain' themselves: to 'make sense' of themselves and their activities and to work out where femaling 'fits' with the rest of their lives.

A number of possibilities are typical of this phase. The femaler may seek professional guidance – a 'cure' – having constituted himself as, for example, a pervert in need of help. He may in, rare cases, construct his own definition of the situation without access to literature or subculture. More typically, he will have chanced upon media references to 'people called transvestites (or transsexuals)', with whom he can identify. Many femalers, either through contact with subcultural literature, or through their reading of the 'scientific' literature, begin to constitute a personalised transvestite or transsexual self-concept within a world of femaling, which is refined as they compare themselves with self-proclaimed transvestites and transsexuals they may meet in the subculture. Some definitions of the situation will be adopted 'ready made' as it were. Others are seen as inapplicable. More typically, the newly confronted constitutions are moulded to fit the particular self-concepts and understandings of self and femaling that the male femaler has constituted thus far.

It is in this phase that meanings begin to crystalise around particular 'namings' (Strauss 1977: 15–30). These are often quite discriminate namings having to do with psychiatric-medical conceptualisations as they have been absorbed into the subculture.

Frequently, much thought and careful consideration is directed towards 'finding the label that fits'. Some come to label themselves as a 'true transsexual'; others as TV (transvestite) with TS (transsexual) tendencies; others as a 'middle-of-the-road transvestite'; while others, as 'primarily fetishistic'. Still others fight shy of medical or quasi-medical categorisations entirely, preferring 'gender bender', 'gender blender' or more idiosyncratic inventions, such as 'gender transient' (see Chapter 9) or 'gender outlaw' (Bornstein 1994).

Having adopted a label, meanings can now be ordered and understood. Once the femaler has sorted out *what* he is (and this is where the emphasis lies), beginnings can be made towards understanding who he is, and towards understanding the meanings of objects to him as variously SSG'd. The emphasis in 'constituting femaling' does, however, tend to be on conceptualisations of self and identity. Once the label has been adopted, past identities are typically re-interpreted in the light of the newly discovered 'condition'. This is especially evident in the context of a consideration of the interrelations between sex, sexuality and gender, the modes of femaling (body, gender and erotic), and the constitution of self and world as being SSG'd. What had been a confusing *mélange* now becomes clear, or clearer. Sally comments: 'I fought it for years, I realise now that I had been TS (transsexual) all along' (newfound 'sex', body femaling identity). Whereas for Annie 'it was always a sexual thing. Now I can meet partners and we can 'rub slips' together, I know that's where I'm at' (erotic femaling identity, constructed around the sexual, with residual gender femaling).

CONSTITUTING FEMALING: PRIVATE AND PUBLIC

It is implicit in the foregoing that constituting femaling takes place variously privately and publicly, within various awareness contexts and with varying use made of literature and of others. This chapter illustrates the major contexts within which constituting takes place, with reference to selected case material chosen to detail the very different major types of constitution available to the contemporary male femaler.

The first example illustrates the possibilities of the lone male femaler constituting a meaning from within his own imaginary and private world. This appears as a serious and sustained constitution which does not draw extensively upon publicly available constitutions. Rather, the solitary male femaler constitutes, *de novo*, as it were, out of the intimate detail of his own life. These constitutions are most easily accessible in the case of individuals labelled psychotic by psychiatry. The private and 'crazy' nature of the constitutions is seen as evidence of psychosis in the language of psychiatry, and of 'madness' in the language of lay folk.

The second example focuses on a dyadic situation – that of the lone male femaler and his professional confidante. I take the particular situation of the patient and psychoanalyst. Here, in the privacy of the psychoanalytic setting, a male femaler comes to an understanding of his male femaling in terms of it being an unconscious attempt to defend against anxieties provoked by heterosexual intimacy. *Pari passu*, with the emergence of this particular constitution, the patient finds himself less inclined to male female. In due course, he considers himself 'cured' of male femaling, and we leave him engaged to be married, 'untroubled' by male femaling fantasying and doing.

The third example considers the case of a young male femaler who comes to accept himself as 'transsexual' after following a route which traverses a general medical practitioner, a self-help group for transsexuals, and a psychiatrist specialising in psycho-sexual 'disorders'. This provides an illustration of a major contemporary conceptualisation of male femaling. Noteworthy, are the interrelations between 'scientific', member and lay knowledge of cross-dressing and sex-changing, as well as the example of self, identity and world being fashioned within those interrelations. The young male femaler forges his private identity in terms of the publicly available category of 'transsexual' as mediated to him both privately and publicly.

The fourth example turns to the constitution of male femaling within private male femaling worlds. It introduces the worlds of private networking amongst male femalers who use the columns of contact magazines to exchange ideas, thrash out meanings and set up meetings. It shows constitutions of male femaling being fashioned in the process of written communication and indicates how self-appointed intermediaries within selected male femaling subcultures may seek to initiate newcomers into their favoured constitutions, with varying success.

Many femalers constitute and re-constitute without ever consolidating around a firm conceptualisation of who and what they are. This final example traces a four-year period of constituting which never reaches a consolidated outcome.

THE LONE MALE FEMALER AND PRIVATE CONSTITUTING

It is a commonplace observation amongst those entrusted with the care of the so-called psychotic that male psychotics frequently think that they are females and vice versa. They may not merely wish to change sex, or think of themselves as female minds in male bodies, but actually believe they are changing sex, or have changed sex. As E. Bleuler would have put it, with reference to schizophrenics, 'schizophrenics are almost invariably, if not indeed invariably, in doubt about which sex they belong to' (Bleuler 1953). Common sense and psychiatry conceptualises these beliefs as delusional.

Opinions differ about how to theorise this commonly observed phenomenon. Despite the very different terminologies developed, there is broad agreement on the basic account. In the process of development, all of us face the task of separating out from our social and physical environment – what Mahler (1968) calls the separation/individuation process. We come to have a sense of ourselves as separate from others and the world. As part of this process of separation, we come to an appreciation of the separation between the sexes and of our own membership of a sex category.

In certain states and on certain occasions, we may experience a fusion with others and the world – often reported in religious and aesthetic experiences, in sexual intercourse and in the state of being in love. Most of us return from these experiences intact. Some, however, become so uncertain of the boundaries between themselves and others that they regularly and involuntarily experience parts of others as being parts of themselves, or parts of themselves as being parts of others. Thus, the psychotic patient may say, 'Doctor, you have my nose today' (an example of appersonation), or 'I have your nose today, Doctor' (an example of transitivism). The patient means the statement literally. Common sense says he is deluded.

By the same token, psychotic patients variously take on the attributes of their opposite sex. During a manic attack the patient finds this experience agreeable because it represents fulfilled wishes. Where, however, there is what psychiatrists term a paranoid symptom complex, 'as at the onset of schizophrenia or paranoid psychosis, the transitivism and appersonation may be alarming and objectionable to the patient' (Freeman 1988: 7). In these cases, particularly, the patient may feel the need to 'explain' his experiences. In doing so, he 'constitutes' their meaning, often in very elaborate formulations.

A particularly sophisticated constitution is the celebrated *Memoirs of My Nervous Illness* by Daniel Paul Schreber (1988). Prima facie, the memoirs read like the tortuous, convoluted meanderings of an insane, albeit very intelligent and cultivated, man. Niederland (1984) has demonstrated persuasively, however, that Schreber has constructed his world from the building blocks of personal biography. Niederland renders public and meaningful what appears to be a mad private world. Particularly relevant in the present context is what Schreber makes of his inital very frightening male femaling experiences, and how he feels compelled to justify what is happening to him, and what he does – all in terms of divine intervention. In doing so, he constructs a complex world view, detailing the significance of his male femaling in 'the Order of the World' (Schreber 1988: 69–79).

It is June 1893 and Schreber is lying in bed one morning, shortly after being informed that he was to be appointed *Senatspräsident* to the Superior Court in Dresden. He has been troubled by dreams which presage a return of his former 'mental illness' when suddenly he is struck by a bolt out of the blue: 'I had a feeling, which, thinking about it later when fully awake, struck me as highly peculiar. It was the idea that it really must be rather pleasant to be a woman succumbing to intercourse' (Schreber 1988: 63).

Schreber is horrified by the thought and declines to accept responsibility for it. First, he attributes it to his half-awake state and later feels inclined to blame others for implanting the thought in him:

The idea was so foreign to my whole nature that I may say I would have rejected it with indignation if fully awake; from what I have experienced since I cannot exclude the possibility that some external influences were at work to implant this idea in me.

(ibid.: 63)

Subsequently, he begins to experience the first signs of communication with 'supernatural powers', particularly that of nerve-contact with his physician Professor Flechsig who spoke to his nerves without being present. Contact with Professor Flechsig is soon replaced by contact with God, who speaks to him 'incessantly'. From this communication, Schreber forms an opinion of:

the tendency innate in the Order of the World, according to which a human being ('a seer of spirits') must under certain circumstances be 'unmanned' (transformed into a woman) once he has entered into indissoluble contact with divine nerves (rays).

(ibid.: 69)

Schreber then devotes a chapter to an exposition of these circumstances. From the initial feelings that it 'really must be rather pleasant to be a woman succumbing to intercourse', Schreber eventually experiences pleasurable sensations *as* a woman who has submitted to intercourse. Indeed, he experiences fertilisation. His 'explanation' of the phenomenon embellishes upon his communication with God: 'I have myself twice experienced (for a short time) the miracle of unmanning on my own body' (ibid.: 74).

I had a female genital organ, although a poorly developed one, and in my body felt quickening like the first signs of life of a human embryo: by a divine miracle God's nerves corresponding to male seed had been thrown into my body; in other words fertilisation had occurred.

(ibid.: 43)

How is Schreber to explain these experiences? His memoirs detail the elaborate edifice of his constitutions. Essentially, they involve three major elements. He has a mission to redeem the world and restore it to its lost state of bliss – he is the saviour, rather than a person in need of being saved. This mission must be preceded by the destruction of the world and by his personal transformation into a woman. Finally, transformed into a female, he – now a woman – would become God's mate, and out of the union a better and healthier race of men would emerge.

At first he is troubled by many questions. 'Are you not ashamed in front of your wife?' he asks himself. 'Fancy a person who was a Senatspräsident allowing himself to be f . . . . d'. However, as he experiences an increasing sense of pleasure in his state of 'high-grade voluptiousness', he decides to accept his new bodily condition without reservation. As he puts it:

Since then I have wholeheartedly inscribed the cultivation of femininity on my banner, and I will continue to do so ... whatever other people who are ignorant of the supernatural reasons may think of me. I would like to meet the man who, faced with the choice of either becoming a demented human being in male habitus or a spirited woman, would not prefer the latter.

(ibid.: 149)

There have been a number of attempts to explain Schreber's constitution ('constituting' constituting femaling). The most celebrated is that of Freud (1911). For Freud, Schreber's second illness was precipitated by his unconscious homosexuality towards his physician Flechsig. The dreams that presaged his second illness were indications of his wish to return to Flechsig as a woman. Frightened by such wishes he negates his wishes towards Flechsig (he does not love him). He comes to hate Flechsig (reversal). He projects his own hatred of Flechsig onto Flechsig – Flechsig hates me and persecutes me – before displacing his thoughts and feelings concerning Flechsig onto God (a father substitute). For Freud, such mechanisms may be uncovered in all similar cases of paranoid illnesses.

Schreber and Freud were both writing long before the constitution and popularising of the diagnostic category of transsexualism. Not surprisingly, perhaps, from the standpoint of contemporary times, others have argued for a different constitution. Critics, for instance, have argued that Schreber's sexual deviation was transsexuality, and his mental illness was schizophrenia, not paranoia (Eysenck 1985: 58). My point, however, is that Schreber constitutes the meaning of his male femaling from the details of his personal biography and his stock of knowledge at hand (Schutz 1953). His seemingly bizarre constitutions can be seen as intelligible in terms of his biography and his theology. In the name of a good education and upbringing, Schreber's father had administered all manner of restraining devices on him – indeed, he had tortured him from a modern humanist perspective. Niederland (1984) translates the content of Schreber's childhood experiences into the content of his 'delusions'. From the standpoint of the atheist, his constitutions concerning God, Jesus Christ and the Resurrection are no more nor less 'crazy' than those of many religious people. Indeed, as a Christian, Schreber is able to use his experiences to illuminate Christian dogma. As he puts it:

On the basis of what I have myself experienced, I am able to give a more detailed explanation of some Christian dogmas and how such things can come about through divine miracles. Something like the conception of Jesus Christ by an Immaculate Virgin – i.e., one who never had intercourse with a man – happened to my own body ... Further, I have reached a fairly clear idea of how the Resurrection of Jesus Christ may have come about; during the latter part of my stay in Flechsig's Asylum and the beginning of my stay here, I have witnessed not once, but hundreds of times how human shapes were set down for a short time by divine miracles only to be dissolved again or vanish. The voices talking to me designated these visions – the so-called '*fleeting-improvised-men*' – some were even persons long ago deceased ... On the basis of these experiences I am inclined to think that Jesus Christ also, who as a real human being died a real death, was subsequently by divine miracle 'set down' anew for a short times as a '*fleeting-improvised-man*'.

(ibid.: 42–3)

CONSTITUTING A 'CURE' IN A DYADIC SITUATION

There is a widespread belief in the male femaling subculture that it is impossible to 'cure' male femaling. One argument is conceptual. A 'cure' suggests a restoration to health or relief from disease. If male femaling is conceptualised as a harmless pleasure or an alternative life style, for example, then to talk of health and disease in this context is inappropriate. Another argument accepts the view that compulsive male femaling is, indeed, a 'condition' – a state of being physically or mentally abnormal – but that a 'cure' is never successful. If it appears to be so, temporarily, then it is never permanently so, and it is better for the male femaler and everyone else to come to terms with that fact.

What this view overlooks is that many male femalers 'begin', 'fantasy' and 'do' male femaling, and then constitute themselves as people needing a 'cure' and embark upon a course of treatment with a professional 'curer' who accepts this definition of the situation. In the course of the 'treatment' the desire to male female may disappear.

Bernard, for instance, referred to his 'transvestite' activities when he sought psychoanalytic psychotherapy. In an early session, he gave his therapist a note which read as follows:

I still have things to say and emotions to express. When I was in my teens I became interested in women's clothes and got really sexually turned on by them, but I hated myself for it and I became really confused. I just didn't know what was going on.

I remember once my mother saying that she used to dress me in girl's clothes when I was a baby-child. I always had a fixation about tights, even at a young age, so maybe that's where it comes from.

I then realised I was using the clothes for a type of female comfort-company, but the fixation 'transvestism?' still continued. Then when I started dating it went away.

It weighs like a black evil cloud over my memories, with the tension, anger, stress and frustration of my youth.

I think that's where a lot of my anger at the opposite sex comes from. It leaves me with a mixed up attitude towards them. I used to think, why were they allowed to wear that type of clothing. Why were only they allowed the privilege, no matter who they were.

Then I took a liking to the feel of men's clothes and felt that I could identify with that style of clothing.

It has left me now that I know my sexual identity which is male orientated, but the boundaries are not fixed, nor am I oppressed by male-female stereotypes – though something is still bugging me, or upsetting me, which I cannot grasp, or understand, as yet. For it is, I think, affecting the way I react to my girlfriend when I get into a relationship. Maybe I am treating them like female sex objects – like what the clothes represented to me.

I hope you understand.

To this note Bernard appended the following:

I have just remembered an old memory of when I was very young. I was with my mother who was shopping. I was about 6 or 7 at the time.

I was looking in a shop window and there was a collection of naked mannequins inside. I remember being or getting excited in a simple sexual way. I started to fantasise about the mannequins – wanting to get inside them and for them to become a second skin, so that I could feel or sense their sexuality.

It was around this time that I had a fixation about women's tights and started to steal and wear my mother's. Though later (at about 11) I forgot the whole episode.

I started to masturbate about this time.

(Personal correspondence)

Bernard's male femaling would return from time to time. As an early adolescent, he occasionally shaved his body hair. Later, he would dress up in his girlfriends' clothes. He felt that these activities acted as a block on his wishes for a closer intimacy with his girlfriends. He was unable to ejaculate inside a woman without fantasies of being cross-dressed himself. Further, he had noticed that his desire to male female, in practice (doing femaling), occurred when he felt let down by an actual or potential girlfriend. He would withdraw into himself, cross-dress and masturbate, and he did not find this satisfying.

As he became better able to accept his vulnerability in the face of an intimate relationship, he felt less need to male female in times of discomfort or stress. After some two years of treatment, his male femaling fantasies and activities had ceased. He still had an interest in women's clothes, particularly under-wear. However, he would indulge his particular interest in 'sexy' underwear by buying his girlfriend various presents. He enjoyed looking at and feeling the underwear on her, rather than the thought or practice of wearing it himself.

The major criticisms made against psychoanalytically based therapies (amongst other therapies) as applied to 'transvestism' and 'transsexualism' are, first, that they are irrelevant – 'a transvestite "has every right to be accepted as a woman" (or man). This is part of personal freedom in a democracy' (Gutheil 1954); second, that they do not work; third, that the therapists' alleged discoveries of 'castration anxiety', 'separation anxiety' and so on, are so much jargon, and unhelpful to those outside the limited circle of the followers of psychoanalysis; and finally, that therapists, whatever their protestations, fit their patients into their theoretical schemas.

Bernard did not want to be accepted as a woman. He found his male femaling unsatisfying. Psychoanalytic psychotherapy did 'work' for him, certainly, at the time. Bernard did experience disgust at the sight of female genitalia (castration anxiety). He was fearful that his penis would not be 'up to the job' of satisfying a woman (castration anxiety). When fearful of losing an actual or potential partner he tended to withdraw into himself and create his own woman by wearing women's clothes, that is, becoming a woman in his fantasies (separation anxiety defended against by identifying with the lost object). Did the therapist fit Bernard into his theoretical schema? The therapist might have said that Bernard provided considerable evidence to confirm the schema. However, had Bernard gone to a therapist of a markedly different theoretical persuasion, he would not have constituted the meaning of his activities in the same way. Moreover, had he sought the advice of a 'transvestite' support group, there is every reason to suppose he would have been encouraged to accept his male femaling. As likely as not, he would have been told that there was no 'cure' for it, nor need there be. Certainly, he would never have come to the constitution he did with his therapist.

THE MAKING OF A MODERN TRANSSEXUAL

Alan provides an excellent example of a male femaler constituting as a 'transsexual' as a result of various interactions with the media, transsexual support groups and the medical profession. It is instructive to compare Alan's account with his psychiatrist's.

When I interviewed Alan he was 21 years of age and living at home with his father. He had been attending a small self-help support group which welcomes anybody who thinks they may be transvestite or transsexual. It was at one of these meetings that I first met him. Petite and fragile looking, with small sharp features, he wore his ginger hair long and dressed sloppily in casual, old-fashioned looking male clothes. He was frequently mistaken for a girl even though he rarely cross-dressed. When I interviewed him he had been attending the support group for some months and had approached a professional for help, for the first time, some six months previously.

He had felt more at home with girls for as long as he could remember and always wished to be one. He had told no one of his wishes and was becoming increasingly sad and tearful about his lonely predicament. He had read about 'transsexuals' in the media some years previously. Although he identified with these people, he had not felt able to make any move which might lead to him 'coming out' as a transsexual. He wasn't sure what he was. Then he chanced upon an advice column in a woman's magazine which listed a number of support groups for transsexuals.

He wrote to a number of these groups, one of which said that he should first see his general practitioner if he felt he was transsexual and wanted to do something about it. He eventually went to his general practitioner, mainly because of his 'extreme depressions' and said he wanted to be referred to a psychiatrist with a view to having a sex-change operation. 'It sort of came out without my really meaning to bring it up'. His general practitioner told him that as far as she knew nothing much could be done about his position and even if it could she wouldn't agree with it as there were other more important priorities for medicine. The general practitioner left him crying in her waiting room.

He then telephoned a local gay help-line and discussed the possibility that he might be homosexual. Here he was given the name of a local psychiatrist with a specialism in psycho-sexual disorders who was known to treat transsexuals. He arranged an appointment with this psychiatrist. At the first visit to the clinic he was given a number of what he referred to as 'diagnostic tests'. He was asked to imagine himself in bed as a male and answered questions relating to masturbatory fantasies. For the last two tests he had to imagine himself as a woman and respond to further questions. On the second visit he was asked for a life history. On the basis of these two sessions he was then told that he was transsexual and that he must behave, act, work and dress as a woman before he would be prescribed hormone pills. His view was that if an expert says he is transsexual, then he is.

At the time of our interviews he was despondent about the fact that his job as a fitter – which he enjoyed – was thought unsuitable and he was told to get a more feminine job. When I introduced the topic of how he would distinguish a transvestite and a transsexual, Alan said: 'You go along to the doctor, and they say what you are. You don't have much choice but to accept it. A transsexual is a woman in a man's body'. Alan is resigned to the fact that he must follow the advice of his doctors but he doesn't really know what that is, except in regard to his job. His psychiatrist told him 'more or less straight out' that he must do everything he was told and then eveything would be all right. If he did not, then that would be an end to treatment. He was told there were certain rules that had to be followed – there would be no surgery until he had lived as a woman and had been taking hormones for two years. The psychiatrist had said this was not her rule, but the general rule.

When I asked him what he said to that, he replied: 'Well, actually, I took along a copy of the SHAFT (Self Help Association for Transsexuals) *Bulletin*, and indicated to her that it referred to differences in treatment elsewhere'. In particular, Alan felt that his psychiatrist was doing things the wrong way round. He wanted to start on hormones before cross-dressing, whereas his psychiatrist would not prescribe hormones until he was living and working as a woman. He continued:

> My psychiatrist read it but seemed to think the rules in general were the same. I realise I must go along with everything they say. They say that if I do they can offer me everything. They have facilities there for offering beauty advice – on how to make-up and on electrolysis. It's great really.

I was not present when Alan was interviewed so I cannot comment on his response to his interviews with his psychiatrist. I did, however, interview his psychiatrist and also read her published work. A rather different picture emerged.

Dr P. considers transsexualism to be a condition in which anatomically normal individuals feel themselves to be members of the opposite sex and earnestly wish to change sex accordingly, although they are well aware of their true biological sex. She subscribes to the view that the gender and sexual identity of an individual are biological in nature and dependent on hormonal brain differentiation at a critical period of intra-uterine development, though she stresses that the case is unproven, as yet. Whilst in her published writings she stresses that transsexualism is often not recognised as such and is diagnosed as transvestism, effeminate homosexuality or as a delusional state, in our personal interview she emphasised that the function of the psychiatrist was to enable transsexuals to accept themselves. 'Maybe they couldn't accept it, or wouldn't, or had been fighting it.'

King (1993: 83–4) suggests that psychiatrists use two very different approaches to determine whether sex re-assignment is appropriate in particular cases. The 'pragmatic' approach places the emphasis upon proven ability to 'pass' in the new role for an extended period of time (Money and Walker 1977; Randell 1971); and the 'diagnostic' approach makes the attempt to diagnose a 'true' transsexual according to some theoretical framework (Stoller 1968; 1975). I put this formulation to Dr P., she was firmly of the 'Randell' view and uses the 'real life' test 'to teach them to be more realistic about the hormonal and surgical outcome'. If they can complete that and they still want surgery then 'that's what we should make available to them', she concluded.

PRIVATE NETWORKING AND THE CONSTITUTION OF MEANINGS

The 1980s saw the publication of a spate of magazines designed both to titillate the casual observer and to make serious communication possible between male femalers – amongst many others with various sexual prefences and identities. Initially, magazines such as *Relate* and *Accord* featured a number of male femaling related advertisements amongst many varied items. The next step was a special 'World of Transvestism' section. Finally, the market was strong enough to support contact magazines like *Transcript*, which placed the emphasis entirely upon various aspects of male femaling.

The advertisements most frequently offered brief details of the advertiser alongside details of the sort of person he wished to communicate with. Often, a photograph of the advertiser was included. The following are typical:

> T4 (Huddersfield, Yorks) Kitty – sensual TV kitten offers her worldly charms to bisexual people, preferably female and other young TVs. Good photography and glamour wear. Correspond, travel or accommodate. Photo essential.
>
> *(Transcript* 1 (2): 27)

> G 171 – TV likes to achieve complete femininity would like to meet a friend (not TV) good figure and would be affectionate with right person. Occasional but regular meetings, discretion expected and given. Phone number for quick contact if possible. St Helens, Southport, Lancs.
>
> *(Rendezvous* 1985, 108: 49)

> T6/3535 – Staffordshire. My name is Paul, femme name Paula. I am a 37 years old heterosexual, closet TV. I am finding life very lonely at the moment and I would love to break out and make contact with other TVs, TSs and sympathetic females. Genuine friendship sought and offered (nothing sexual). ALA.
>
> *(TV Friend* 6: 14)

These magazines feature advertisements from male femalers at various stages within various phases of male femaling. They do, however, presuppose a knowledge of the favoured short-hand for male femaling of TV and TS, either pre-op, or post-op. These are, of course, particular 'namings' having to do with psychiatric-medical conceptualisations as they have been absorbed into the subculture.

The great merit of the contact columns for many male femalers seeking contacts is that those using them can both mask and tier their disclosures. Thus the private male femaler, uncertain about disclosing his male femaling to another, can do so via the contact system, initially using such protective devices as femme names, assumed names, post office box numbers and so on. Having tested the waters in early introductory letters, decisions can be made later about how far to pursue the contact, where and how.

Those with no knowledge of the private networking enabled by the contact magazines often assume that the advertisers are not genuine. It is true that many advertisements are placed by 'professionals' seeking to earn or supplement their livelihoods, and this is often not made explicit, initially. It is true also that a number of advertisers get 'cold feet' and do not follow up their potential contacts. Most advertisements, however, are genuine and many lead to life-long and fruitful contacts. Jonathan, for instance, was an architect who lived a very private life with a sexual life centred around various solitary sado-masochistic male femaling rituals. He was terrified of public disclosure but very lonely. He placed an advertisement and eventually met a more outgoing cross-dressing quantity surveyor who (for a while) saw himself as bisexual. The pair hit it off immediately and became close friends.

What advertisers complain of most frequently is the number of so-called 'timewasters' – particularly those who make all sorts of promises in their letters to the advertisers, but break appointments when the time comes for a first meeting. Most usually, it is a case of the respondents getting cold feet at the last moment rather than deliberately deceiving the advertiser. Many are testing their own responses to the situation as it develops.

While a number of advertisers and respondents have very definite ideas of what they want – they have 'consolidated' their male femaling (Chapter 9) and are using the contact columns accordingly – many enter the private networks in a spirit of tentative enquiry. These cases make particularly good material for an analysis of 'constituting' femaling. As we follow the progress of these networkers, we see them making sense of their experiences and activities as their contacts deepen and widen. Over a period of time they may 'constitute' and 're-constitute' their male femaling many times over.

To illustrate, I draw upon a series of letters written over a four-year period between 1989 and 1993 from Josephine to Phaedra. It is just one of many such correspondences in the Trans-Gender Archive. Phaedra has 'consolidated' as a 'gender transient' (see Chapter 9) and is keen to initiate the 'constituting' Josephine into her philosophy. Josephine is uncertain of what she is, what her femaling means to her and where it fits into the rest of her life. I focus on her letters to Phaedra and only introduce Phaedra's letters in so far as they are necessary to make sense of the developing dialogue.

When we take up the story, Josephine is cross-dressing in the privacy of her home. She has made a few tentative contacts with members of a self-help group for TVs and TSs, and has begun a number of correspondences with male femalers. One of them has suggested that she write to Phaedra, who has a reputation for helping male femalers to 'make sense' of their experiences and activities. Josephine feels very isolated and is very lonely, feeling that there is something about her that puts people off her. She is in a state of despair about her ability to make friends. She is in her early 30s. She has one brother and one sister who have married and live many miles away. Her father and mother have been dead for many years. She dislikes her job and has no friends at work. She is spending more than she can afford on photographic equipment to photograph her male femaling. She alternates between fantasying a female partner – someone to talk to, touch and hold on to – and cross-dressing and masturbating, fantasying that she, herself, is the woman of her dreams. She is torn by conflict – by guilt at what she is doing: 'it is wrong' – and by an increasing addiction to her activities. She uses her femme name throughout the correspondence, and seldom refers to her male identity.

Her first letter is designed to make contact and introduce herself. For this she uses her photocopied standard 'letter of introduction' first written in June 1989. At this time, Josephine is describing herself as 'TV' and is 'doing male femaling' in various ways:

These few notes are a way of introducing myself to other correspondents without having to rewrite so much long-hand . . .

I joined the TRI-ESS (a United States TV group) about a year ago. Some of you may well be surprised why someone so far away would wish to join. Well I joined mainly to make contact with girls in other countries and to broaden my horizons. Anyway I like very much to write letters, exchange photos, experiences, common problems, etc. I belong to a TV group in G— which is about 100 miles from where I live. The numbers that attend meetings are small – about 10–15 at each meeting on average. This is hard to understand when one realises that there are thousands of TVs in G— alone. I suppose in larger towns and cities, TVs tend to join informal groups, etc. and don't feel the need for corresponding or belonging to a group.

As regards myself, I am single, 34, and very tall (6' 2") so I have problems with clothes. However, I am fairly slim, but still height is a problem. As regards problems, I probably have less than many TVs, as I live alone and can dress regularly, as often as I want. However, even though I am only 100 miles from G—, I feel isolated a bit as I have no contacts in the local region. I am a very keen photographer. I like most types of music and also like outdoor sports.

At the moment I am trying to build up a suitable wardrobe, mainly through mail order firms which are not very good here. One or two TVs in G— have offered to help with shopping, as any time I have tried to buy anything myself I have 'frozen', even in big stores in G— which has a population of over 1 million. Hopefully, after one or two excursions, with a bit of help from my friends, I will be able to shop myself, as I really would enjoy that. It would be so different from mail order.

I live in a relatively small town and although some people know I am TV, it would not be acceptable to go around in public dressed, even if my standards of dress, make-up, etc. were of a much higher quality. In all these areas I am really a raw beginner and like most TVs have to learn the hard way. There is little chance that I could ever pass in public due to my height, but this does not worry me unduly but I would like to get to a standard acceptable for socials, etc.

It is really only in the last year that I have decided to enjoy being a TV and stop trying to repress feelings which I have had as long as I can remember.

If you are interested in corresponding, I would love to hear from you about yourself, your country or the area of it you live in, and what the general scene is for TVs in your area.

With her standard 'letter of introduction', she adds a personal letter written to Phaedra, dated 31 September 1989.

I am writing to you to try to establish contact with some TVs. I correspond fairly regularly with Gillian G. who gave me your name and address . . . I have gone through most of the ups and downs of being a TV. Recently, I went into a bit of a nose dive, got a lot of feeling sorry for myself, etc. So Gillian G. gave me a few other addresses to write to.

I have now determined to make improving myself a priority which is at least a decision.

As you can see from the few details listed that improving myself is not going to be easy, but as Gillian G. says, 'make the best of what you have'. The group in G— has sort of fallen apart. It was never much of a group as regards numbers or organising help for raw beginners who were willing to pay for knowledge re cosmetics, make-up, clothes, etc. . . The more I experiment with cosmetics the worse I seem to become.

Assuming I get over make-up and clothes difficulties, the main problems really are body hair and height.

Phaedra, in her first letter, had introduced Josephine to her theorisation of male femaling in terms of 'gender transience'. In this view, the male femaler deliberately puts his gender in transience to study and enact it (see Chapter 9). This entails getting in touch with both the man and the woman within. Phaedra also suggested various techniques to draw out the woman within linking her theories to various ancient Greek, religious and anthropological data. She also tells Josephine of her group – the Gender Transient Affinity – a group of male femalers who accept Phaedra's theorisations and reject the categorisations of TV and TS for themselves.

Josephine is impressed. In her reply of 14 October 1989, she comments:

What you say about marrying the mind of man and woman together in one body is a real eye-opener. I tried to follow your explanations about Gender Transient and it fits in better to my state than describing me as TV or TS (if I knew twelve to fifteen years ago what I know now).

After various details concerning their similar height and a consideration of tips for taking better photographs, Josephine concludes:

I would like to know more about your group of friends and your outlook in the Gender Transient Affinity . . . Your first letter was so interesting and it made me feel more relaxed.

In her next letter, Phaedra develops her view which links gender transience with Shamanism.

Josephine replies on 28 October 1989:

> I am trying to get a book on your faith, i.e., *Shamanic Voices* ... I relax now in the way you describe and I guess I do feel better. The way you explain things has made me less self-centred.

However, the relaxation about her male femaling remains precarious. She continues:

> When I go down the main street, I feel or hear a voice hammering inside my head 'I'm mad', 'I'm mad', when I see all the 'normal people'.

She then gives more details about herself, particularly as regards her life-long shyness:

> The shyness I have never been able to cope with. I know it is a form of selfishness. Also it has meant I have never had much success with the opposite sex, i.e., girls.

However, Josephine soon returns more specifically to the 'constituting' theme of trying to make sense of her male femaling, particularly as regards the new ideas Phaedra is introducing her to and their relationship with more mainstream ideas:

> Like you I feel slightly TS. I often wish I was born a girl. I have corresponded with a TS society but your conception of being is more meaningful to me than any definitions of TV or TS that I have come across. I think that ever since your first letter I have made some progress towards self acceptance, but some of your terms ... I don't fully understand, so try to put up with my questions ... For example – transforming. The first step I understand as relaxing and letting the woman in me come out ... I agree with you about beauty coming from within – this one hopes to bring about by relaxing and meditating on being the woman, as you say.

Josephine is also seeking to put into practice Phaedra's hints for taking better photographs of herself (further developments in doing femaling, in tandem with constituting femaling).

> I will try to take photos as you suggest, i.e., looking above camera ... I will have to shave all this blinking hair off, but I am scared of the reaction of other people. I would have to shave once a week at least, I would say. It's going to be some job, but once it is done it should be easier to keep down. I tried shaving my chest with a Gillette razor and it just clogged up, so I need an old type razor (knife-type).

But her struggle with meanings is never far away. The letter continues:

I am having a problem transforming and in meditation. The Christianity that I have soaked up all my life is saying – This is wrong ... over and over. Maybe when I start some reading things will sort themselves out better, but it is a loud voice.

Josephine then confides about her experiments with pornography:

One other area I have not touched on much is sex. I mentioned my failures with girls. This came to a head about last June after three successive failures, I said f... it. I hired out a video machine and bought some pornographic tapes to help me, or help satisfy me more when I have the only sex I have, i.e., by masturbating. I hope this does not offend you too much, as it is really a degradation of womanhood, but I was desperate and fed up. Any pleasure they bring is only of a transitory nature, as I feel even more empty and alone after watching them and acting out my fantasies. I think sex fantasies are no harm, but the way I am using them is negative. I hired out a video and it is due for renewal in a few weeks time. I think I will chuck it out as it is a waste of time and money really. I don't really know why I am writing in this vein but it helps to let someone else know.

She concludes:

I know I have covered a lot of ground, but trying to be at peace with myself is important and I really would be grateful for advice.

By now, Josephine is signing her letter off with 'all my love', and Phaedra is clearly making a big impact on her.

In a letter of 16 November 1989 she thanks Phaedra for her encouragement, talks about wanting to wander around 'transformed' (Phaedra's terminology), which makes her feel so much better, and is thinking about visiting Phaedra:

It is really only beginning to dawn on me now, but you certainly are unlike any TV/TS, or whatever, I ever met or wrote to, but that really is great as you give a full meaning to life.

There is so much to do and know to help understand myself better. I sure am glad I wrote to you as you really have given me hope. I was going downhill for the past 3 years and fast, in the last 9–12 months, but now hopefully with your help I can sort myself out.

Phaedra had raised the topic of homosexuality in her previous letter, and once again we see Phaedra's impact on Josephine:

You mentioned homosexuality. I am not homosexual but due to general loneliness, etc., etc., I had considered having a relationship just to feel close to someone, even though I think the homosexual act is not good. Meeting you through your letters and photos has given me the start of a new courage, however, and I have no intention of pursuing such a relationship now.

Two months later Josephine is feeling very depressed. Her photography is not going right for her. She is having money problems. She has no video and is unable to sell her tapes. In a letter of 8 January 1990, she writes:

Pornography is still my escape route and safety valve which I indulge in maybe once a week, or more frequently, or I might not look at magazines for weeks. I use them when masturbating. Most of the time I wish I was the girl in the photo even though it is a 'man's world'.

Reflecting her desperation for a new beginning, perhaps, Josephine adds a postscript about changing her name:

I have been thinking of changing my name again, but at this stage it is like changing around the furniture. I thought maybe a more feminine name.

But a couple of weeks later (23 January 1990), Josephine is wrestling, again, with her wish to find a woman for herself, with her lack of confidence in actualising the wish, and with a falling-back on the development of herself as a woman:

I had intended last year to make a special effort to get a girl to go out with . . . I don't know what happened. Anyway if I really knew there was no future for me with a woman I would nearly be better off and go and develop my female side more, and allow it to develop.

Phaedra has reprimanded her for not shaving for the last set of photographs and Josephine replies:

Why didn't I shave? Well I did a little for those few photos, but I let it re-grow in case I got going with one of my dream girls.

On 25 February 1990, Josephine writes saying she is unable to make the proposed trip to meet Phaedra. Another period of terrible uncertainty has intervened.

Thanks for all your comments and help all along but I seem unable to come to terms with myself or the world around me and can't decide what to do, nor probably ever will.

In a long letter of 3 May 1990, Josephine relates how though Phaedra's ideas are right in theory, in practice she is unable to effect them. She reports, too, how she has become worried about the possibility of catching AIDS from touching the video tapes. She has begun to wash her apartment down with disinfectant and asks for information and help from Phaedra in dealing with her worries.

A few weeks later (27 May 1990) Josephine is still preoccupied with the possibility of contracting AIDS – this time from second-hand women's clothes she has bought, or from new ones that might have been tried on in the shop, previously. She is hoping, again, to visit Phaedra (on the Isle of Wight) and, indeed, is considering the possibility of retiring to the Isle of Wight when she may be offered voluntary redundancy in a year or so's time.

There is then an almost year long break in the correspondence. Josephine, once again, has been unable to go through with her plans. Instead, she has turned to the TV group in G—. In a letter of 25 April 1991 she updates her progress. She has been 'doing femaling' with renewed vigour, going on shopping trips and having her first beauty treatment. She has changed her name to Anthea. 'For the first time I know this is it – this is what I am', she says, but feels herself to be a '3rd rate TV' because most other TVs she knows don't have the tremendous problem with body hair that she has. Her plucked eyebrows are getting the attention of acquaintances. She is, however, desperately dependent on the support of others for her male femaling, and, without it, is racked by uncertainties:

> The girls in the salon were very helpful for my morale, but . . . when cut off from support I get real or imagined sicknesses in my stomach . . . I wonder and sometimes worry myself sick as to how I will be judged, yet I feel in my soul I am right . . . at long last, after all the wasted years I feel I am something. I make no resolutions, as I can – and do – lapse back, so I have to take it day by day.

And still, the loneliness and uncertainty persist:

> I wish I had a girl to sleep with, to talk to or go for a walk with, but unless I stop being so shy there is no hope of that.

Two months later, however, (28 June 1991) Anthea – the male femaler who knows what she wants is rapidly asserting herself. As the emphasis on 'doing femaling' continues, she seems to be accepting her femme self, more and more. The agonising about her precise status has gone, and she is more concerned to get on and enjoy her 'doing':

> I feel much better and am really beginning to enjoy being what I am in the last 4–6 months, as I finally accept the fact of what I am, and I am feeling good, really good about it for a change . . . Now I love more than ever being as female as I can be, wearing perfume, getting my nails right, wearing make-up – in fact I truly feel the people who don't are missing out.
>
> Actually the biggest breakthrough was plucking my eyebrows as it announced to everyone that this is it, take it or leave it . . . I have missed out for too long on being what I want to be.

As she develops her femininity she finds herself wanting to be 'feminine' rather than 'sexy':

Actually, I'm going to spend little if any money in future on sexy mini-skirts, etc. and concentrate on trying to get nice skirts, blouses, etc. . . .
I will try to portray my femininity more.

Another year lapses, before her next letter of 21 June 1992. Josephine/
Anthea has now become Josephine again. It is as though Anthea was needed
to help Josephine out of the closet, but now that she is increasingly out,
Josephine can pick up where Anthea left off. A printed name and address
sticker in the name of Josephine now features on her letters. She is developing
her femme self, more and more, but it is still not clear where it is all leading
to:

I feel at ease with myself today as it is Sunday and I am relaxed and
dressed. I have been re-reading some of your letters . . . Things in
general have improved for me I think! I am developing my femme self
more and more.

Now she is not afraid to differentiate herself from Phaedra:

It may be different to you, as James (his male self) is someone I don't
dislike, but I prefer to be Josephine. Forgot to mention – back to
Josephine again, I think for keeps.

She distinguishes her world of femme development from her world of work
as James:

I have tried to adapt, etc. but the peace and happiness that I find in being
my feminine self is so out of touch with the hypocrisy of paper figures
and 'facts', no one believes. The level of rubbish is getting worse daily.

Josephine is now advertising again in the contact magazines:

I put several ads in a contact columnn and answered some. The results
were . . . maybe average. A couple of TVs (separately) came here recently.
Things did not go well again, so you begin to wonder maybe I am totally
odd-ball. It must be me and, maybe it is, but I have met a good few TVs
now and there are only a couple that I have any time for or they for me . . .
Nothing much physical developed on these visits. I fancied making
love with one of them but she said no – I felt an awful idiot.
   I no longer feel a fraction as guilty about what I am, or the wanking
(DIY). There are a few contradictions though, e.g., my liking for some
porn. I just like it. It helps relieve tension, stress, etc. Usually, if I am
using it at DIY, I dissolve into myself or the girl in the photo – I like
lesbian shots or ones of girls, as I identify better with them, and usually
mentally I end up with the girl in the photo or mag.

Many male femalers constitute themselves as 'transvestites', and then
become more and more preoccupied with 'doing femaling'. As they do so,
they find the possibilities of constituting as 'transsexual' increasingly attract-

ive. This seems to be the path that Josephine is heading down. She is beginning to see herself as TS, though she is still very uncertain. On one occasion (in the letter of 21 June 1992), she writes of her 'friends' disappearing 'although they may seem to tolerate my being a TS, or whatever I am'. On another occasion, in the same letter, she describes herself as 'TV/TS'. On yet another occasion, she refers to her 'accepting being a TV, TS or GT – what do you think I am?'

Ever present, however, is the longing for a female friend and her despair at ever being able to have one. Josephine (as James) had been in town one afternoon, when 'two gorgeous Swedish girls on motor cycles' had pulled up and asked her for directions:

> I still think of them. Imagine, I will go through the world and never see them again. I blew it. I could have started something, even a short chat as they cut their 'motors'. They were very nice, also both were good looking. I hope they make love with each other. I would hate to think of them in the arms of some of the males that I know.

But still the increasing 'doing femaling' persists. In her next letter (5 January 1993) Josephine relates her further steps to feminise herself. She has had a couple of sessions of electrolysis – 'If I got really going on getting rid of hair, it would mean a lot to me', and she has started to regret the thinning of her male head of hair:

> The wigs are fine and that's going to be it for ever more now, so there is no point regretting the hair I once had – it was better than many of the girls I saw locally, once it grew long. I had it for years and used to treat it carefully, etc. I should have started on hormones as lack of hair is in the family.

In her penultimate letter of 8 January 1993, she is thinking of moving to the Isle of Wight to live near Phaedra. At the same time she is still hankering after the Swedish motorcyclists. Maybe if she went on holiday to Sweden, she might meet them, she ruminates.

In her final letter of 6 June 1993, she is still uncertain of both her future and her identity, but her horizons have widened considerably. She is entering a world-wide network of TV/TS correspondents. She is buying an electrolysis machine:

> I do hope they contact me as I like to write and exchange views with TV/TSs from many parts of the world – not just on being a TV/TS, or whatever I am, but to find out more about their own country, location, etc. . . I am ordering an electrolysis machine to do some parts of my body.

In a final postscript, she rues the rivalries that have broken out between different TV/TS groups in G—, and agrees with Phaedra's pleas for

co-operation between the various male femaling groupings. The sentiment
fits well both with Josephine's wish to be less isolated, and her uncertainty
as to her own identity and how she might consolidate in the future:

> I agree we should all support each other – the rivalries even between
> the two groups in G— are a turn-off. We are all minorities. I wonder
> sometimes if all the minorities were put together would we have a
> majority – of GT, TV/TS, etc. I dislike too closed a labelling system as
> maybe not many fit in but straddle several 'definitions'. For instance, *I
> am not yet sure who or what I am* [italics added]. I used the term TV/TS
> loosely above. I know I am Josephine. I adore being my femme self, but
> definitely, although my sex drive is towards women, I feel my male side
> is becoming less and less important to me.

With that, the correspondence breaks off. In effect, Josephine has been
constituting and re-constituting for years. Maybe she will never consolidate.
As Strauss (1977: 25) so aptly puts it:

> The naming or identifying of things is, then, a continual problem, never
> really over and done with. By continual I do not mean continuous –
> one can lie in a hammock contentedly watching the moon rise and
> raising no questions about it, the world, or oneself. Nevertheless, some
> portion of one's classificatory terminology, the symbolic screen through
> which the world is ordered and organized, is constantly under strain –
> or just has been – or will be.

Josephine's dilemma is that her concerns about the meaning of her male
femaling make it hard for her to lie in the hammock for any length of time.

It is often puzzling to those with no intimate appreciation of the lives of
cross-dressers and sex-changers why so many of them spend so much time
engaging in what might be seen as a kind of obsessive taxonomising. The fact
is that most male femalers initially find their male femaling confusing and
often distressing. Adopting an identity which makes sense of things – 'finding
oneself' as it is sometimes put – can therefore be immensely liberating. As
April/Ashley put it, 'You cannot imagine the comfort in knowing that one is
something, and not merely monstrous' (Fallowell and Ashley 1982: 76).

Most of my informants did not doubt the existence of a special group of
people characterised by a condition to which the terms transvestite and
transsexual had some reference, despite doubts about their own or others'
'correct' identity and despite some controversy over the central characteristics of the conditions.

Schreber, as a lone male femaler living before the 'scientific' categories of
'transvestite' and 'transsexual' were available, necessarily, perhaps, had to
construct his private system of 'namings'. Bernard, Alan and Josephine/
Anthea had available to them the medical profession's creation of a discourse
by means of which they could apprehend their male femaling (King 1996b).

Bernard rejected the categorisation 'transvestite' for himself and set about ridding himself of his wishes to male female. He left the male femaling career path. Josephine/Anthea vacillated between different medical ways of categorising self and other, and an alternative discourse constructed by Phaedra. Alan, on the other hand, was content enough to accept the label 'transsexual', if that was what his psychiatrist decreed. He may not have been entirely happy about the 'treatment' that the categorisation involved, but his acceptance of the categorisation did enable him to set about the task of 'consolidating femaling'. And it is to this task that we are now ready to turn.

9

CONSOLIDATING
MALE FEMALING

This final chapter details the phase of consolidating femaling. It also seeks to consolidate the approach of the book as a whole. Early chapters detailed the theoretical and methodological approach of the study and were followed by a detailed account of a number of phases in the ideal-typical career path of the male femaler – using selected case material to illustrate throughout. Immersion in the real lives of male femalers enabled the generation of a conceptual schema that 'fits and works'. Inevitably though, an approach which isolates phases and stages, and uses selected vignettes to illustrate them, fails to do justice to the fact that in actual lived experience, development and order are constructed *post facto*, and anew from the standpoint of each new present.

What counts as an incident of a particular phase is likely to be negotiable depending on present problems and future intentions. Certainly, the meaning of that incident will be negotiable. What counts as the interrelations between the phases will take on different nuances. Moreover, in actual lives, the phases, or parts of phases may be circled and cycled again and again. Individuals may stop off at different points, on different occasions.

Furthermore, all life history material is, in an important sense, the product of its occasion – in its reporting, in its publication and in its reception. Thus, for example, a male femaler who publishes an erotic account of his 'beginning femaling' for an audience of erotic femalers may well report a 'first incident' very differently if, on another occasion, he is addressing an audience who he thinks might find overt eroticism inappropriate. He will certainly report the incident differently if he is using it to illustrate a point unrelated to the erotic. Again, if a researcher asks that same male femaler for his 'first incident' of cross-dressing, the male femaler may find himself recalling a different event altogether. Frequently, new memories emerge in the course of life history interviews. Certainly, except in the most rehearsed of interviews, it is the rule rather than the exception that a particular twist to an 'old' memory emerges. How much more so at other times and in other places.

Symbolic interactionism has a clear standpoint on all this. All meanings emerge from within particular presents. All pasts are reconstructed from the standpoint of each present (Mead 1932). This is inevitable and cannot be avoided. Appropriately, therefore, I make a virtue of that necessity in this 'consolidating'. chapter. I take three lives as illustrative of the three major modes of consolidating – what I term 'aparting', 'substituting' and 'integrating' (see next sections) – and freeze frame the life, rather than the incident. The interviewees had been informants for many years, but for the purposes of this chapter an interview situation was specially set up in which each informant was invited to present a chronological account of their lives as cross-dressers and/or sex-changers. The interviews were tape recorded with minimal intervention from me, each lasting 1½–2 hours. The material is presented from the standpoint of 'consolidating male femaling', setting the interview material within the context of my knowledge of the biographies of the three informants as set within the particular symbolic interactionist and grounded theory approach of this study. This chapter uses the material collected in the interviews to example the informants' constructions of their pasts from the standpoint of the particular present of the interview. Each life history is compared with the ideal-typical career path, commenting on the extent to which the former 'fits' the latter.

Consolidating male femaling marks the stage where a more full-blown constitution of femaling self and world is established. This phase provides the individual with a more or less comprehensive and coherent framework within which to consolidate or develop his femaling self and world, and will also provide him with the means to relate these systematically to his 'everyday' non-femaling world, where this remains – as it most usually will.

The consolidation may be centred around body femaling, erotic femaling or gender femaling, with the emphasis upon the corresponding features and facets of sex, sexuality or gender. Various combinations over time are possible, but, typically, having constituted self and world, 'consolidating' sees reconstructions of pasts, consolidations of presents and moves made towards intended futures, clustering around 'chosen' foci.

Thus a consolidating body femaler having come to see that 'really' she was transsexual all along (sexed identity), takes stock of herself, and embarks upon a programme of appropriate body feminisation, which may be seen as culminating in 'the op.', now defined in terms of becoming as near as is possible and practicable to what she should have been all along. She now dresses as a woman, because she *is* a woman. Her presentation of self is herself. As Carol puts it: 'Richard, this *is* me!' She's not merely expressing parts of herself, or play acting. Thus, the meanings of what might have been conceptualised in terms of gender or sexuality are now re-defined and may take on different career paths of their own, all, in a sense, as adjuncts to the major focus of her femaling. As regards gender issues, she develops her personal style much as a genetic woman would have done – the difference being that she is starting rather late, has to do it rather quickly, and is likely to be hampered by residues of her maleness. As regards her sexuality, as

131

hormonal treatment continues, she loses what male sexuality she has, and is effectively desexualising her old sexuality concurrent with the construction of a new sex and sexuality.

The erotic femaler having consolidated his femaling around the erotic/sexual, may now look to new ways to develop his erotic femaling. He may build up collections of subcultural literature and exotic paraphernalia. He may experiment with a view to finding what most 'turns him on'. He may begin to conceptualise what 'turns him on' in a fairly fine-tuned way. His female style may take on sado-masochistic variants which would normally be considered fetishistic and which may take increasingly bizarre forms, for he is not so much interested in the subtleties of femininity as he is with his personal sexual excitement. The role and meaning of body and gender femaling are re-defined and clarified accordingly. Serious and sustained body femaling has no appeal at all. It would entail the loss of his eroticism and his pleasure-giving penis. Likewise, orthodox gender femaling may come to be seen as having prissy, drab or effete connotations.

Another tack lies in the developing of subcultural contacts that will lead to a conscious celebration of the erotic. Erotic femalers may advertise for partners in subcultural magazines such as *The World of Transvestism* or *Transcript*. They may provide the magazines with photographs, personal details and accounts of some of their sexual exploits carried out with other 'TVs (transvestites)' or 'TV punters' (apparent 'straights' who fancy and hang around TVs and TSs) met through the magazine. Many erotic femalers build up something of a cult following through this procedure. Some may get further excitement from being paid for their services. In this case the erotic femaler gets maximum sexual excitation by becoming the stereotypical erotic female, the 'sexy hooker'.

The gender femaler, on the other hand, tends to move in the opposite direction. Residual fetishisms may recede. In this case his fascination with the whole world of the feminine now knows no bounds. He wants to look like and behave like a 'real' woman (as he sees women), not some stereotypical male fantasy of one. This may entail the steady development of his femme self with her own personality, tastes and enthusiasms. Many will model themselves on admired 'RGs' (real girls); others will study deportment, voice production, fashion, make-up and the like.

Body femaling and erotic femaling are now re-defined in terms of the gender foci. It is not necessarily true that a consolidation around gender femaling entails no body femaling. In fantasy there may be much of it. Similarly, the gender femaler may adopt every bit of the sex role paraphernalia his ingenuity can dream up. He may, for instance, insert tampons in his fantasied vagina (rectum), or occasionally 'go on the pill'. But he does these things 'because that is what RGs do', not because he thinks he is one, or is becoming one, or because of any very obvious erotic kick he gets out of doing it – 'That wouldn't be feminine'.

Typically, his relationship with the erotic is likely to be ambiguous. While there are gender femalers who are asexual, or increasingly become so, and who female for 'reasons of tranquillity' or even aesthetic reasons, the eroticism is more likely, perhaps, to be attenuated and dispersed and may indeed become increasingly so. We might say eroticism is adjuncted to gender femaling in these cases. For some, with increasing gender fine-tunedness, an ever-increasing number of objects in the world of women become mildly eroticised – but at the same time, their own sexuality becomes increasingly genderised. This can lead to a distaste for sexuality except as expressed in gender form. Sexual intercourse, for example, is fantasied in terms of gender femaling role play. Another possibility is that past gender femalings which were not erotic femalings at the time, come to form material for erotic scripts in subsequent episodes of fantasy femaling.

Sometimes the consolidating centres around a particular 'Damascus Road' experience. With other male femalers it may emerge more slowly. For instance, after a period attending various groups for transvestites and transsexuals Liz was seeing TV as a 'bit of an amorphous thing, with TV sort of merging into TS'. After she had been to Martine Rose's 'House for Transvestites' in Sheffield and heard Martine's theories about cross-dressing and sex-changing, and met a number of TVs there, she began to accept a TV identity. She recognised her transsexual thoughts as fantasies.

Sometimes a particular 'doing femaling' might be a major factor in the consolidation. Lara had recently had her first photo session whilst dressed as a woman. She had just received the prints, framed them and had placed them by her bedside. Later that day, she was on the telephone to another crossdresser and she found herself referring to herself as a 'transvestite' for the first time. Previously, she had been unable to name herself in this way. She wondered whether the photographs had in some way established her identity as a transvestite. Similar reports abound. Thus Julia Grant says in her TV documentary (BBC-TV Inside Story, 1980) that she had 'the bust operation' to prove to herself that she was serious about having the (re-assignment) operation in the future. It is as though Lara's photographs and Julia's breast operation provide proof of identity and, as such, are instrumental in introducing consolidating or a new phase of consolidation.

It is instructive to organise the major modes of consolidating around three possible 'solutions' to the problems posed by disjunctures between male and male femaling selves and worlds. These I term 'aparting', 'substituting' and 'integrating'. In 'aparting' the emphasis is upon maintaining rigid boundaries between male worlds and male female worlds. In 'substituting' the male femaling world increasingly takes over from the male world. It is, in fact, to a greater or lesser extent, substituted for it. Finally, in 'integrating', the attempt is made to transcend previous positions which entailed disjunctures between male and male femaling selves and world, in order to foster the emergence of an 'integrated' position which seeks to transcend the conventional arrangement between the sexes.

Male femaling entails, as we have seen, the participation within particular meaning frames (and their constituent objects) that are at variance with 'everyday' (common-sense) meaning frames. In the earlier phases of the male femaling career path this may not cause the male femaler too much of a problem. The problems are merely embryonic. Thus, as we saw, for example, in the beginning femaling phase, re-involvement within the meaning frames of 'normal' everyday life follows the cross-dressing incident and leaves 'normal' self-concept and world more or less intact. Again, in the fantasying femaling phase the male femaler can keep his fantasies separate from his everyday world, thus keeping this everyday world more or less 'normal' and enabling its development more or less boundaried from the incipient femaling world. The doing phase is likely to be marked by an increasing strain on the separation of worlds with the increasing pressure for the male femaler to 'explain' himself leading to the phase of 'constituting'. Once the male femaler has sorted out who and what he is, however, he is likely to feel an increasing pressure or desire to make clear to himself and others the precise relations between his various worlds. This will entail reconstructions of pasts which will consolidate past life histories.

APARTING

In 'aparting', the male femaler seeks to maintain a strong boundary between his male and his male femaling self and worlds. 'Aparting' may take place between private worlds, between private and public worlds and between variously public worlds. Thus the male femaler may, for instance, seek to consolidate a strong boundary between his 'fantasying femaling' and his non-femaling fantasies accompanying his sexual relations with his wife or girl-friend. Fred/Freda would habitually cross-dress in private, look at herself in the mirror and masturbate to the fantasy that she was a beautiful woman. When Fred had sexual relations with his wife, however, he would never allow himself male femaling fantasies as part of their lovemaking. He felt that would be 'unfaithful'. Instead, he would find himself conjuring up images of his wife scantily clad in provocative poses (private 'aparting'). He did not find this entirely satisfactory but it did enable him to maintain arousal and an erection to the point of orgasm without drawing upon his private male femaling world.

The male femaler may disclose his male femaling to no one, but consolidate his male femaling self and world in isolated, secret activity (private/public 'aparting'). Finally, he may consolidate his male femaling activities within a male femaling subculture which constitutes a separate, possibly core, recreational world. Only subcultural members will know of his male femaling activities, while they may know nothing of his domestic, work, or other recreational social worlds. Conversely, participants within his non-male-femaling worlds know nothing of his male femaling identity or his involvement in male femaling worlds (public [social] 'aparting').

SUBSTITUTING

In substituting, the male femaling meaning frames and their constituent objects increasingly take over from the non-male-femaling world and their related objects in such a way that the male femaling life becomes the new 'everyday life'.

If the 'solution' of 'aparting' is adopted, the male femaler maintains his participation in non-male-femaling related domestic, work and recreational worlds. In 'substituting', however, the male femaler develops his participation in male femaling related worlds at the expense, and ultimately to the exclusion, of his participation in non-male-femaling related worlds.

He may go 'full time', that is, dress permanently as a woman and live accordingly. Where the consolidation has focused on body femaling he may consolidate his identity as a post-operative transsexual, or 'new woman', change his documents accordingly, and live his life entirely as the genetic woman he may appear to be. There are many male femalers who live as women with male partners who know nothing of their previous lives as men. They may go through ceremonies of marriage with these partners, adopt substitute families and for all practical purposes expunge their life as males entirely. Their friends, colleagues and acquaintances just assume they are genetic women. Here, the male femaler seeks to substitute self and world entirely. This 'solution' entails full-time participation as a woman in female worlds and male/female worlds and may entail avoidance entirely of any and all male femaling related worlds – most notably any involvement in male femaling subcultures or any contact with any male femalers. Furthermore, as many male femalers taking this route consider they were 'really' female and not 'really' male all along, their substituting is a private retrospective 'reality' as well as a public social 'reality'.

This sort of substitution of self does entail participation in the conventional arrangement between the sexes, but as a substituted self. An alternative 'solution' is for the male femaler to 'full time' as a 'woman', but maximally substitute his male femaling social worlds for those of his non-male-femaling related worlds. He may dress full time and socialise with other male femalers more. Many such male femalers turn their domestic settings into resting places and safe havens for male femalers who need counselling, or 'changing facilities', or whatever. Eventually, a stage may be reached where almost all the male femaler's social worlds and social circles will be male femaling related. Betty, for instance, for many years worked in a male identity to earn a living, but spent an increasing amount of her time in a transvestite/ transsexual subculture. In time, she gave up the job in her male identity, and set up a professional 'dressing service' for 'transvestites'. Interestingly, in Betty's case, her consolidating was focused on gender femaling both as regards herself and others. She adopted the label 'transgenderist' for herself, did not take hormones or seek surgical intervention, had no erotic sexual life whatsoever, and gained great pleasure and satisfaction in living as a full-time male femaler servicing the gender femaling requirements of others.

INTEGRATING

Integrating arises when the male femaler subjects his existing notions of sex and gender related behaviour to scrutiny and attempts to transcend what he comes to see as the constraints of sex and gender role stereotyping.

'Social integrating' can be seen embryonically in the activities of the radical and activist transvestite and transsexual groupings such as TAG (Transsexual Action Group), a British group of the late 1960s, and in the activities of the flourishing groups of this type in the United States of the 1990s (Mackenzie 1994). Such groups seek societal reconstruction which finds a space for greater integration between what is conventionally separated into male/female, masculine/feminine.

A good example of 'personal integrating' is the account published by John Pepper as *A Man's Tale* (1982). After much 'aparting', much 'fusing' (see next section), and a rejection of 'substituting', Pepper tells how 'he came to unearth his feminine self – the anima in all men'. The book is seen as 'an account of a struggle for "men's lib"; for freedom from a conventional masculinity'. Pepper's particular solution 'struck gold – at the feet of the lamas of Tibet, first glimpses of the ancient mystical secret of the androgynous impulse'. Others take less esoteric pathways to the same end. But many male femalers come to see the impulse behind male femaling related practices as being essentially liberated.

The extent, mixture and type of aparting, integrating and substituting to be found in any particular life history, at any particular time, will, of course, vary. 'Solutions' tend to be precarious. At any time, there might arise the possibility or actuality of intended apartings, integratings and substitutings being torn asunder, either voluntarily or involuntarily.

FUSING

'Fusing' arises when the boundaries between the meaning frames of male femaling worlds and those of 'everyday life' begin to break down. This may entail the interpenetrating of social worlds and social circles which the 'aparting' male femaler might prefer to keep separate. Involuntary fusing may be a perpetual fear for aparting male femalers. They fear the humiliation that may result. On the other hand, integrating femalers may voluntarily fuse in the service of their integrating. Again, the particular style of substituting is likely to be very much influenced by the view of fusing held by the male femaler. Thus many male femalers who consolidate as post-operative transsexuals prefer that their pasts be known only by selected intimates – they do not want to deny their past – and to that extent are happy enough to fuse. Other transsexuals, often as a result of their political activism, become what might be termed 'professional transsexuals'. It becomes almost impossible for them to be taken as genetic women except by those who do not know them well. While their 'fusing' enables a particular public identity, it does, concomitantly, restrict their possibilities of 'substituting' more completely.

Fusing may involve private or variously public worlds. Examples of fusing which might be consolidated would include the following. The 'transvestite' might find that he enjoys sexual relations with a woman most when he is fantasying himself as a woman (voluntary or involuntary private fusing). He may disclose his 'transvestism' to selected members of his domestic world such as wife or girlfriend, who may participate in domestic male femaling or in the subculture (voluntary public fusing through voluntary disclosing). On other occasions, his work, recreational or domestic worlds may involuntarily interpenetrate. He may meet a supposed 'straight' friend in a transvestite setting. He may be spotted 'dressed' in public and recognised by workmates. This may lead to renewed attempts at 'aparting' and to self directions to be more careful in future, or to lie low for a while. It might, on the other hand, lead towards re-consolidating and an attempt at integrating.

A major clue to the explanation of particular career paths and 'solutions' adopted – and the prediction of future outcomes – lies in the examination of the particular attachments and commitments of individual male femalers.

By 'attachments' I refer to 'a human being's capacity to become affectively involved with another person and hence sensitive to his/her thoughts, feelings and expectations, particularly in regard to their relevance for his/her own behaviour' (Box, 1981: 123). 'Commitments', on the other hand, refer to the rational, rather than the affective, elements in social bonding. A commitment is 'the awareness of the impossibility of choosing a different social identity or rejecting a particular expectation because of the imminence of penalties involved in making the switch' (Stebbins 1971: 35).

Consolidating femaling may entail the consolidation of existing commitments and attachments. More likely, however, it will entail – sometimes sooner, sometimes later – very drastic shifts in existing attachments and commitments.

In the constituting phase, these shifts can be postponed. It is evident that Josephine, in the previous chapter, was doing just that. Josephine undertook paid employment in her male identity, while increasingly male femaling in her home and leisure worlds. She was never able to abandon the hope of a 'straight' heterosexual relationship and, in consequence, the penalties for consolidating as a full-time transvestite or transsexual were too great. She remained too committed to her male identity and too attached to the prospect of a female partner to do this. In her case, the fact that she was never able to make a satisfactory attachment to a female partner was, arguably, the major factor in her continuing male femaling. She became her own partner – but that attachment was not satisfactory either. So the merry-go-round continued. She was unable to get off it or stop it.

As the male femaler becomes involved in the social worlds and social circles of domesticity, of work and of non-male-femaling related recreation, he is likely to become progressively 'committed' and 'attached' to them. When then faced with male femaling impulses, these will be suppressed, managed or developed from within the backdrop of existing commitments and attachments. Thus, the individual with no opportunity to provide a wife with credible reasons for periodic absences from home will 'do femaling' rather infrequently, relative, say, to the sales representative whose 'opportunity structures' for cross-dressing are much greater. The single male femaler with no family commitments and attachments, on the other hand, may well become more attached and committed to male femaling related worlds as he participates more freely in them.

There are a range of possibilities and permutations. Those engaged in 'substituting', for instance, may slowly come to perceive existing attachments and commitments differently, and deliberately engage in more 'substituting'. On the other hand, many male femalers only gain self-knowledge of existing attachments and commitments when toying with giving them up. Commonly, these individuals backtrack ('backsliding'). They return to families and compromise their male femaling activities. Others more committed to an overly masculine style in their work worlds might see their activities as males as funding their femme selves. They come to celebrate the excitements of 'dual worlding' and 'aparting'. They may see themselves as 'having the best of both worlds' and develop both worlds in tandem.

In brief, the possiblities are manifold. Understanding, explaining and predicting necessitates the detailed examination of individuals, their possible career paths, their existing attachments and commitments, their existing and projected participation in social worlds and social circles, together with examination of their relevant domestic, recreational and work worlds.

To this end, I detail life history material collected from three male femalers who have consolidated, respectively, as a 'transvestite', a 'post-operative transsexual/new woman', and a self-styled 'gender transient'. Tom, the transvestite, consolidates around an 'aparting' style which, in retrospect, can be seen as omnipresent throughout his entire male femaling career. Gail, the transsexual, consolidates around 'substituting' after periods of 'aparting' and semi-voluntary 'fusing'. Finally, Bruce/Phaedra, the gender transient, consolidates around 'integrating' – an outcome which, in retrospect, might have been predicted quite soon in his/her male femaling career.

TOM – THE 'APARTING' TRANSVESTITE

Tom is an unmarried 40-year-old teacher. He has been with his present girlfriend for twelve years and has been sharing a house with her for the last five years. She knows nothing of his 'transvestism'. They rarely have sexual relations and his sexual life is centred upon masturbating to video tapes of transvestite cabaret shows and transvestite beauty contests. In addition to collecting and watching the tapes, he copies them and makes them commercially available. His girlfriend does not know that he owns a video machine – far less the fact that he has a collection of such tapes, and access to sophisticated copying equipment. He corresponds with male femalers and video producers and sales persons through a PO Box number which he operates under an assumed name from a distant town. He has not cross-dressed for many years.

In terms of our ideal-typical career path, Tom has presently consolidated around erotic fantasying femaling – the content of his fantasies being moving images of glamorous transvestites which he alternatively identifies with and takes as his fantasy object choice. He has adopted this particular 'aparting' consolidation after protracted and varied episodes of doing and fantasying male femaling.

His beginning phase was short and only vaguely remembered. As a 4- or 5-year-old, Tom would put on one of his mother's fur coats and on occasions go to bed in it. He is not sure why – 'possibly because there was no central heating in my room . . . or there may have been something more to it . . . but there was a great sort of comforting feeling, a great warm feeling about wearing this fur coat'.

Whatever the reasons, it was his perception of his mother's response which was to set the stage for his subsequent 'aparting' style:

I can recall being discovered by my mother on two or three occasions and being told off. 'You mustn't wear the coats, again', she would say. I think in some way she was, perhaps, sort of discouraging me but not discouraging me strongly enough or something. But I can't remember. I was too young to remember.

His mother's disapproval was enough, however, to stop his male femaling until puberty. With the emergence of adolescence, though, we see Tom entering his doing femaling phase:

When I was around 12 – maybe 11 – somehow I managed to be at home on my own. I remember going into mum's bedroom . . . you know . . . trying on the clothes. The shoes, of course, are too big and nothing fits, but nevertheless I was getting the idea of what it's like to wear female clothes . . . trying on mum's stockings and things like that.

He 'aparts' from the outset.

This dressing continued occasionally – probably only during the school holidays as this would have been about the only time I could have guaranteed being on my own, with mother out – perhaps, one day a week when she was out at work.

Nevertheless, having experienced the doing femaling, he has his memories to draw upon in his subsequent erotic fantasy femaling.

Tom's constituting femaling phase comes suddenly and is short:

I was in a bookshop, when I was about 13, and I came across the word 'transvestite'. It caused me tremendous excitement and, of course, I then went about looking up every possible book in the library – every sociological and psychological book – trying to learn more about the subject.

Tom accepted the label for himself immediately. Unlike so many other male femalers he has no difficulty with the term. 'I've never been concerned about being a label. To me a transvestite is somebody who gets a thrill out of wearing women's clothes and I do.' Nor does he see himself as in any way transsexual. For him the matter is straightforward. From his reading of the 'scientific' literature as supplemented by his personal experiences he opines:

A transsexual is somebody who does not feel very happy being a man and thinks that they are either really women, or wants to become a woman and have a re-assignment operation. I sometimes wondered when I was younger . . . it would have been quite nice to take hormones . . . to know what it was like to have breasts on your chest and having to wear a bra. But I think one of the results of hormones is the reduction in the male sex drive and I don't think having a problem with an erection, as a side effect of hormones, would have appealed at all.

It was, however, to be another three or four years before a chance incident was to set the course for Tom's subsequent male femalings. From thenceforth, Tom was to become principally preoccupied with glamorous female impersonators or fantasy female impersonators both as sources of identification and of object choice:

I think I was about 16, or, perhaps, 17. I had a part-time job in the holidays as a hospital porter and on the way home popped into a shop selling magazines. And there was a magazine there which featured some pictures of female impersonators. It was around 1968. There were pictures of Holli White, Coccinelle, people like that. I smuggled it home and started using the pictures as a masturbation aid.

This theme of erotic excitement at the visual depiction of glamorous female impersonators soon became a core thread of Tom's sexual life. So taken is he with them that he begins to fantasy genetic girls as female impersonators:

Figure 9.1 Tom's fantasy *alter ego*, Holli White, c.1968

I can rememember using pictures of girls from *Parade* and *Tit Bits* and things like that. Pictures of pretty girls or girls in bikinis – possibly even topless shots – using them as masturbation aids – but pretending they were boys dressed up as girls. And pretending also that this was me dressed up. What excited me particularly was taking these pictures of girls and imagining they weren't girls, but they were incredible female impersonators, looking incredibly glamorous.

Sent to boarding school for a year at 17, Tom ceases his episodic doing femaling and continues his fantasy femaling, masturbating to the images of glamorous female impersonators. At school there is no opportunity to cross-dress undisclosed and he lacks the will to engineer episodes where it might have been possible. Again, in retrospect we can see Tom's tendency to emphasise fantasy femaling at the expense of doing femaling as his safest way of 'aparting'.

Throughout his teens and early twenties, Tom is attracted to girls. He feels no attraction to boys. After leaving university and working as a ski instructor in Europe, he feels the need to 'prove' his heterosexuality. 'I think I was beginning to get concerned that although I found it easy to get on with girls, I wasn't getting as much sex as I thought I should be having'. Likeable and attractive, Tom has no difficulty in securing a string of female partners visiting the ski resort where he works. However, he makes sure to bring with him a couple of magazines of female impersonators which he continues to use as a masturbation aid:

> I think in some way what I was trying – this is my sort of analysis – was sort of demonstrating to myself that I was blue-blooded (sic), strongly heterosexual, that I could establish relationships with girls ... get them into bed on a regular basis ... on a casual basis without too much difficulty. Perhaps, I didn't want to admit that I was happier sitting around in a mini-skirt and a pair of high-heels.

Many were the times he was tempted to drop his 'aparting'. Always, however, the fear of humiliation led him to draw back from the brink of disclosing:

> On many occasions I came close to revealing to the girls that ... gosh! I'd really like to see what it's like wearing your shoes. Or I'd like to try your mini-skirt. But I never actually did because, of course, you've got a sort of position there. You're the sports teacher, people look up to you. And, of course, I was terrified that they would run screaming to the manager. And say ... you know ... your sports teacher is an absolute nut-case. He wants to wear my blouse. You should sack him. So, of course, I would be humiliated and sacked. And that lasted for about three or four years.

Meanwhile, when engaging in sexual intercourse with these girls he would find images of female impersonators coming into his mind to facilitate orgasm. Here, Tom's femaling and non-femaling worlds are fusing, but it is a private fusing, as opposed to public fusing, thereby enabling him to maintain his 'aparting' both intimately to the girls, and publicly to others. He continues:

> So I think we've covered my sort of attempted analysis of the situation ... sort of trying to demonstrate to myself and to other people that there was absolutely no question but that this person would be completely heterosexual – because he was – gosh – he's out with another – bloody hell – he was out with that nice little brunette last week, and now he's got this older one. God, this man's got something ... he never stops going out with girls.

Following his return from continental Europe, Tom lives for a while in London, giving him the opportunity to increasingly experiment with 'doing femaling' without a great risk of the fusing of his male femaling and his everyday worlds. In short, he begins to socially apart, with doing taking precedence over fantasying. Sometimes his sexual partners are male femalers, sometimes he cross-dresses himself.

To enable maximum 'aparting', Tom begins to lead what, in effect, are two separate lives in two separate worlds (dual worlding). He contacts the Beaumont Society (see Chapter 7). However, he finds this a stuffy organisation with an elderly membership and quite unsuited to his needs. He prefers the London drag ball scene and soon meets his first 'real' female impersonator. Not surprisingly, perhaps, he has a brief affair with her.

> I was at one of these balls and there was a very very attractive Malaysian boy there. I took her to be a girl originally and I had a chat with her and discovered that she was a boy. And I suppose in some ways against my better judgement and all that sort of thing, we went down into the basement area and kissed a bit. It was really quite an extraordinary sensation to be extremely attracted to somebody, but at the same time thinking – well, gosh, underneath this very sexy outfit and the wig, whatever it was, there was a young boy. But she was so sexy and charming that I was able to put that to one side.

Tom's intimate relations with a male femaler gives rise to refinements of constituting. Tom has no doubt that he is a transvestite attracted to other transvestites, but in his fantasies he is relating to girls – albeit girls who are boys. Once intimate with a boy/girl who is all boy in body, he has to make sense of where he stands as regards homosexuality. It was a liaison that made a major impact on him:

> He was completely homosexual as far as I was concerned. The night we spent together, he was passive and I was active. It was just an extraordinary experience to have sex with another man. I think he kept his wig on and still had make-up on and he had a very feminine body. Though he hadn't taken any hormones or anything he was quite soft and curvaceous – and was young – and was absolutely lovely. We had anal sex with me as the active partner which I found surprisingly enjoyable. If someone had said ten years before, you'll really enjoy sucking another man's penis I would have been quite stunned. But that was very pleasant. He was then keen to penetrate me, but I said, 'No, I think that's enough for one night'. You know my illusions and various aspects of my life had been shattered. But on a later occasion he did penetrate me, which I must say I didn't really enjoy.

The close connection between the pleasures of having and being (Freud 1941: 299) is all too frequently ignored outside of the psychoanalytic literature. Tom's oscillations between having and being were seldom far away: 'Soon after that I got the drive to dress up again.' Next he is advertising in contact magazines for a girlfriend who will accept him as a girl, help him dress and so on. Soon he has met such a partner and they are going to drag balls as two girls. Tom gives his new-found girlfriend no inkling of his life beyond his male femaling. Aparting must be maintained. He continues:

> It may seem bizarre but I was getting dressed up to satisfy myself more than anything else. I wasn't interested in getting dressed up to go out and attract a man. Ideally what I would have liked, I think, was to get dressed up as a sexy girl and go out with a girl and for another real girl to come over and say 'Gosh ! You look really nice. I've always been interested in transvestites. Would you like to dance?'

Once again in his doing femaling, Tom is refining his constituting.

It should be recalled that all through this period Tom is dual worlding and is careful to keep his male femaling and 'everyday world' apart. He was enjoying seeing his female drag ball companion every six or eight weeks. As he put it: 'whenever I was able to get away from my girlfriend. It's a horrible thing to say but you know what I mean.'

But the lure of glamorous female impersonators is never far way. In 1985, Tom manages to have a holiday in Thailand. There he is able to visit the beach resort of Pattaya, well-known for its transvestite cabaret acts. He has his first sexual experiences with male cabaret club performers who live as girls taking whatever female hormones they can get hold of and in many cases having breast augmentation surgery. (Tom's first intimate contact with body femalers.)

At the end of the performance the cabaret performers come out to meet the public and Tom pays two of them to come back to his room and have sex. Now that his fantasy figures have become 'realities', however, the elusive nature of his search reveals itself – not least because it is 1985 and he is aware of the AIDS scare:

> AIDS really brought me up short and I did not have anal or penetrative sex. I was only prepared to get involved in mutual masturbation and some very gentle kissing. I certainly would not perform oral sex and I wasn't too keen to have oral sex performed on me which has really caused a problem ... because you're there with somebody you're very attracted to and having to keep saying – don't let her do that. It's not a very nice feeling.

Being in close proximity with these body male femalers excites Tom beyond his wildest dream: 'I sat there with a beer in my right hand and my left hand round this beautiful girl thinking have I died and gone to heaven?' Yet, such excitement, he feels, should lead to an orgasm, 'and the right place to have an orgasm seems to be inside a vagina'. His experiences leave him in a confused state, illustrating how 'constituting' is never really over and done with.

He reflects upon what might have been:

> I think possibly if it had not been for AIDS then I might have gone in a different direction. I might have really tried to find a beautiful pre-operative transvestite to have a relationship with, like the one with the Malaysian boy in the early 1980s. And I think I might possibly have gone along the route of wanting to try to find a transsexual to have a relationship with.

Tom perceives a problem with this 'solution', however, as he thinks transsexuals want relationships with 'real' men – not transvestite-inclined ones. In any event, the matter has become academic to him. Faced with such difficulties he finds himself reverting to his fantasies. He begins to cease 'doing femaling' altogether. Inevitably, perhaps, increasing fantasying femaling fills the void he feels.

He returns home to his partner and decides to live with her. His partner suffers from a gynaecological problem which may inhibit her (and him) from enjoying coitus together – a contributory factor, perhaps, in his increasing consolidating around erotic fantasy femaling. He masturbates more and more to the moving images of the video tapes he collects with an increasing tenacity. Tom is, however, very attached to his girlfriend. He does not want to lose her and is committed to staying with her for a while yet. His, he feels, is a somewhat unsatisfying and uncertain 'consolidating' femaling. 'It does rather begin to worry me, you know, that my sexual life is sitting in front of the television screen'.

Nevertheless, he cannot contemplate disclosing his male femaling to his partner. This would hurt her and humiliate him. His fear of involuntary disclosure has led to him refraining from doing femaling for several years and this is the position in which we leave him. His collection of female clothes are stored, undisturbed, with a former confidante, and he has no intention of compromising his 'aparting' by leaving such clothes around his own home. Indeed, when I visit him in his home for the purposes of an interview, he provides me with an elaborate alibi for my knowing him should his girlfriend ever wonder who I am. In short, 'aparting' and the fear of involuntary disclosure governs his male femaling life. He has now consolidated as a fantasying femaler both identifying with, and desirous of, the moving images of glamorous female impersonators that the video revolution has enabled him to enjoy.

As he surveys his male femaling life from the standpoint of his present 'consolidating', he is happy enough. He has his memories of his 'doings' (both his own 'doing femaling' and his 'doings' with other male femalers). His valedictory words provide a fitting temporary summary and end point:

I'm very pleased, indeed, that I've had the experience of getting dressed up as a girl. And I've had the experience of going out with another girl while dressed. And I've had sex with a post-operative transsexual, so I know what that is like. And I've had sex with another man. I've performed oral sex on another man ... it's been done to me, so I know what that's like. And I've had the experience of this Malaysian boy screwing me – which I didn't enjoy. But at least I tried it.

GAIL – THE 'SUBSTITUTING' TRANSSEXUAL

Gail is a divorced 37-year-old care assistant. She has been living full time as a woman for eighteen months and became a 'new woman', as she calls herself, six months ago, following her sex re-assignment operation. She lives alone in a small apartment flat and has a regular boyfriend, whom she sees mainly at weekends. They have a full and active sexual life together. Gail presents as an intelligent, engaging and feminine young woman several years younger than her actual years – with none of the preoccupation with a glamorous self-presentation shared by many male femalers.

Gail has been consolidating as a transsexual for the last four years. During that period, as a direct result of this consolidating, her wife has divorced her, she has been sacked from her former job as a quantity surveyor, and she has been forced to sell her family home. Since her re-assignment surgery her wife has denied her access to their only child. Her mother and brother, her sole remaining close family, have refused to see or speak to her for the last two years.

Gail's substituting has been steady and sustained – a four-year period following some seventeen years of episodic doing femaling and difficulties in constituting – far less consolidating – as either transvestite or transsexual. The seventeen years were marked by a particular aparting style: a terror of discovery, with a doing style that invited it; a denial of her cross-dressing when confronted with it but a recurring wish to be confronted so that she would have someone to talk to.

As Gail records it, her 'beginning femaling' was as belated as it was sudden:

On my 17th birthday, completely out of the blue, I went downstairs and to this day I'll never know why, I put on some of my mother's mascara and eye-shadow and lipstick. And I've still got my old diary, that has got in big capital letters – OH MY GOD! WHAT AM I? WHAT'S HAPPENING TO ME?

We cannot be certain Gail never cross-dressed before, but she has no recollections of any such incidents. Just before she was nine her father died suddenly and she feels that the trauma of her father's sudden death led her to blank out much of her early childhood.

Gail did, however, fantasy herself as female as an adolescent. It seems possible, therefore, that in her case significant fantasying femaling preceded beginning femaling, reversing the order of our ideal-typical career path. For Gail the fantasying was related to adolescent masturbatory fantasies and it took on a particular twist:

> I hadn't really had very many girlfriends – well, any really. I was always a bit shy with girls but never had any gay feelings in childhood or puberty. But, when I began masturbating, I did for some reason fantasise that I was female. I remember doing this when I was in my early teens. Initially, I used to cut pictures out of magazines and papers and things like that. I used to masturbate to them, but I used to imagine I was the girl in the picture. Certainly, I wanted to be the girl in the picture.

It was, however, the later first cross-dressing incident, rather than the masturbatory fantasy femaling, that left Gail in such a confused state. 'As you can imagine, I was very confused. I had never heard of the word transvestite or transsexual and I didn't know what I was, or what was happening to me.'

Notwithstanding her confusion, she progresses with her doing femaling, as the opportunity arises, when she is left alone in the house with her younger brother and mother out. In contrast, say, to Tom, it is doing femaling, rather than fantasying femaling which is so important for Gail:

> Over the next few months, indeed, the next couple of years, rather than just putting on mascara, it progressed to blusher and foundation. In those days my skin was a lot better than it is today, so I didn't need so much.

Soon the experimenting with make-up is insufficient. 'I began to dress in some of her clothes. My own hair was reasonably long. I used to put curlers in it and try and style it.'

Meanwhile her self-questioning leads her to the local library – as it did with Tom: 'I really didn't have a clue what the hell I was doing, so I started to go to the library and I started looking at the word 'transvestite' – seeing what it meant'.

Unlike Tom, however, she is unable to embrace the term 'transvestite' in an uncomplicated way. We might say, she is unable to constitute herself around the term transvestite. She prefers not to think what she might be, and turns, rather, to elaboration of her doing:

> The feeling of total isolation crept upon me, and I dressed in secret. I used to send off for things that I'd seen advertised in Sunday papers and ask for them to be sent in someone else's name. They would come to the house and I would say: 'Oh this has come with the wrong address on, I'll stick it in the post on the way out'. Of course, it was actually addressed to me in a pseudonym.

Gail then develops a variant of a particular 'aparting' style. Unlike many male femalers who seek to destroy the evidence of their male femaling once the incident of cross-dress is over, Gail would habitually commit to writing her ponderings concerning what she found herself doing. 'I used to write about the feelings, about the feeling of being a girl ... how nice it was.' And it was this that led to a pattern of near-discovery and subsequent denial that was to continue for many years. As she would put it later, it was as though she really wanted to be discovered, although the reality of discovery would send her into renewed denials.

She incorporates her own male femaling into her adolescent games:

> I used in those days to recreate war games, and things, in a fairly realistic manner with figurines, and so on. I would devise a set of rules from a particular period in history. I was continually writing on bits of paper. One day my brother appeared with some friends and they found what I'd written – about being a girl and wearing make-up. When they started laughing and making fun of her and saying, 'Oh! he's a transvestite', I realised what they'd found. I immediately denied it, saying, 'Oh no! it's just a fantasy', and grabbed the paper off them, ripped it up and threw it away. And really, I guess that was the start of my denials about what I was – the start of my denials publicly and then inwardly, even to myself.

And still the doing continues as Gail dresses as often as she can. She is casual about returning her mother's clothes exactly as she found them and soon the inevitable arises. Her mother who has long suspected Gail of dressing in her clothes eventually confronts Gail about it. Her response serves only to reaffirm Gail's aparting style:

> She stormed into the living room. I can still see her face now, spittle in the corner of her mouth, in a blue rage, saying, 'you've been wearing my stuff again'. Her reaction was so negative that I immediately denied doing it. She was impossible to talk to. And I think that was the drastic turning point in my life, actually, in the way the next few years of my life developed. It became such a disgusting, perverted secret that I couldn't tell anyone about it. My brother had laughed at me. My friends had laughed at me. And my mother had been disgusted by me. So consequently, I tried to deny it. And really that was the pattern – the set pattern for many years to come – dressing, denying and yet secretly always wanting to be found out and to be able to talk to someone.

Emerging in these memories is the picture of someone who, having constituted himself later as a transsexual, recalls many lost opportunities to constitute as a transsexual earlier. It is reconstructed biography from the standpoint of a presently consolidating transsexual who feels herself to have inexorably reached her present point after years of denial of the 'truth' about herself.

At around the age of 21, Gail begins a relationship with the woman who will become her wife. At the same time she is making tentative steps to contact other cross-dressers. Once again comes near discovery, followed by denial and a putting-off of the (retrospectively) inevitable:

> I had given an old jacket to my prospective father-in-law. In the pocket I'd left all the information on the Beaumont Society and he found it. I knew instantly what he'd found. Jane (Gail's fiancée) got a glimpse of things and again I was terrified. I still had this deep-seated terror of being discovered, so I ripped it up quickly, ran upstairs and put it down the toilet. And I said to her, 'Oh, it was just a fantasy I had. I was a bit concerned that I might be transvestite but I wasn't.' And, again that was a chance to change the course of my life. But I think because of the reaction of my mother and the deep-seated fear of being some sort of pervert, I couldn't face up to it. And yet another potential turning point was missed.

Missing the turning point, Gail marries, thus committing herself still further to the life she will eventually disentangle herself from. Even as she does so, she is contriving to meet her first transsexual:

> I remember saying to her (the transsexual), 'If I had my time over again' – and I'm only 23 at this stage – 'I think I would have tried living as a woman'. But I felt there were too many people I could have let down, that I was committed now to a marriage and so on. Basically, I didn't have the courage – or, I guess, the conviction at that stage – to do what I think in my heart I knew, even then, I should have done.

And so a pattern continues: unsatisfactory sexual relations with her wife, continued cross-dressing, and the simultaneous wish for disclosure and fearfulness of its consequences for existing attachments:

> I was never particularly sexual. I didn't particularly enjoy intercourse – certainly, I didn't do anything other than the basic act because for some reason it almost disgusted me. I found I could not go down on her. It just didn't seem right. And she found out a few times that I was cross-dressing because I used to leave things under the bed in an unlocked suitcase. I was desperate to be found out to be able to talk to someone. But unfortunately she was fairly rigid in her attitude and was disgusted, so everything was thrown away. Then dressing started again, secretly. And it was found, and it was thrown away. That happened two or three times over the next eight years and each time I denied it, because of her reaction and because of my fear. Of course, it didn't go away. It got stronger. This really carried on for a long time and I was confused, a bit scared and very sad.

Once again, Gail commits herself further to her non-femaling world. She and her wife decide to have a child:

> But unfortunately his birth didn't, perhaps, have the desired effect. I was now a family man. I was in private practice in surveying and earning good money. We had a house in the country and I had a very good social life. We had holidays, once, sometimes twice a year, but actually I was more unhappy than I had ever been.

Gail's apparent attempts to consolidate as a family man confronted her with the prospect of a pre-ordained life ahead. The prospect was horrifying to her. 'And, of course, I was still cross-dressing, secretly'. This period was also marked by a shift in the significance of her cross-dressing to her, a movement from erotic to gender femaling:

> The sort of sexual kick had gone – not completely, but to a great extent. Now cross-dressing gave me an inner peace or calm, a tranquillity. It was like a room to go to, to be on my own, to be safe.

With the demise of the erotic in her femaling, and her unsatisfactory sexual life with her wife, Gail finds herself seeking out a possible sexual partner outside her marriage. Feeling herself female and heterosexual, she yearns for male company:

> For the first time I began to wonder what it would be like as a woman with a man. These weren't gay feelings because when I was dressed, certainly, I was a woman. I started to phone up contact lines, to listen to people. Then I talked to a few people and managed to meet a guy who wanted to meet a TV. It turned out that he was TV as well – a young chap and he came up from Sussex and we met in a lay-by. I was shaking like a leaf. I was dressed as Gail. We went back to where I lived and we chatted. He said he found me attractive and I didn't know what to do. Later, on the way back to the lay-by, I remember this desperate urge to stop his car and say thank you for coming up to see me and to kiss him and that's what I did. I just kissed him on the cheek. Then he kissed me on the lips. And that was it. I never saw him again.

Very frequently, new 'doing femaling' leads to new constituting. Responses are monitored and compared with existing constitutions which often leads to re-constitutions or refinements of existing constitutions. In Gail's case this single incident had dramatic consequences for her:

> I stood in the road for twenty minutes and thought 'My God! Am I gay?' I thought, 'No I am not. I was a woman kissing a man.' And really I think that was the first time, when I thought, 'My God. Perhaps, I'm not transvestite. Perhaps, I'm transsexual.' Well, you can imagine for the next few months I didn't know what to do with myself.

150

The ground has been prepared for Gail to constitute herself as transsexual, though she is not quite ready to take that step. It takes the intervention of a professional counsellor, contact with declared transvestites and transsexuals, and endorsement from within the medical world (constituting within the interrelations of 'member' and 'expert' worlds) before she is able to do so.

Soon after this incident her wife finds out that Gail is still cross-dressing. Now that they have a son, both Gail and her wife feel the cross-dressing to be more serious, and they see a Relate counsellor. This 'expert' advocates allowing Gail to attend Beaumont Society meetings. The consequences were to be dramatic and speedy.

Initially, there is great relief. It was the first time Gail had spoken to a third party 'about my transvestism – because I was still calling it that – and for the first time somebody didn't laugh or vilify me. They were understanding and compassionate.' Her wife, too, is able to view Gail's cross-dressing with less disgust as a result of the professional intervention.

Gail is soon attending Beaumont Society meetings and is able to compare herself with the self-proclaimed 'transvestites' and 'transsexuals' she meets there. She feels 'different' to the transvestites: 'they were still men, even if some looked fine'. For Gail, on the other hand, dressing entailed becoming the woman she increasingly felt herself to be. For a period she takes her wife's contraceptive pill. The increasing doing femaling reaches a climax when she meets a sympathetic transsexual at a Beaumont Society weekend with whom she feels she can identify. Someone gives her the telephone number of a psychiatrist specialising in gender disorders who is well known in the subculture. Within a month she has started electrolysis, referred herself to the psychiatrist and been put on a course of hormones.

And then began, as Gail puts it: 'probably the most traumatic two years of my life, or, I think, without being too dramatic, most other people's lives'.

As she attends counselling sessions at a TV/TS support group, and continues with her hormone treatment and electrolysis, her conviction of herself as transsexual is confirmed. After a very short period within the male femaling subculture and contact with medical 'experts', she is able to say – 'and I knew that I was transsexual'.

> But how could I tell my wife? I didn't know what to do. It was a time of utter confusion. And terror – about losing everything I'd ever had, including myself – because myself wasn't really the true me.

The terror comes, of course, from the dawning on Gail that consolidating as a transsexual will entail the collapse of previous selves and worlds. What is to take their place?

Initially, all Gail has, 'is a deep-seated conviction that I was going to live the life I should have been born to'. She reduces her 'aparting' and begins what very soon becomes a steady and rapid 'consolidating' through 'substituting'. Domestic substituting comes first. She tells her mother and is met by hostility and blank incomprehension. Gail has only seen her a couple of times since. Her wife can take no more of it and Gail is forced to leave home and begins living a dual-role – in retrospect a preparation for full-time substituting.

Gail works as a man, and lives at home as a woman. Having accepted herself as transsexual, her doing femaling takes on a new impetus and renewed resolve. 'I was letting my hair grow, electrolysis was coming on, and so on. My appearance was beginning to change. Small breasts were developing and my skin was getting softer' (early consolidating/body femaling focus).

Inevitably, her maling and non-femaling worlds begin to fuse: 'I think people at work still had no idea – I think they thought I was gay'. Others begin to take her for a woman even when she is dressed as a man.

As she puts it: 'I knew I was beginning to change and it was quite satisfying.'

As Gail sees it, the woman within is now coming more and more to the surface. The increased body femaling enables her to present herself as female full time. She now feels able to embark on a systematic substitution. She has professional photographs taken of Gail and takes them into work. Her employers, initially, keep her on, but transfer her to another office. An uneasy four months follows, after which she is eventually sacked. She does, however, receive her last salary cheque in Gail's name. A month before this she had changed all her documents into Gail's name.

So it was that 'a little before I'd wanted to . . . I became Gail. I told the local residents and shop keepers and so on, and the next year lived as a woman.

The full force of the degree of 'substituting' is poignant. She recalls: 'Although I'd lost my self, my wife and my family, I had found myself . . . and I was happy'.

By now Gail has lost most of her old friends. She begins to make new ones as Gail (continuing substitution). Moreover, the stage has now been set for a boyfriend – for her to relate to a man as a woman:

> We had a relationship and actually it was wonderful. For the first time
> I realised that that was where my sexual orientation was, as well. And
> that was a huge change as well, because I'd never thought of myself as
> gay. But I was totally happy as a woman with a man. And the pleasure
> I got was immense. I was happier to do sexual acts, to go down on a
> man as I could never have gone down on a woman. At last everything
> was blossoming and it was actually easy, really, to transform.

By now Gail has obtained a job as a woman. Six months later, Gail has her re-assignment operation. In an interesting twist she pays for it privately out of the funds obtained from an out of court settlement obtained from her employers for unjustifiablly dismissing her because of her male femaling (substituting).

It remains for Gail to determine her position on the matter of fusing. Her particular solution is pragmatic. She feels transsexuals should stand up for

Figure 9.2 Gail Hill 1995
Source: © Gail Hill

their rights. In this capacity she is bringing legal proceedings against her local authority for not considering her application for NHS funding for sex re-assignment. She is fighting, through the courts, for access to her son. In short, she does not wish to deny her past as a man. On the other hand, she does not broadcast her past. Most people take her for the genetic woman she appears to be, and she is happy for that. Her consolidating has, she feels, been a great success:

> My life as a woman is complete – at work, in my social life and in my relationship. I have a good home life and I'm accepted as a woman. And so really life is better than it ever has been. I hope I get my son back. I have not seen or spoken to my brother and mother for nearly two years. This is sad, but, ultimately it is their loss. I'm not sure I could ever forgive them for not supporting me in the years I needed them most.

She leaves us with a sadness, but with an ultimate optimism. I have no reason to suppose her consolidating will not continue further along the path she has set herself – substituting in so far as she intends to consolidate her new life as a woman, voluntary fusing in so far as she feels it necessary to maintain integrity with her past life as a man; and also fighting for her rights and those of male femalers like herself.

PHAEDRA – THE 'INTEGRATING' GENDER TRANSIENT

Phaedra Kelly is the alternate personality of Bruce Laker. She is a 42-year-old married writer and transgender activist who lives with her wife and step-daughter on the Isle of Wight in a home which doubles as The Museum of International Gender Identity. From the same address she directs the International Gender Transient Affinity, the first working world-wide trans-gender human rights organisation.

Phaedra terms herself a 'gender transient' – a person who puts their gender in transience in order both to study it and to live a life which maximally integrates the masculine and feminine in one's personality. The International Gender Transient Affinity (IGTA), a largely postal network of like-minded gender transients, an outgrowth of the Transconscient Art Movement, serves as her power base within the transgender community. Through it, she promulgates her ideas concerning the importance of integrating masculine and feminine 'gender polarities' in both the individual and society, and seeks to extend her influence both inside and outside the international transgender community.

Phaedra began consolidating as a gender transient some fifteen years ago after a lifetime of cross-dressing and sexual and gender experimentation with accompanying constituting and re-constituting. For her, the integration of the private and the personal with the public and the political is an essential part of what it means to be gender transient. It is reflected in both her domestic and work worlds which are all of a piece. She considers Bruce Laker and Phaedra Kelly as alternative personalities and will adopt either depending on the purposes at hand. At home, Bruce (dressed as a man) is a 'house-husband' keeping house for his wife, Vanda, who runs her own business locally and is the family breadwinner. Dressed as Bruce, he writes from home as Phaedra. Nowadays, Bruce tends to 'transform' (adopt the outer appear-ance of Phaedra) only in pursuit of his various public 'missions'. These might be locally based – a photographic shoot, or an entry for a carnival queen competition, for instance. They might be nationwide – as with Phaedra's fund raising for various charitable causes. Most recently, the focus of his/her attention has been his/her various world-wide missions to document the global position of the transgendered, to foster locally based organisations and to extend the influence of the IGTA.

'Never doubt that a small group of thoughtful, committed citizens can change the world; indeed, it is the only thing that ever does', wrote Margaret Mead: 1995: 9). Bruce/Phaedra seeks to do just that through his/her particular mix of personal and social integrating.

Phaedra's memories of female clothes go back very early – to the time she was 2 or 3 years old. She describes what might be termed a proto-beginning phase:

> There were clothes strewn around the room I used to sleep in. One of them was my mother's ball-gown – for going out to parties, cocktails and so on. It was a cold material on the outside, a sort of silk weave garment. It was the 1950s so it was very flared and pleated and there were sundry petticoats with it. And, of course, they were cold on the surface and then I was interested in the tactile sensations, and the coldness that warmed to the body and the perfumes that arose off it. I used to crawl out of my cot and get into it and sit in it and stand up in it.

She recalls her mother's tolerant attitude to this 'short phase':

> Mother was very warm and tolerant about it. Sometimes she would come in and find me doing it. I didn't look up or become startled by her arrival in the room. She would walk over and pick me up and smile, put me back into my cot and say, 'now go to sleep'. And that was it.

By the time she is 6 years old, however, Phaedra is dressing in female clothes, as opposed to merely getting inside them as an infant (beginning femaling), but her embarrassment at the reaction of her family soon leads her to stop it. She had found a dress-up box in the attic which contained her mother's old props from the theatre:

> My mother let me play around in this petticoat thing ... and I used to twirl in it. Then mother and grandmother used to call me out of my room to see me doing it. And that embarrassed me, so I stopped doing it.

From that time, to when Phaedra was around 11 years old, there were no incidents of cross-dressing but Phaedra recalls a great fascination with the intricacies of female attire throughout that period.

As is so frequently reported by cross-dressers, it was at puberty – at around twelve – that cross-dressing became linked with the overtly sexual. It was at this time that Phaedra would seem to be entering her doing femaling phase. In Phaedra's case it took a particularly idiosyncratic twist. She discovered masturbation whilst climbing a smooth barked pine tree. As she was practising pull-ups to develop her muscles she suddenly experienced 'this free fall sensation that goes with ejaculation and I wasn't sure what it was, but that was the way I masturbated for some time thereafter'.

Phaedra then incorporated into her masturbatory routine, a ritual which involved dressing as an impromptu Maid Marion in a pair of green tights. In retrospect, she sees her interest in the assertive Maid Marion as accounting for 'why later on Phaedra Kelly evolved into quite an assertive male woman – with the glamour by day and the adventure by night'. She explains:

> At the time, you see, there was the series on ITV of *Robin Hood* with Maid Marion who dressed in all these long flowing garments by day when she was in the Sheriff of Nottingham's castle. And when she nipped out of the back door to be with Robin, she was in these green tights with this short jerkin kind of micro-skirt thing. I sort of recreated the appearance of Maid Marion swinging from a tree.

There was other idiosyncratic experimenting during her early adolescent years:

> I was a bit of a mermaid, at 12 or 13. I used to go swimming a lot and used to swim out to the rocks where I couldn't be seen and turn my bathing costume into a bit of a bikini by rolling it up and giving it a bit of a thong. I would create myself a mermaid from seaweed. I would make a seaweed wig and put the long tentacles of seaweed through the bathing costume and then swim around the rocks being a mermaid.

Phaedra also pursued more orthodox male femaling, dressing in skirts and stockings, which she would borrow from a young woman of eighteen who used to stay with the family. Predictably, perhaps, she tends to dismiss this more conventional 'doing femaling' as of less significance.

Meanwhile, Phaedra was reading about 'transvestism' and 'transsexuality' – gleaning what information she could from press reports, from the semi-scientific texts on sexual perversions prevalent in 'adult' bookshops at the time (Wolfgang 1964), and from autobiographies written by transsexuals. She recalls being particularly impressed by *I Changed My Sex: The Autobiography of Stripper Hedy Jo Star Formerly Carl Hammonds* (Star 1955).

Whilst her mother and grandmother had been tolerant – even encouraging – of her cross-dressing in the pre-pubertal period, they became anxious now that it was continuing into puberty. Matters reached a head when Phaedra showed her mother a book on sexual perversions. She was about 12 years old at the time:

> I'd been reading this book on various sexual perversities (sic). There was actually no transgender in it. I don't think mother found it. I think I showed it to her for some reason, I can't remember why. And she ceremoniously tore it up and threw it on the fire and asked me very anxiously – probably anxiously more than angrily – 'Do you want to be a woman, or something?' And I thought for a good twenty minutes and then I said, 'No, no, I don't think so'.

Forced to focus on the significance of her cross-dressing by her mother's intervention, Phaedra recalls a period of confusion and anger, followed by a clear (negative) 'constituting' that she did not want to take a transsexual route ('It was too arduous a journey'). While she was clear that she did not want to be a woman, however, she did, she says, 'want to be a good tran', but at that time she was not sure what that would entail. Rather, she stopped cross-dressing entirely for seven years and decided 'to discover what being male was all about' (an alternating pattern, in her case as a prelude to later integrating).

There followed a period of sexual activity with both men and women, both being precipitated by rape, or near-rape. At 12, Bruce was seduced by a woman in her thirties. At 13 he was raped by a middle-aged man.

At her school, at the time, there operated a clique of semi-rent boys who were made available to older men for homosexual sex. Phaedra avoided the clique but it seems they decided she was too pretty to go uninterfered with. The precise circumstances are unclear. What is certain is that Phaedra was walking through her local park one day when she was set upon by a middle-aged man and anally raped.

She feared the incident might mean that she was homosexual, but felt very confused about this. Did the incident make her homosexual in some way she wondered. A friend advised her to put her fears to the test, so she joined the other rent boys hanging around the public toilets and began to monitor her reactions to her experiences.

Later, at 17, she tries 'a little experiment', her first transformation for almost five years, and her last until she is 20:

> I went into this shop in Bournemouth and bought some female underwear – a suspender belt, and other frills. I went back to the toilets and locked the cubicle door, slipped off my male clothes and trans-formed. And they were beating the door. They had lost all discretion. They didn't care whether they were arrested or not. There were eyes through every spy hole, feet under the door. They were banging on the door and whispering. They were getting really excited. I thought, 'Yes, you bastards, I've got the power now. I'm not up for rent any more. Nobody buys me. Nobody owns me.' I took the clothes off, chucked them back in the bag and walked out through them and never went back. And then it came to me. I'm a tran. What kind of tran, I don't know, but I'll discover later.

Phaedra's non-femaling pursuits were carried out in a similarly experimental style. Her masturbatory fantasies were eclectic: some were sadistic, some masochistic. A few incorporated male femaling. Her heterosexual relationships were wide and varied:

> I was busy discovering that particular woman that was in my arms. Each woman was different and what works for one, doesn't work for the

157

other. I tried this and I tried that and I was open to them telling me I was doing it wrong.

And then came a marriage in which Phaedra was 'mind-numbingly bored'. There followed sporadic incidents of what Phaedra refers to as 'single-garment fetishism' but these were she says, 'merely the exercises of a cage-bored animal'.

It was following the divorce that Phaedra decided to develop what she felt was always there – the female within. She felt that having experimented with 'transforming' in her childhood and early adolescence, and having deliberately explored her male side for the duration of her teens, the time had now come to explore and develop her female side: 'I made the conscious decision, from my first full transformation, that now was the time for her. She was going to have my full attention.'

Moreover, from the start there was to be no 'aparting': 'Anybody who came into my life – male or female – would have to live with it. I wasn't going to hide it. I had an open public career right from the start.'

In her life as a male she had always sought to construct her own 'third way':

You see I've have always been between two things. When my father left, the money went down, so mother was maintaining a cottage in the upper middle-class area of Sandbanks. I was going to a private school and living most of the time with my grandmother under the gas works with fishermen's kids. So I was living two lives, in two accents, and in two modes of behaviour. And I thought: 'fuck this for a game of sailors. I'll live the third way.' So I took the best of whatever was available and threw in a few things of my own. I've always done this. I've constructed my own third way.

Similarly, Phaedra set about constructing her own third way in her male femaling. Consolidating began, we might say, with her first 'full transformation' at the age of 20, when she transformed for a fancy dress disco at a local youth club. It was a great success for her: 'The DJ fell in love with me and the boys protected me. They created a special category of prize for me and it was great fun.'

Soon she was basking in the local celebrity status her transformation had enabled her to achieve. There followed a period of correspondence and sexual liaisons with variously transgendered people met through contact advertisements and drag balls. Phaedra was appalled by the lack of vision and any sense of transgender history shared by most of the male femalers she met. During this period she wrote to the Beaumont Society. Her query and its response is telling:

I wrote to the Beaumont Society asking them what their frame of reference was on any kind of 80s minded transvestite or transsexual, and asked them if there were such things in their groups and how could I meet 80s minded trannies. A very curt reply came back on headed paper. 'There is no such thing as an 80s minded transvestite or transsexual.' And the date on the letter was 1983. They didn't even appreciate the irony!

She continues:

I would have been patient with them, but I found they were radically different from the way their culture appears to be. I have explored through comparative religion, through philosophy and many other cross-currents what I identify as the culture – nationally and internationally – of transgendered people, of whatever particular stripe: transvestite, transsexual, eonist, travesti, hijra, berdache and so on. I then found that there was a community in Britain that was completely and utterly divorced from all that culture and unaware of it; a community that didn't even recognise it, let alone adopt it. As they had adopted a male woman role I thought it would naturally follow that they would adopt their cultural heritage. But I found that they were locked into a stagnating culture. It was all very interesting, all this fascination with 50s frocks, mini skirts, schoolgirl clothes and things like that, but it was a limit.

Gradually, Phaedra finds other innovators who feel an affinity with her 'consolidating': 'Suzanne was exploring herself through music and poetry. Boudicca was exploring herself through art and music and myth.' And so the Transconscient Art Movement was born. A group of like-minded people met, exchanged ideas and transformed themselves into the embodiments of their mythical, literary and artistic heroines. At the same time, they exhibited their 'transconscient art' at local exhibitions and published in local and subcultural outlets.

In due time, what had been conceived as an art movement metamorphosed into the Gender Transient Affinity and later the International Gender Transient Affinity. Phaedra explains:

I started to perceive transconscience as too long a word for a designation of identity, and more of an artistic movement than a gender identity. Also, of course, I had a passing interest in quantum physics and its relation to Newtonian thought. I perceive of transvestite and transsexual as being Newtonian and finite – swapping from one half to another half, from one polarity to another polarity. Whereas gender transience is in motion and, therefore, through a simple discipline of duality it can achieve a monist gender continuum. Because nobody else around us lives that way, we have to do it for ourselves.

Meanwhile, Phaedra was putting her theories into practice in her relationships with women as well as male femalers. She had met Vanda (a genetic

Figure 9.3 Phaedra Kelly with her wife Vanda 1982
Source: © Phaedra Kelly

girl) who was to become her second wife. Incorporating sexual experimentation – including male femaling– into their relationship, they were fooling
around one day with a bit of S & M (sado-masochism) with Vanda 'dollied
up' as Kitty, a male femaling friend, when Vanda 'popped the question'.
Shortly afterwards they married with Phaedra dressed in traditional bridal
attire and Vanda dressed as the groom. Appropriately, after their registry
office marriage, they married again with Phaedra as a Shaman priest/priestess
marrying the male and female in Phaedra and the female and male in Vanda.

Secure in her personal integrating, Phaedra has increasingly turned her
attention to the international transgender community since her marriage. She
concludes:

> I want to discover my sisters and brothers in every country of the
> world. I want to unify them and help them form organisations of their

own; help them communicate with each other and to meet each other as a broader school; to feel their strength and to discover what they are and to find their world culture, their identity as a nation within every nation.

In this she has made a striking beginning, as the reports on her world-wide missions amply testify (Kelly 1992a; 1992b; 1993a; 1993b; 1994a; 1994b; 1995a; 1995b).

This has been a long chapter which serves both as a summary of the male femaling career path and as a summary of the book itself. As we saw, Tom had no difficulty accepting the term 'transvestite' for himself once he came across the term. The problems his 'doing femaling' entailed, however, eventually led him to a less than satisfactory consolidating around fantasying femaling. How permanent this will be, we do not know. Gail, on the other hand, after years of putting off the retrospectively inevitable, embraced a transsexual identity wholeheartedly. As I write, she has just been appointed Public Relations Officer of the major United Kingdom organisation for

Figure 9.4 Phaedra and her travesti sisters, Athens, 1995
Source: © Phaedra Kelly

transsexuals – The Gender Trust. How far this modest 'social integrating' interferes with her attempts to live as a woman, rather than as a transsexual woman, remains to be seen. Phaedra, on the other hand, is a male femaler whose time may well have arrived.

In a final update before this book went to press, I discussed with Phaedra the gender 'paradigm shift' alleged by some transgendered activists to be occurring right now. As Denny puts it:

> With the new way of looking at things, suddenly all sorts of options have opened up for transgendered people: living full-time without genital surgery, recreating in one gender role while working in another, identifying as neither gender, or both, blending characteristics of different genders in new and creative ways, identifying as genders and sexes heretofore undreamed of – even designer genitals do not seem beyond reason.
>
> (1995: 1)

'What do you make of all this?' I asked Phaedra. 'Well, you see, Richard', she replied, 'there are a lot more of us than you think. It's just that I was the first!' . . . Maybe.

10

CONCLUSION

This study has been concerned to generate grounded theory in the substantive area of male cross-dressing and sex-changing. Re-conceptualisation of the area in terms of the basic social process of male femaling has enabled justice to be done to the processual and emergent nature of much cross-dressing and sex-changing phenomena. Specifically, it has generated a number of conceptualisations which have highlighted facets of male femaling hitherto not studied. The study has explored some of the major possible and neglected shifting interrelations between facets of human sex, sexuality and gender; considered these in terms of the interrelations between self, identity and world; and situated both sets of interrelations within the interplay of scientific, member and common-sense knowledge. These issues are highly salient to the lives of cross-dressers and sex-changers, who consequently provide excellent case histories and case studies with which to examine them. We omit to study these matters at the risk of ignoring fundamental problems of relevance to us all.

People often think that male femaling is a rather minority and unimportant matter. In fact, it is both widespread and fundamental to each of our lives. The 'depth psychologists' have long realised this, as have many before them. As far back as 1899 Freud was accustoming himself to regard 'every sexual act as a process in which four individuals were involved [the male and the female in each partner]' (Masson 1985: 364). Later analysts have had to posit a drive to become both sexes to make sense of what comes up on the analyst's couch (Kubie 1974). Off the couch, it is no coincidence that the contemporary pop star Michael Jackson's post-plastic surgery face is frequently likened to the face of his idol Diana Ross. Indeed, Segal (1994: 198) comments: 'it becomes hard to propose a single Western icon, from Valentino to Elvis, from Mae West to Madonna who does *not* emanate a type of sexual ambiguity (often both as feminized *and* hypermale, or vice versa)'. Also, look at the popularity of Dame Edna Everage, Julian Clary, Eddie Izzard, RuPaul or Lily Savage. Why, too, the sort of 'Stop it, I like it' treatment of cross-dressing and sex-changing in the popular press?

Even as I have been writing this book, I seem to have been riding on the crest of a wave of interest in cross-dressing and sex-changing. *Orlando, Mrs Doubtfire, Priscilla, Queen of the Desert, The Crying Game, Ed Wood, To Wong Foo, Thanks for Everything Julie Newmar* all became cultural top sellers. A major television advertisement for Levi jeans in 1995 featured the gender bender/transgenderist Zaldy. The family game *Trivial Pursuit* featured a clique of drag performers in a newspaper advertisement widely published in the period coming up to Christmas 1995. Not coincidentally, perhaps, the period saw a spate of new publications on cross-dressing and sex-changing, ranging from popular health and medicine reports such as Coleman (1996), to volumes aimed at a specialist homosexual market, such as Nataf (1996). New editions of old classics appeared (Baker 1994) and academic books on cross-dressing and sex-changing proliferated (Bornstein 1994; Herdt 1994; Mackenzie 1994; Lewins 1995; Ekins and King 1996a). A further three collections are in press (Bullough and Bullough; Denny; Ramet).

Given that my research began in 1979 and has spanned seventeen years, inevitably, perhaps, this lengthy time span had a bearing on matters of emphasis. Had I started the study in the early 1990s, for instance, I might well have been more sensitive to the idea of gender as performance as opposed to category or identity (Butler 1990; Bornstein 1994). Had I begun as late as 1995, when the book was in its final stages, I might well have been influenced by Ken Plummer's important *Telling Sexual Stories* (Plummer 1995). Again, back in the 1980s, the significance of the decoupling of sex, sexuality and gender had not been grasped. I had to labour hard on this. It may be that this decoupling will become the common currency of those working in the vanguard of the emerging field of 'transgender studies' (Bolin 1994; Mackenzie 1994, Whittle 1996, Ekins and King 1996b). Whatever, this book is the first theorisation of these issues that has a sound and systematic empirical base.

Grounded theory is concerned principally with core problems and how they are processed. In large measure these are beyond personal prejudice, preference or fashion. 'Core variables, particularly basic social processes, have lasting qualities . . . They are abstract of time and place' (Glaser, 1993: 1). However, the grounded theorist can only theorise on the basis of intimate appreciation of what s/he *has* studied and not what s/he *might* have studied. My focus has been on male cross-dressers and sex-changers in contemporary Britain. Moreover, my presentation of data has been guided by publishing requirements which called for a monograph, not an encyclopedia or essay in cultural studies. Inevitably, I have raised a host of important issues that were peripheral to my focus, but which would profit from further work. Principal amongst these are the following:

1 I touched upon a number of sub-worlds within male femaling worlds which have never been systematically researched. Particularly significant in this regard is the topic of sissy maids introduced in the context of 'dyadic doing femaling'. Those sissy maids who male female to become

neither male nor female (unsexed) in effect variously sexualise housework and genderise the erotic in their femaling. These issues raise a host of interesting questions for, *inter alia*, a sociology of housework and a social psychology of the eunuch. Likewise, the adult male femaling babies I touched upon in the context of 'fantasy femaling' would repay extensive study. Such study might tell us much about polymorphous infantile sexuality in both the child and the adult, and about mother–baby bonding.

2 In certain substantive arenas I opened up new research domains but did not pursue them past preliminary work. Notable in this regard is my treatment of erotic fantasy femaling which drew on the recently emerged male femaling telephone sex-lines. Random sampling of telephone sex-lines suggests that every conceivable erotic fantasy will be available in principle. The social process/grounded theory approach adopted in this study might be extended to the full range of scripts. Content analysis of the major themes is needed. Again, the meanings of telephone sex-lines will be different to different users, as will the use made of the scripts. This warrants comprehensive investigation, both inside and outside the specific area of male femaling.

3 The focus of my conceptualisations was on the ordering of myriad male cross-dressing and sex-changing phenomena in terms of social psychological process. Necessarily, I had to set process within structure in order to understand and explain the different ways male femalers process their problems. This was done by introducing the social structural unit of the masked awareness context. Nevertheless, social structural matters remained undeveloped throughout the study. A focus on social structure, with a subsidiary theme of social process, would have produced a very different book which might well be worth writing. Again, personal predilections, training and abilities led me to favour the methodology of what Glaser calls traditional grounded theory, particularly the 'basic social process' approach (Glaser 1992; 1994). Had I followed more closely the methodology of Strauss (1987), and Strauss and Corbin (1990), a rather different study would have emerged. While it would probably have included much less detailed empirical material, it would certainly have been conceptually more dense.

4 In my detailed illustrative material, the focus was on male femalers who consider themselves heterosexual or bisexual. Although homosexual male femalers are quoted, such material is sparse. The emphasis is, in part, a feature of the arena, but was also, once again, of my predilections, training and abilities. Certainly, the gay studies literature is a vast one and it largely fell beyond the scope of this study. I leave to others the possibility of applying the conceptual framework developed here to predominately homosexual male femalers.

5 Despite the increasing use of the term gender dysphoria (Fisk 1973; King 1996b), and, indeed, the term transgendered, the psychiatric-medical

literature is still marked by disputes as to whether transvestism should properly be considered a sexual or gender anomaly, and whether transvestism and transsexualism should be considered as discrete clinical syndromes. These disputes might well be illuminated if considered in the light of male femaling as a basic social process.

6 More fundamentally, a major task lies ahead for the researcher who would do full justice to the complexities, consequences and ramifications of the interrelations in practice between psychiatric-medical conceptualisations and categorisations of cross-dressing and sex-changing, and those of the male femalers themselves. Male femalers tend to be sceptical of medics and psychiatrists and, indeed, all so-called experts, whilst frequently existing in an umbilical relationship with them. This warrants a comprehensive investigation.

7 Of major interest to sociologists might be the exploration of male femaling as a case study in the sociology of secrecy. My theory and 'findings' were illustrated with data which suggested that certain femalers come to adopt the label 'transvestite' and come to gender female at the expense of overtly celebrating the erotic; whilst others come to adopt the term 'transsexual', and then body female, re-defining their gender femaling, and underplaying facets of male eroticism to extinction. Both of these routes provide rich material for work on the management of stigma and related issues.

8 Systematic study of the particular relationship male femalers have with their bodies would provide valuable case material for the fast developing sociology of the body. There are signs that this is being grasped as regards 'transsexuals' (Stone 1991; Lewins 1995). But what about other male femalers?

9 Of potential importance and relevance outside the substantive area of male femaling are a number of highly complex issues that need to be explored further. In the process of male femaling, identity, selves and objects become variously – and with varying degrees of inter-connectedness – sexed, sexualised and gendered. If any social psychology and sociology (cf. social anthropology, Herdt 1981) of sex, sexuality and gender is to be based upon firm foundations, we need to know much more about this process, both inside and outside the specific area of male femaling.

10 Finally, I raise another far reaching issue. To what extent would our understanding and explanation of the behaviour of all 'males' and 'females' be enhanced by using the sort of conceptual framework proposed in this book? In my judgement, we urgently need substantive grounded theories of 'male maling' (cf. cultural theory, Simpson 1994), 'female maling' and 'female femaling'. Then, and only then, will we be in a position to begin the task of generating adequately grounded formal theories of 'gendering'.

NOTES

2 A REVIEW OF THE LITERATURE FROM THE STANDPOINT OF GROUNDED THEORY

1 *All* grounded theory is formal, in this sense. Grounded theory may be substantive or formal – the former developed in a substantive area of enquiry, the latter developed in a conceptual area of enquiry (Glaser and Strauss 1967b: 33). 'Male femaling' is a 'basic social process' (BSP), a particular type of 'generic social process' (Prus 1987), developed in the substantive area of male cross-dressing and sex-changing (see Chapter 4). Since the analytic focus of a BSP is a generic process, formalisation of theory can be readily accomplished (Bigus, Hadden and Glaser 1982: 39).

7 DOING MALE FEMALING

1 The Membership Secretary, asked to give her view of the Beaumont Society on the occasion of its thirtieth birthday, wrote:

> At thirty then we are a mature young lady with a caring nature, solvent, smart and well groomed, with an active social life and many friends. I am sure at fifty we shall have matured into a glamorous gran, but hopefully still having the youthful ambition and spirit of our founding members.
>
> (Paula Frost 1996: 11)

BIBLIOGRAPHY

Alice, L100 (1991) 'A history of the Beaumont Society', *Beaumont Bulletin* 23 (3): 37–9.

Angie (1991) 'SHE', *Rose's Repartee* 7: 15.

Anne (1993) Book review: 'Vested Interests: Cross-Dressing and Cultural Anxiety by Marjorie Garber', *International TV Repartee* 15: 13.

Baker, R. (1994) *Drag: A History of Female Impersonation on the Stage*, London: Cassell House.

Beigel, H. and Feldman, R. (1963) 'The male transvestite's motivation in fiction, research and reality', in H. Beigel (ed.) *Advances in Sex Research*, New York: Harper and Row.

Benjamin, H. (1966) *The Transsexual Phenomenon*, New York: Julian Press.

Berger, M. and Watson, B. (eds) (1995) *Constructing Masculinity*, London: Routledge.

Berger, P. and Luckmann, T. (1966) *The Social Construction of Reality: A Treatise in the Sociology of Knowledge*, Garden City, NY: Doubleday.

Bernstein, R. (1976) *The Restructuring of Social and Political Theory*, Oxford: Basil Blackwell.

Berry, J. (1993) Personal communication, 14 January, Emah Ltd, Halcyon Associates.

Bigus, O., Hadden, S. and Glaser, B. (1982) 'Basic social processes', in B. Glaser (ed.) *More Grounded Theory Methodology: A Reader*, Mill Valley, CA: Sociology Press, 1994.

Billings, D. and Urban, T. (1982) 'The socio-medical construction of transsexualism: an interpretation and critique', *Social Problems* 29: 266–82.

Birrell, S. and Cole, C. (1990) 'Double fault: Renée Richards and the construction and naturalization of difference', *Sociology of Sport Journal* 7: 1–21.

Bleuler, M. (1953) Personal communication, cited in Daniel Paul Schreber (1988) *Memoirs of My Nervous Illness*, (trans. and eds) I. Macalpine and R. Hunter, Cambridge, Massachusetts: Harvard University Press, 1988.

Blumer, H. (1956) 'Sociological analysis and the variable', *American Sociological Review* 21: 683–90.

—— (1969) *Symbolic Interactionism: Perspective and Method*, Englewood Cliffs, NJ: Prentice-Hall.

Bockting, W. and Coleman, E. (1992) *Gender Dysphoria: Interdisciplinary Approaches in Clinical Management*, New York: Haworth.

Bogdan, R. and Taylor, S. (1975) *Introduction to Qualitative Research Methods: A Phenomenological Approach to the Social Sciences*, New York: John Wiley and Sons.

Bolin, A. (1994) 'Transcending and transgendering: male-to-female transsexuals, dichotomy and diversity', in G. Herdt (ed.) *Third Sex, Third Gender: Beyond Sexual Dimorphism in Culture and History*, New York: Zone Books.

Bornstein, K. (1994) *Gender Outlaw: On Men, Women and the Rest of Us*, New York: Routledge.

Box, S. (1981) *Deviance, Reality and Society*, London: Holt, Rinehart and Winston.

Brake, M. (1976) 'I may be queer but at least I'm a man: male hegemony and ascribed versus achieved gender', in D. Barker and S. Allen (eds) *Sexual Divisions in Society: Process and Change*, London: Tavistock.

Brierley, H. (1979) *Transvestism: A Handbook with Case Studies for Psychologists, Psychiatrists and Counsellors*, Oxford: Pergamon Press.

Buckner, H. (1970) 'The transvestic career path', *Psychiatry* 33: 381–9.

Buhrich, N. and McConaghy, N. (1976) 'Transvestite fiction', *Journal of Nervous and Mental Disease* 163: 420–7.

Bullough, V. and Bullough, B. (1993) *Cross Dressing, Sex, and Gender*, Pennysylvania: University of Pennysylvania Press.

—— (eds) (in preparation) *Gender and Transgender Issues*, New York: Garland Publishing.

Burgess, D. and Ekins, R. (1986a) 'Transsexualism, birth registration and the right to marry: schedule of legislative and case law developments in Europe', interim paper for the 2nd International Congress on Psychiatry, Law and Ethics, Tel Aviv.

—— (1986b) 'Transsexualism, birth registration and the right to marry: proposals for a friendly settlement in Europe', interim paper for the 2nd International Congress on Psychiatry, Law and Ethics, Tel Aviv.

Butler, J. (1990) *Gender Trouble: Feminism and the Subversion of Identity*, New York: Routledge.

Caughey, J. (1984) *Imaginary Social Worlds: A Cultural Approach*, Lincoln: University of Nebrasaka Press.

Charmaz, K. (1983) 'The grounded theory method: an explication and interpretation', in B. Glaser (ed.) *More Grounded Theory Methodology: A Reader*, Mill Valley, CA: Sociology Press, 1994.

—— (1995) 'Grounded theory', in J. Smith, R. Harré and L. Van Langenhove (eds) *Rethinking Methods in Psychology*, London: Sage Publications.

CIC (1993a) 'Girls' changing room', PO Box 1650, B1 1AA.

—— (1993b) 'TV dream line', PO Box 1650, B1 1AA.

Cindy (1993) 'Love of taffeta', *International TV Repartee* 14: 52–3.

Coleman, V. (1996) *Men in Dresses: A Study of Transvestism/Crossdressing*, Barnstable, Devon: *European Medical Journal* – A *European Medical Journal* Special Report.

Concise Oxford Dictionary of Current English, 7th Edn, (1975) Oxford: Oxford University Press.

Cornwall, A. and Lindisfarne N. (eds) (1994) *Dislocating Masculinity*, London: Routledge.

Costa, M. (1962) *Reverse Sex*, London: Challenge Publications.

Crimson (1993) 'TV wedding belles', PO Box 540, CH3 5YU.

Crossdresser's International Shopping Guide (1995) Burbank, CA: JMPG, PO Box 7217.

Curtis, J. and Petras, J. (eds) (1970) *The Sociology of Knowledge: A Reader*, London: Gerald Duckworth.

Dekker, R. and van de Pol, L. (1989) *The Tradition of Female Transvestism in Early Modern Europe*, London: Macmillan Press.

Denny, D. (1994) *Gender Dysphoria: A Guide to Research*, New York: Garland Publishing.

—— (1995) 'The paradigm shift is here!' *Aegis News* 4: 1.

—— (ed.) (forthcoming) *Current Concepts in Transgender Identity: Towards a New Synthesis*, New York: Garland Publishers.

Devor, H. (1989) *Gender Blending: Confronting the Limits of Duality*, Bloomington: Indiana University Press.

Docter, R. (1988) *Transvestites and Transsexuals: Toward a Theory of Cross-Gender Behavior*, New York: Plenum Press.

Eazee Come (1993a) 'Girls must work', PO Box 649, EC1U 9UU.

—— (1993b) 'So you want to be a girl – like me?' PO Box 649, EC1U 9UU.

Ekins, R. (1978) 'G.H. Mead: contributions to a philosophy of sociological knowledge', unpublished Ph.D. thesis, University of London.

—— (1983) 'The assignment of motives as a problem in the double hermeneutic: the case of transvestism and transsexuality', paper for the Sociological Association of Ireland Conference, Wexford, Ireland.

—— (1986) 'Theorising sex changing: some medico-legal formulations in relation to the "solution" from human rights', in M. Haslam (ed.) *Psycho-Legal Aspects of Sexual Problems*, Burgess Hill, Sussex: Schering.

—— (1988) 'News from around the world – in their own words: interview with Dr Richard Ekins of the Trans-Gender Archive, University of Ulster', *Renaissance News* 1 (5): 4–5, [The Chrysalis Interview].

—— (1989a) 'Archive update: interview with Dr Richard Ekins of the Trans-Gender Archive, University of Ulster', *Fanfare* 41: 9–12.

—— (1989b) 'Trans-gender biography: a guide to the literature with an annotated bibliography', *Archive News: Bulletin of the Trans-Gender Archive* 1 (2): 12–28.

—— (1990a) 'A trip to Morocco: a note on the early history of "sex changing"', *Renaissance News* 4 (1): 1 and 9.

—— (1990b) 'Building a trans-gender archive: on the classification and framing of trans-gender knowledge', in Alice (ed.) *The Beaumont Trust International Gender Dysphoria Conference Report*, London: the Beaumont Trust.

—— (1990c) 'Half worlds between the sexes: popular press coverage of transvestism and transsexuality, 1949–1959, Part I', *Archive News: Bulletin of the Trans-Gender Archive* 2 (1): 3–23.

—— (1992a) 'Half worlds between the sexes: popular press coverage of transvestism and transsexuality, 1949–1959, Part II', *Archive News: Bulletin of the Trans-Gender Archive* 3 (1): 26–8.

—— (1992b) 'The work of Peter Farrer: women's clothes and cross-dressing with a provisional list of novels in which mention of cross-dressing is made, 1901–1951', *Archive News: Bulletin of the Trans-Gender Archive* 3 (1): 3–20.

—— (1993) 'On male femaling: a grounded theory approach to cross-dressing and sex-changing', *Sociological Review* 41: 1–29.

—— (1996) 'Male femaling, telephone sex and the case of intimacy scripts', in R. Ekins and D. King (eds) *Blending Genders: Social Aspects of Cross-Dressing and Sex-Changing*, London: Routledge.

Ekins, R. and King, D. (eds) (1996a) *Blending Genders: Social Aspects of Cross-dressing and Sex-changing*, London: Routledge.

—— (1996b) 'Blending genders: contributions to the emerging field of transgender studies', in D. Denny (ed.) (forthcoming) *Current Concepts in Transgender Identity: Towards a New Synthesis*, New York: Garland Publishing.

Ellis, A. and Abarnel, A. (1961) *The Encyclopedia of Sexual Behaviour, Vol. II*, London: Heinemann.

Epstein, J. and Straub, K. (1991) (eds) *Bodyguards: The Cultural Politics of Gender Ambiguity*, Routledge: New York.

Eysenck, H. (1985) *Decline and Fall of the Freudian Empire*, New York: Viking.

Fallowell, D. and Ashley, A. (1982) *April Ashley's Odyssey*, London: Jonathan Cape.

Farrer, P. (ed.) (1987) *Men in Petticoats: A Selection of Letters from Victorian Newspapers*, Liverpool: Karn Publications Garston.

Feinbloom, D, (1976) *Transvestites and Transsexuals: Mixed Views*, New York: Dell.

Fisk, N. (1973) 'Gender dysphoria syndrome (the how, what and why of a disease)', in D. Laub and P. Gandy (eds) *Proceedings of the Second Interdisciplinary Symposium on Gender Dysphoria*, Palo Alto, CA: Stanford University Medical Centre.

—— (1974) 'Gender dysphoria syndrome: the conception that liberalises indications for total gender reorientation and implies a broadly based multi-dimensional rehabilitative regimen', *Western Journal of Medicine* 120: 386–91.

Foucault, M. (1979) *The History of Sexuality, Volume 1: An Introduction*, London: Allen Lane.

Freeman, T. (1988) *The Psychoanalyst in Psychiatry*, London: Karnac Books.

Freud, S. (1911) 'Psycho-analytic Notes on an Autobiographical Account of a Case of Paranoia (Dementia Paranoides)', in *The Standard Edition of the Complete Psychological Works of Sigmund Freud, Vol. 12*, London: Hogarth, 1958.

—— (1933) *New Introductory Lectures on Psycho-Analysis*, in *The Standard Edition of the Complete Psychological Works of Sigmund Freud, Vol. 22*, London: Hogarth, 1964.

—— (1941) [1938] 'Findings, ideas, problems', in *The Standard Edition of the Complete Psychological Works of Sigmund Freud, Vol. 23*, London: Hogarth, 1964.

Frost, P. (1996) 'Reflections on a thirtieth birthday', *Beaumont Magazine* 4 (2): 11.

Fry, J. (1993) 'Your attitude is everything', *Cross-Talk* 44: 8.

Gagnon, J. and Parker, R. (1995) 'Conceiving sexuality', in R. Parker and J. Gagnon (eds) *Conceiving Sexuality: Approaches to Sex Research in a Postmodern World*, New York: Routledge.

Garber, M. (1992) *Vested Interests: Cross-Dressing and Cultural Anxiety*, Routledge: New York.

Garfinkel, H. (1967) 'Passing and the managed achievement of sex status in an intersexed person', in H. Garfinkel, *Studies in Ethnomethodology*, Englewood Cliffs, NJ: Prentice-Hall.

Gender Trust, UK (1990) *A Guide to Transsexualism, Transgenderism, and Gender Dysphoria*, London: Gender Trust.

Giddens, A. (1976) *New Rules of Sociological Method*, London: Hutchinson.

Ginger (1980) *Female Mimics International* 2.

Glaser, B. (1978) *Theoretical Sensitivity: Advances in the Methodology of Grounded Theory*, Mill Valley, CA: Sociology Press.

—— (1992) *Basics of Grounded Theory Analysis*, Mill Valley, CA: Sociology Press.

—— (ed.) (1993) *Examples of Grounded Theory: A Reader*, Mill Valley, CA: Sociology Press.

—— (ed.) (1994) *More Grounded Theory Methodology: A Reader*, Mill Valley, CA: Sociology Press.

—— (ed.) (1995) *Grounded Theory, 1984–1994, Volumes 1 & 2*, Mill Valley, CA: Sociology Press.

Glaser, B. and Strauss, A. (1967a) 'Awareness contexts and social interaction', *American Sociological Review* 29: 669–79.

—— (1967b) *The Discovery of Grounded Theory: Strategies for Qualitative Research*, Chicago: Aldine.

Goffman, E. (1959) *The Presentation of Self in Everyday Life*, Harmondsworth: Penguin.

—— (1968) *Stigma: Notes on the Management of Spoiled Identity*, Harmondsworth: Penguin.

—— (1974) *Frame Analysis: An Essay on the Organisation of Experience*, New York: Harper and Row.

—— (1979) *Gender Advertisements*, London: Macmillan.

Goldin, N. (1993) *The Other Side*, Manchester: Cornerhouse Publications.

Gould, M. and Kern-Daniels, R. (1977) 'Towards a sociological theory of gender and sex', *The American Sociologist* 12: 182–9.

Green, R. (1974) *Sexual Identity Conflict in Children and Adults*, London: Duckworth.

—— (1987) *The 'Sissy Boy Syndrome' and the Development of Homosexuality*, New Haven: Yale University Press.

Green, R. and Money, J. (1969) (eds) *Transsexualism and Sex Reassignment*, Baltimore: Johns Hopkins Press.

Greenson, R. (1966) 'A transvestite boy and a hypothesis', *International Journal of Psycho-Analysis* 47: 396–403.

Gutheil, E. (1954) 'The psychologic background of transvestism and transsexualism', *American Journal of Psychotherapy* 8: 231–9.

Halcyon (1993a) 'Husband enslaved', Emah Ltd.

—— (1993b) 'Maid for the dildo', Emah Ltd.

—— (1993c) 'Transvestite spanking!', Emah Ltd.

Harré, R. and Lamb, R. (eds) (1986) *The Dictionary of Personality and Social Psychology*, Oxford: Blackwell.

Haworth, A. (1993) 'Samoa: where men think they are women', *Marie Claire*, 57: 50–3.

Heap, J. and Roth, P. (1973) 'On phenomenological sociology', *American Sociological Review* 38: 354–67.

Henwood, K. and Pidgeon, N. (1995) 'Grounded theory and psychological research', *The Psychologist* 8: 115–18.

Herdt, G. (1981) *Guardians of the Flutes: Idioms of Masculinity*, New York: McGraw-Hill.

—— (ed.) (1994) *Third Sex, Third Gender: Beyond Sexual Dimorphism in Culture and History*, New York: Zone Books.

Hermaphrodites with Attitude: The Quarterly Publication of the Intersex Society of North America (1995) Spring.

Hirschauer, S. (1996) 'Doing sex and doing gender in medical disciplines', in A. Mol and M. Berg (eds), *Differences in Medicine* (in preparation), Cambridge, Massachusetts: Harvard University Press.

Hirschfeld, M. (1910) *Transvestites: The Erotic Drive to Cross-Dress*, trans. 1991, New York: Prometheus Books.

Hoenig, J., Kenna, J. and Youd, A. (1970) 'Social and economic aspects of transsexualism', *British Journal of Psychiatry* 117: 163–72.

Kadushin, C. (1966) 'The friends and supporters of psychotherapy: on social circles in urban life', *American Sociological Review* 31: 786–802.

Kando, T. (1973) *Sex Change: The Achievement of Gender Identity Among Feminized Transsexuals*, Springfield, Illinois: Charles C. Thomas.

Kelly, P. (1987–90) (ed.) *Chrysalis International: Gender Transient Affinity Magazine*, Freshwater, Isle of Wight.

—— (1992a) 'Transgender in Turkey', *International TV Repartee* 12: 24–7.

—— (1992b) 'Russian project', *International TV Repartee* 12: 28–9.

—— (1993a) 'Storm over Russia', *International TV Repartee* 14: 26–8.

—— (1993b) 'Hellenic travesti', *International TV Repartee* 16: 11–13.

—— (1994a) 'Hellenic travesti: Part 2', *International TV Repartee* 17: 18–21.

—— (1994b) 'Phaedra in China', *International TV Repartee* 18: 12–13.

—— (1995a) 'Croatia/Slovenia mission', *International TV Repartee* 20: 36.

—— (1995b) 'The beautiful dolls of Rio', *International TV Repartee* 22: 42–4.

—— (1996) 'London grandeur: the Porchester Ball', in R. Ekins and D. King (eds) *Blending Genders: Social Aspects of Cross-Dressing and Sex-Changing*, London: Routledge.

Kendall, D. (1993) 'Pampered in panties', *International TV Repartee* 15: 44–5.

Kessler, S. and McKenna, W. (1978) *Gender: An Ethnomethodological Approach*, New York: Wiley.

King, D. (1981) 'Gender confusions: psychological and psychiatric conceptions of transvestism and transsexuality', in K. Plummer (ed.) *The Making of the Modern Homosexual*, London: Hutchinson.

—— (1984) 'Condition, orientation, role or false consciousness? Models of homosexuality and transsexualism', *Sociological Review* 32: 38–56.

—— (1990) 'Male cross dressing, sex changing and the British press', in Alice (ed.) *The Beaumont Trust International Gender Dysphoria Conference Report*, London: Beaumont Trust.

—— (1993) *The Transvestite and the Transsexual: Public Categories and Private Identities*, Aldershot: Avebury.

—— (1995) unpublished manuscript.

—— (1996a) 'Cross-dressing, sex-changing and the press', in R. Ekins and D. King (eds) *Blending Genders: Social Aspects of Cross-Dressing and Sex-Changing*, London: Routledge.

—— (1996b) 'Gender blending: medical perspectives and technology', in R. Ekins and D. King (eds) *Blending Genders: Social Aspects of Cross-Dressing and Sex-Changing*, London: Routledge.

Kirk, K. and Heath, S. (1984) *Men in Frocks*, London: Gay Men's Press.

Koranyi, E. (1980) *Transsexuality in the Male: The Spectrum of Gender Dysphoria*, Springfield, Illinois: Charles C. Thomas.

Kroker, A. and Kroker, M. (1993) *The Last Sex: Feminism and Outlaw Bodies*, Houndmills, Basingstoke: Macmillan.

Kubie L. (1974) 'The drive to become both sexes', *Psychoanalytic Quarterly* 43: 349–426.

Kulick, D. and Willson, M. (eds) (1995) *Taboo: Sex, Identity and Erotic Subjectivity in Anthropological Fieldwork*, London: Routledge.

Lee, V. (1995) 'Dragnet compiled by David Taylor', *Thud: The Urban Diversion* 40, 18–20.

Lemert, E. (1951) *Social Pathology*, London: McGraw-Hill.

—— (1972) *Human Deviance: Social Problems and Social Control*, Englewood Cliffs, NJ: Prentice Hall.

Lewins, F. (1995) *Transsexualism in Society: A Sociology of Male-to-Female Transsexuals*, Melbourne: Macmillan.

Lukas, M. (1978) *Let Me Die a Woman: The Why and How of Sex-Change Operations*, New York: Rearguard Productions.

McGoldrick, F. (1985) 'Boys will be girls: a participant observation study of cross-dressing in Belfast', unpublished B.Sc. dissertation, University of Ulster.

Mackenzie, G. (1994) *Transgender Nation*, Bowling Green: Bowling Green State University Popular Press.

McKinney, J. (1955) 'The contribution of George H. Mead to the sociology of knowledge', *Social Forces* 34: 144–9.

Mahler, M. (1968) *On Human Symbiosis and the Vicissitudes of Individuation, Vol. 1*, New York: International Universities Press.

Masson, J. (ed.) (1985) *The Complete Letters of Sigmund Freud to Wilhelm Fleiss, 1887–1905*, Cambridge, Massachusetts: Harvard University Press.

Mead, G. H. (1932) *The Philosophy of the Present*, La Salle, Illinois: Open Court Publishing Company.

—— (1934) *Mind, Self, and Society: From the Standpoint of a Social Behaviorist*, Chicago: University of Chicago Press.

—— (1938) *The Philosophy of the Act*, Chicago: University of Chicago Press.

Mead, M. (1995) *Hermaphrodites with Attitude*, newsletter, p. 9.

Mills, C. Wright (1940) 'Situated actions and vocabularies of motive', in *Power, Politics and People: The Collected Essays of C. Wright Mills*, New York: Oxford University Press.

Money, J. (1969) 'Sex reassignment as related to hermaphroditism and trans-sexualism', in R. Green and J. Money, (eds) *Transsexualism and Sex Reassignment*, Baltimore: Johns Hopkins University Press.

Money, J. and Ehrhardt, A. (1972) *Man & Woman, Boy & Girl*, Baltimore: Johns Hopkins University Press.

Money, J. and Walker, P. (1977) 'Counselling the transsexual', in J. Money and H. Musaph (eds) *Handbook of Sexology*, Biomedical Press: Elsevier/North-Holland.

Morris, J. (1975) *Conundrum*, London: Coronet Books.

Nataf, Z. (1996) *Lesbians Talk Transgender*, London: Scarlet Press.

Neil, L. (1987–93) (ed.) *Transcare: A Magazine for Trans People*, Wellington, New Zealand: The Minorities Trust.

Newton, E. (1979) *Mother Camp: Female Impersonators in America*, Chicago: University of Chicago Press.

Niederland, W. (1984) *The Schreber Case: Psychoanalytic Profile of a Paranoid Personality*, Hillsdale, NJ: The Analytic Press.

Nikki (undated) *The World of Transvestism*, supplement 1: 15.

Peel, C. (1992) 'Seven brides but not a brother in sight!', *Beaumont Bulletin* 24 (5): 30.

Pepper, J. (1982) *A Man's Tale*, London: Quartet Books.

Person, E. and Ovesey, L. (1974a) 'The transsexual syndrome in males: I primary transsexualism', *American Journal of Psychotherapy* 28: 4–20.

—— (1974b) 'The transsexual syndrome in males: II secondary transsexualism', *American Journal of Psychotherapy* 28: 174–93.

Plummer, K. (1975) *Sexual Stigma: An Interactionist Account*, London: Routledge and Kegan Paul.

—— (1979) 'Symbolic interactionism and sexual differentiation: an empirical investigation', Final Report on Grant HR 4043 to the SSRC.

—— (ed.) (1981) *The Making of the Modern Homosexual*, London: Hutchinson.

—— (1983) *Documents of Life: An Introduction to the Problems and Literature of the Humanistic Method*, London: Allen and Unwin.

—— (1984) 'Sexual diversity: a sociological perspective', in K. Howells (ed.) *Sexual Diversity*, Oxford: Blackwell.

—— (ed.) (1991) *Symbolic Interactionism, Vols I and II*, Aldershot: Gower.

—— (1995) *Telling Sexual Stories: Power, Change and Social Worlds*, London: Routledge.

Prus, R. (1987) 'Generic social processes: maximising conceptual development in ethnographic research', *Journal of Contemporary Ethnography* 16: 250–93.

Ramet, S. (forthcoming) *Gender Reversals and Gender Cultures*, London: Routledge.

Randell, J. (1971) 'Indications for sex reassignment surgery', *Archives of Sexual Behaviour*, 1: 153–61.

Raymond, J. (1980) *The Transsexual Empire*, London: The Women's Press.

Rees, M. (1984) Application No. 9532/81 Mark Rees against United Kingdom, *Report of the European Commission of Human Rights*.

Renaissance Education Association (ed.) (1987–96) *Renaissance News*, King of Prussia, PA: Renaissance Education Association.

Roberts, J. (1995) *Who's Who & Resource Guide to the Transgender Community*, King of Prussia, PA: Creative Design Services.

Rose, M. (1993) 'A rose by any other name – TV v. CD', *International TV Repartee* 15: 6.

Rubington, E. and Weinberg, M. (eds) (1973) *Deviance: The Interactionist Perspective: Texts and Readings in the Sociology of Deviance*, London: Macmillan.

Sagarin, E. (1969) 'Transvestites and transsexuals: boys will be girls', in *Odd Man In: Societies of Deviants in America*, Chicago: Quadrangle Books.

Schreber, D. P. (1988) *Memoirs of My Nervous Illness*, I. Macalpine and R. Hunter (trans. and eds) Cambridge, Massachusetts: Harvard University Press.

Schutz, A. (1944) 'The stranger: an essay in social psychology', in A. Schutz, *Collected Papers II: Studies in Social Theory*, The Hague: Martinus Nijhoff, 1967.

—— (1953) 'Common-sense and scientific interpretation of human action', in A. Schutz, *Collected Papers I: The Problem of Social Reality*, The Hague: Martinus Nijhoff, 1967.

—— (1967) *Collected Papers I: The Problem of Social Reality*, The Hague: Martinus Nijhoff.

Scott, J. (1992) 'President's report', *Beaumont Bulletin* 24 (3): 6–7.

Seeley, J. (1966) 'The "making" and "taking" of problems', *Social Problems* 14: 382–9.

Segal, L. (1994) *Straight Sex: The Politics of Pleasure*, London: Virago.

Shively, M. and De Cecco, J. (1977) 'Components of sexual identity', *Journal of Homosexuality* 3: 41–8.

Simmel, G. (1908) 'The stranger', in D. Levine (ed.) *Georg Simmel: On Individuality and Social Forms*, Chicago: University of Chicago Press.

—— (1955) *The Web of Group Affiliations*, New York: The Free Press.

Simpson, M. (1994) *Male Impersonators: Men Performing Masculinity*, London: Cassell.

Sinclair, Y. (1984) *Transvestism Within a Partnership of Marriage and Families*, London: TV/TS Group.

Smith, J., Harré, R. and Van Langenhove, L. (1995a) *Rethinking Psychology*, London: Sage Publications.

—— (1995b) *Rethinking Methods in Psychology*, London: Sage Publications.

Star, Hedy Jo [Carol Rollins Hammonds] (1955) *I Changed My Sex: the Autobiography of Stripper Hedy Jo Star Formerly Carol Hammonds*, Allied, A Novel Book.

Stebbins, R. (1971) *Commitment to Deviance*, Westport, Connecticut: Greenwood.

Stein, A. and Plummer, K. (1994) '"I can't even think": "queer" theory and the missed sexual revolution in sociology', *Sociological Theory* 12: 178–87.

Steiner, B. (ed.) (1985) *Gender Dysphoria*, New York: Plenum Press.

Stoller, R. (1968) *Sex and Gender: Volume 1, The Development of Masculinity and Femininity*, New York: Science House.

—— (1970) 'Pornography and perversion', *Archives of General Psychiatry* 22: 490–500.

—— (1973) 'Male transsexualism: uneasiness', *American Journal of Psychiatry* 130: 536–9.

—— (1975) *The Transsexual Experiment*, London: Hogarth Press.

—— (1985) *Presentations of Gender*, New Haven: Yale University Press.

Stone, G. (1962) 'Appearance and the self', in A. Rose (ed.) *Human Behaviour and Social Processes: An Interactionist Approach*, London: Routledge and Kegan Paul.

Stone, S. (1991) 'The *empire* strikes back: a posttranssexual manifesto', in J. Epstein and K. Straub (eds) *Body Guards: The Cultural Politics of Gender Ambiguity*, New York: Routledge.

Strauss, A. (1977) *Mirrors and Masks: The Search for Identity*, London: Martin Robertson.

—— (1978) 'A social world perspective', in N. Denzin (ed.) *Studies in Symbolic Interaction, Vol. 1*, Greenwich, CT: JAI Press.

—— (1982) 'Social worlds and legitimation processes', in N. Denzin (ed.) *Studies in Symbolic Interaction, Vol. 4*, Greenwich, CT: JAI Press.

—— (1987) *Qualitative Analysis for Social Scientists*, Cambridge: Cambridge University Press.

—— (1993) *Continual Permutations of Action*, New York: Aldine de Gruyter.

—— (1995) Personal communication.

Strauss, A. and Corbin, J. (1990) *Basics of Qualitative Research: Grounded Theory Procedures and Techniques*, Newbury Park: Sage Publications.

Talamini, J. (1982) *Boys Will be Girls: The Hidden World of the Heterosexual Male Transvestite*, Lanham Maryland: University Press of America.

The Tranny Guide (1996) London: The Way Out Publishing Company.

Thomas, W. (1923) *The Unadjusted Girl*, Boston: Little Brown.

Unruh, D. (1979) 'Characteristics and types of participation in social worlds', *Symbolic Interaction* 2: 115–29.

—— (1980) 'The nature of social worlds', *Pacific Sociological Review* 23: 271–96.

Wålinder, J. (1967), *Transsexualism: A Study of Forty-Three Cases*, Goteborg: Scandinavian University Books.

Warren, C. (1977) 'Fieldwork in the gay world: issues in phenomenological research', *Journal of Social Issues* 21: 93–107.

Warshay, L. (1980) *Symbolic Interaction* 3(1):6

Webb, T. (1996) 'Autobiographical fragments from a transsexual activist', in R. Ekins and D. King, *Blending Genders: Social Aspects of Cross-Dressing and Sex-Changing*, London: Routledge.

Weeks, J. (1981) *Sex, Politics and Society: The Regulation of Sexuality Since 1800*, London: Longman.

Weigart, A. (1983) 'Identity: its emergence within sociological psychology', *Symbolic Interaction* 6: 183–206.

Wheelwright, J. (1989) *Amazons and Military Maids: Women Who Dressed as Men in Pursuit of Life, Liberty and Happiness*, London: Pandora.

Whittle, S. (1996) 'Gender fucking or fucking gender? Current cultural contributions to theories of gender blending', in R. Ekins and D. King (eds) *Blending Genders: Social Aspects of Cross-Dressing and Sex-Changing*, London: Routledge.

Who's Who & Resource Guide to the Transgender Community (1995) King of Prussia, PA: Creative Design Services, PO Box 61263.

Winch, P. (1958) *The Idea of a Social Science*, London: Routledge and Kegan Paul.

Wolfgang, M. (1964) *Male and Female Deviations*, Los Angeles, CA: Sherbourne Press Inc.

Woodhouse, A. (1989) *Fantastic Women: Sex, Gender and Transvestism*, Basingstoke: Macmillan.

Woodlawn, H. with Copeland, J. (1991) *A Low Life in High Heels: The Holly Woodlawn Story*, New York: St. Martin's Press.

Zerubavel, E. (1980) 'If Simmel were a fieldworker: on formal sociological theory and analytical field research', *Symbolic Interaction* 3: 25–33.

INDEX

177